Etlatongo

Social Complexity, Interaction, and Village Life in the Mixteca Alta of Oaxaca, Mexico

Jeffrey P. Blomster
Brandeis University

 Case Studies in Archaeology: Jeffrey Quilter, Series Editor

THOMSON
™
WADSWORTH

Australia • Canada • Mexico • Singapore • Spain
United Kingdom • United States

Anthropology Editor: *Lin Marshall*
Assistant Editor: *Analie Barnett*
Editorial Assistant: *Amanda Santana, Kelly McMahon*
Marketing Manager: *Diane Wenckebach*
Project Manager, Editorial Production: *Rita Jaramillo*
Print/Media Buyer: *Rebecca Cross*
Permissions Editor: *Kiely Sexton*

Production Service: *Buuji, Inc.*
Copy Editor: *Linda Ireland, Buuji, Inc.*
Cover Designer: *Rob Hugel*
Cover Image: *Jeffrey P. Blomster*
Text and Cover Printer: *Webcom*
Compositor: *Buuji, Inc.*

The logo for the Archaeology series is based on ancient Middle Eastern and Phoenician symbols for house.

Printed in Canada
1 2 3 4 5 6 7 07 06 05 04 03

For more information about our products, contact us at:
Thomson Learning Academic Resource Center
1-800-423-0563

For permission to use material from this text, contact us by: **Phone:** 1-800-730-2214
Fax: 1-800-730-2215
Web: http://www.thomsonrights.com

Library of Congress Control Number: 2003108209

ISBN 0-534-61281-4

Wadsworth/Thomson Learning
10 Davis Drive
Belmont, CA 94002-3098
USA

Asia
Thomson Learning
5 Shenton Way #01-01
UIC Building
Singapore 068808

Australia/New Zealand
Thomson Learning
102 Dodds Street
Southbank, Victoria 3006
Australia

Canada
Nelson
1120 Birchmount Road
Toronto, Ontario M1K 5G4
Canada

Europe/Middle East/Africa
Thomson Learning
High Holborn House
50/51 Bedford Row
London WC1R 4LR
United Kingdom

Latin America
Thomson Learning
Seneca, 53
Colonia Polanco
11560 Mexico D.F.
Mexico

Spain/Portugal
Paraninfo
Calle/Magallanes, 25
28015 Madrid, Spain

*To the people of Etlatongo, past and present,
who taught me so much. And to my parents.*

Contents

Foreword

ABOUT THE SERIES

These case studies in archaeology are designed to bring students, in beginning and intermediate courses in archaeology, anthropology, history, and related disciplines, insights into the theory, practice, and results of archaeological investigations. They are written by scholars who have had direct experience in archaeological research, whether in the field, laboratory, or library. The authors are also teachers, and in writing their books they have kept the students who will read them foremost in their minds. These books are intended to present a wide range of archaeological topics as case studies in a form and manner that will be more accessible than writings found in articles or books intended for professional audiences, yet at the same time preserve and present the significance of archaeological investigations for all.

ABOUT THE AUTHOR

Jeffrey Blomster is an anthropological archaeologist specializing in social complexity, interregional interaction, and approaches to style, ritual, and ideology. His regional and spatial research interests lie primarily in Mesoamerica, where he has focused on Mixtec, Zapotec, and Olmec cultures. In addition to Mexico, he has also performed fieldwork throughout the United States, from the Four-Corners region of the Southwest to eastern Pennsylvania. He received undergraduate training in anthropology and political science at Washington and Lee University, and graduate training in anthropology and archaeology at Yale University. For nearly a year, he conducted archaeological fieldwork in the Mixteca Alta of Oaxaca, Mexico. This fieldwork, and subsequent laboratory analysis in Oaxaca, examines the emergence of social complexity in the Nochixtlán Valley and explores the impact of interregional interaction in this area. His academic writings have focused on manipulation and movement of style, looking at both traditional stylistic analyses as well as petrographic approaches. He recently received a grant from the Foundation for the Advancement of Mesoamerican Studies, Inc., to explore diachronic change in obsidian procurement and utilization in the Nochixtlán Valley and the Valley of Oaxaca. He has taught a variety of courses in the anthropology departments of both Muhlenberg College and Brandeis University.

ABOUT THIS CASE STUDY FOR *ETLATONGO*

As if continuing the practices of the late prehistoric petty kingdoms of southern Mexico, the archaeologists who work in Oaxaca and vicinity tend to be a contentious lot. There are factions, rivalries, alliances, attempts at empire, and other intrigues aplenty. Bringing a new perspective comes Jeffrey Blomster with this book and a strong argument for his own view of past cultural dynamics in the Mixteca Alta, internally, in relation to the Valley of Oaxaca and beyond.

Following standard policy for the *Case Studies in Archaeology* series, a well-presented, reasonable argument is the criterion for publication, bounded by the extremes of arguments for lost continents or alien interventions. I leave it to others to argue the fine points of whether or to what degree the specific perspective taken by Blomster on issues of emerging complexity, relations with "centers" and "peripheries," and the like is compelling. As someone who has never been to southern Mexico and who has no strong opinions on the fine points of arguments regarding its prehistory, I must note, nonetheless, that Blomster's arguments make sense to me. Furthermore, he has done a very fine job of producing an excellent *Case Study* because he has addressed so many important issues for the reader of this book.

Blomster thoroughly covers various theoretical schools in archaeology, gives a comprehensive review of the "Olmec problem," discusses problems in interpreting the past in general, and provides us with a view of the dust and dilemmas of field-work. It is a masterful example of how theory, method, and technique link together in the doing of archaeology, from the library, to the field, to the laboratory, and to the office. Blomster is willing to work with a large theoretical tool—a world systems perspective—but at the same time fully realizes that the "devil is in the details."

The issue of whether the Olmec was a "mother culture" for Mesoamerican civilizations was raised decades ago and is still with us. Blomster approaches the question but realizes that it can never fully be answered, or, more precisely, he clearly understands that the question is overly general. By concentrating on how specific material expressions of Olmec and Formative period goods that reflect ideology were produced and distributed in Mesoamerica, Blomster provides archaeology with a more sophisticated view of cultural dynamics. While he is not alone in this approach, his efforts are yielding results that will provide scholars and the interested public with more detailed and sophisticated views of ancient Mesoamerican prehistory. We are beginning to learn the fine points of how societies began to develop rank, hierarchy, and eventually, class in ancient Mexico. We are learning how the kinds of ideas and symbols that first emerged in some regions were accepted or rejected by people in other parts of a world with sustained and complex economic, political, and social interactions. As this process continues, the question of whether the Olmec was the "mother culture" of ancient Mesoamerica will not so much be finally answered as it will become irrelevant. The final statement (if there ever is one) likely will be "in some ways, yes, and in some ways, no," and we are starting to learn in what ways the answer is in the affirmative and in what ways it is negative.

Jeffrey Blomster's book is written with skill, imagination, erudition, and wit. It offers much for the undergraduate, graduate, and professional. In many ways, it is the ideal *Case Study* in the breadth of its appeal, the depth of its discussions, and the clarity of its writing. It is a pleasure for me to introduce it as a member of the series.

Jeffrey Quilter, Series Editor
Garrett Park, Maryland

Preface

The rise of social complexity—how some people in a society assume greater priority in a variety of sociopolitical and ideological realms—has been a primary focus of my research since I first became interested in archaeology. While numerous studies exist on contemporary societies for which we have a mosaic of data at our disposal, often these studies appear as "snapshots"—moments frozen in time. They lack the kind of time depth that archaeology provides. Through archaeology, it is possible to gain new insights and perspectives on the development and trajectory of social complexity. This volume attempts to provide such insights and data that will be of interest to both colleagues and students.

In order to explore this issue, I elected to focus my research in southern Mexico. Well known because of the ancient state centered at Monte Albán in modern Oaxaca state, many of the antecedent processes have also been studied in the surrounding Valley of Oaxaca. Yet, while well-known for the centuries prior to the Spanish invasion, the Mixteca Alta—lying northwest of the Valley of Oaxaca—had received comparatively limited attention. Indeed, perhaps it was the scant information available that led some scholars to characterize this area as peripheral to the kinds of inter-regional interaction and developing social complexity that occurred from approximately 1200 to 500 B.C. in the Valley of Oaxaca, prior to the founding of Monte Albán. Deciding that limited data do not necessarily indicate minimal cultural and social activity, I selected an ancient village in the Mixteca Alta for the focus of a multidisciplinary project. Some of the results contributed by this project appear in this monograph.

As the director of a multidisciplinary project, I had many choices to make on how to best allocate the resources, primarily a Fulbright (IIE) Fellowship, that I had at my disposal. While I had registered for many courses on archaeological method and theory as both an undergraduate and graduate student, there was clearly no one way in which to craft a research design—nor should there be. As I scanned the literature as part of the background research for my own project, what I really wanted to see were explications of research designs from their planning to implementation, and to see how such plans evolved in the field. In addition to providing and interpreting data relevant to the development of social complexity and village life in ancient Mexico, this book is also an effort to provide such a perspective. It is not meant to serve as a "cookbook" approach (add three test units to a robotage excavation, stir in a transit, and bake), but merely to provide one example of how the process of research design began and changed due to circumstances in the field. I hope it will provoke thought and discussion as both students and colleagues plan and evaluate their own excavations, whether real or imaginary.

An additional goal of this book is to explain how I arrive at certain interpretations often based on stratigraphic and ceramic data. I assure readers they will find no lack of detail in these realms; readers will be able to assess for themselves the veracity of my conclusions. I believe this small project has made, and will continue to make, a significant impact on how we understand early social complexity, interregional interaction, and village life. As archaeologists have a responsibility to report the results of their findings, I am pleased to do so in the format provided by the Case Studies series, which has the potential for reaching a great number and various types of readers.

ACKNOWLEDGMENTS

One of the most pleasant tasks in writing this volume is reflecting on the numerous individuals and institutions that have helped me bring this project to fruition. In addition to the Fulbright (IIE) Fellowship mentioned earlier that funded the fieldwork, several Josef Albers Fellowships, the Charles J. MacCurdy Endowment, Yale University, the Department of Anthropology, Brandeis University, and a Jane's Grant from the Latin American Studies Program, Brandeis University, supported subsequent research and technical analyses. In Mexico City at the Instituto Nacional de Antropología e Historia (INAH), permission to carry out the research and support were provided at differing times by Lorena Mirambell, Marí Carmen Serra Puche, and Joaquín García-Bárcena; in Oaxaca City, Ernesto González Licón and Eduardo López Calzada provided support in their roles as directors of the Oaxaca INAH office. At San Mateo Etlatongo, Magdaleno Rodríquez F., then Presidente Municipal, provided support and permission for the fieldwork. I gratefully acknowledge the support, interest, and tolerance of the townspeople of San Mateo Etlatongo.

In the field, I was fortunate to have an exceptionally gifted and dedicated crew of field assistants from San Mateo Etlatongo and volunteers. In length of time with the 1992 project, these were: Hugo Cruz Rodríguez, Francisco Zárate Cruz, Tomás Rodríguez González, Joaquín Casas Hernández, Apolinar José Ramírez, Sixto Rodríguez González, Antonio José García, Juan José García, Juan Rodríguez Serna, Antonio Serna Cruz, Kevin Thuesen, Justin Glass, Trey Beck, Betty and George Havers, Damon Peeler, Frank Crohn, and Oswaldo Chinchilla. Many of these individuals contributed directly to the drawings of features and stratigraphy produced in the field. Additional laboratory work was aided and abetted by: Hugh Robinson, Juan and Eduardo Nolasco Martínez, Elisabeth Hildebrand, Jessica Hedgepeth, and Ryan Arp.

In terms of technical contributions, Pedro Antonio Juarez and Alec Christensen examined all human remains. The instrumental neutron activation analysis discussed in Chapter 6 was directed by Drs. Hector Neff and Michael Glascock, both of the Missouri University Research Reactor, and supported by a National Science Foundation grant to the reactor (DBS-9102016 for the obsidian, and SBR-9503035 for the ceramics). Elisabeth Hildebrand drew the lithics in Figure 4.14, Juan Cruz Pascual created Figure 7.16, Hugo Antonio Dominguez Figure 8.1, and Jason Trout Figure 8.3. The expertise in various computer programs (and patience!) of Paul Blomster, Javier Urcid, and Andrew Workinger vastly improved many of the final figures. I wish to thank Michael Coe for permission to publish Figures 4.13 and 6.3, and Dumbarton Oaks for Figure 6.2.

My dissertation committee guided much of this research: Michael Coe, Richard Burger, and Ronald Spores, who first recorded Etlatongo as part of his survey of the Nochixtlán Valley. In Oaxaca, I owe a great debt to Marcus Winter for his advice and support in all stages of this research. He provided a constant stream of borrowed equipment, volunteers, and expertise in all aspects of Oaxaca archaeology. Support and advice in Oaxaca constantly comes from Cira Martínez López, Raul Matadamas,

Nelly Robles García, Roberto Zárate Morán, Susana Ramírez Urrea, and Robert Markens. Too many colleagues provided advice and commentary on various issues, or even read select passages, related to this manuscript to include here, but I do wish to thank John Clark, Elizabeth Ferry, Scott Hutson, Janet McIntosh, Richard Lesure, Javier Urcid, and Mark Varien.

In addition to providing a peer review, Jeffrey Quilter, general editor of the Case Studies series, provided the initial encouragement to write this volume. I also thank the editorial staff at Wadsworth who greatly facilitated the production of the book, especially anthropology editor Lin Marshall; assistant editor Analie Barnett; project manager Rita Jaramillo; and copy editor Linda Ireland of Buuji, Inc.

Finally, I thank my family and friends for their patience, encouragement, and indulgence for my long absences.

1/The Mixtecs of Oaxaca

An Introduction to Complexity, Interaction, and Formative Mesoamerica

Mixtec. Variations of this word refer to a land (the Mixteca Alta), a people (the Mixtec or Mixtecs), and a language (Mixtec). In the Mixteca Alta—the land of the Cloud or Rain People—Mixtec-speaking people have lived for millennia. While commonly used, Mixtec is a name given to these people by the Aztecs, an expansive empire in the century prior to the Spanish invasion based in the vicinity of modern Mexico City. Like many Aztec names for people and places, *Mixtec* approximates the indigenous term. The Mixtecs call themselves—Ñuu Dzavui, land or people of the rain (Jansen and Pérez Jiménez 2000). Naming confers great power. The Aztec names for many peoples and places remain prevalent today, as they were the ones first recorded by the invading Spanish beginning in 1519—a hegemonic legacy of the Aztec perpetuated by their conquerors.

The Mixtec region, in the southern highlands of Mexico, lies today primarily in Oaxaca state, as well as parts of adjoining Pueblo and Guerrero (see Figures. 1.1, 1.2). This region has been the nexus for the cultural developments distinctive to Mixtec culture, a thriving complex of competitive city-states referred to as *cacicazgos* or *señorios* at the time of the Spanish Conquest. While today erosion scars the land and imposing colonial churches dominate the landscape, the Mixteca Alta remains a sacred landscape to its inhabitants. Powerful spirit forces inhabit the mountains, lakes, and other natural features that surround Mixtec communities (Pohl et al. 1997). Mixtecs have long infused features on the landscape with sacred and historical significance. The Mixtec people, or at least the elite, originated from a tree within the Mixteca Alta, at Apoala; this tree died only recently. The Nochixtlán Valley, the location of the site of Etlatongo and the focus of this volume, is the largest valley in the Mixteca Alta.

Archaeologists have gained only a limited understanding of the long occupation of the Mixteca Alta by these people. A sequence that ties in with that known for Mesoamerica as a whole has been established (see Table 1.1). Much of what is known about ancient Mixtec culture is based on the final pre-Hispanic era, when indigenous artists created painted books prior to and after the arrival of the Spanish. These rich texts contain information pertaining to the last 600 years of pre-Hispanic

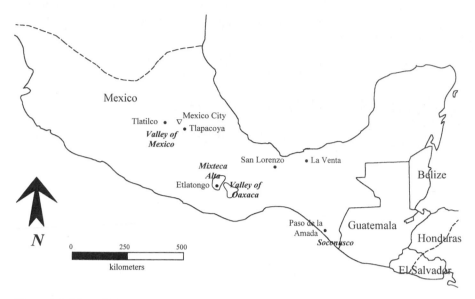

Figure 1.1 Map of Mesoamerica, showing the locations of many of the Formative period sites referred to in the text, as well as modern boundaries of countries included within Mesoamerica. Regions are indicated by boldfaced, italicized type. The dashed lines show the boundaries of Mesoamerica. © 2003, J. Blomster.

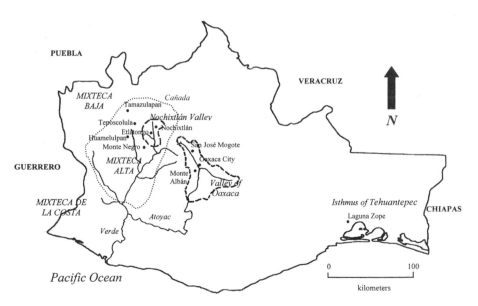

Figure 1.2 Map of contemporary Oaxaca state that shows river systems, the locations of the Valley of Oaxaca (indicated by dashed line), and the three foci of Mixtec culture: the Mixteca Alta (indicated by dotted line), the Mixteca Baja, and the Mixteca de la Costa. An additional dashed line demarcates the Nochixtlán Valley. Contiguous Mexican states are indicated by boldfaced, capitalized text. © 2003, J. Blomster.

TABLE 1.1   CHART COMPARING THE PREHISPANIC
CERAMIC CHRONOLOGIES OF THE VALLEY OF OAXACA
AND THE NOCHIXTLÁN VALLEY*

| Time | Period | OAXACA REGIONAL SEQUENCES | |
		Valley of Oaxaca	Nochixtlán Valley
1400	Postclassic	Monte Albán V Late (Chila)	Natividad
1200	Postclassic	Monte Albán V Early (Liobaa)	Natividad
900	Postclassic	Monte Albán V Early (Liobaa)	Natividad
500	Classic	Monte Albán IIIb-IV (Xoo)	Las Flores
	Classic	Monte Albán IIIa (Pitao)	Las Flores
200	Classic	Monte Albán II (Niza)	Ramos
A.D. 1	Classic	Monte Albán II (Niza)	Ramos
200		Monte Albán I Late (Late Pe)	Ramos
	Formative	Monte Albán I Early (Early Pe)	Yucuita
500	Formative	Rosario	Late Cruz
	Formative	Guadalupe	Late Cruz
850	Formative	San José	Middle Cruz
1150	Formative	San José	Middle Cruz
	Formative	Tierras Largas	Early Cruz
1500	Formative	Tierras Largas	Early Cruz

*Dates are placed in the context of the major periods defined for Mesoamerica: the
Formative, Classic, and Postclassic. Such is the contentious nature of Oaxaca
archaeology that disagreement remains on ceramic-based phase names. In this chart
I have combined traditional phase numbers, based on the Monte Albán sequence,
with newer phase names (indicated in parentheses). Adapted from Blomster
1998a:Table 2.1; Lind 1996; Martínez López et al. 2000:Table 2.

Mixtec history, and give voice to the ancient Mixtecs. In the final pre-Hispanic centuries, the Mixtecs are known for their polychrome ceramics and their mastery of
crafts such as gold working; they also appear in colonial documents. The earlier
achievements of the Mixtecs, however, have received less attention. The focus has
been on a period in their long history that dates back to half a millennia or more
before the Spanish Conquest.

    Although the genesis of Mixtec city-states can be seen in the first Mixtec urban
centers, the initial emergence of complex society in the Mixteca Alta has received

limited attention (Dahlgren 1966; Winter 1989). Because of the lack of data relevant to the preurban era in the Mixteca Alta, the Mixtecs have often been consigned a peripheral role in the initial emergence of complex societies in Mesoamerica (a cultural area including most of Mexico, Guatemala, Belize, and parts of Honduras and El Salvador; see the "Digging Deeper" section in this chapter). This book attempts to augment our understanding of the Mixtecs during the Formative period of Mesoamerica primarily through the themes of social complexity and interregional interaction.

THE ANTHROPOLOGY OF SOCIAL COMPLEXITY AND INTERREGIONAL INTERACTION

All archaeologists follow some kind of theoretical paradigm, no matter how much they may deny it. The days when archaeologists were "slightly reformed antiquarians," as one cultural anthropologist claimed (Kluckhohn 1940), have long since ended. The past is no longer considered self-evident. The normative view, that artifacts directly express cultural norms or values, has been largely abandoned. Although archaeologists are closely associated with fieldwork, they frame such excavations within a larger theoretical context. An overview of such major theoretical perspectives (Processualism, Postprocessualism, Marxism, etc.) is beyond the scope of this volume (see Johnson 1999). Rather than lashing myself too firmly to the mast of any one theory, I prefer a more eclectic approach. Here I explain the major issues investigated by the Etlatongo research and the theoretical perspectives that inspire and inform this research.

The two primary issues addressed in this volume are the development of social complexity and the development of interregional interaction; in addition, I explore the possible relationship between them. A third issue is changing occupation of the site through time. Interaction is viewed through a world systems perspective (Wallerstein 1974; Hall 1999), which has not previously been employed for Early Formative Mesoamerica. Both complexity and interaction are further informed through "practice" or agency theory (Ortner 1984) in order to promote an action-based theory of change, rather than a reactionary—and ultimately functionalist view—of change. The intellectual background of these concepts will be discussed here.

Social Complexity and Inequality

Equality in all aspects of human society is a social impossibility; various actors play different social roles depending on age, gender, and physical endowments (McGuire 1983; Miller and Tilley 1984). Egalitarian society may occur when as many positions of prestige exist as qualified persons to fill them, but all people may not be equal in every role. In rank society, status positions are limited so qualified individuals outnumber positions (Fried 1967). Rather than focusing on cultural complexity—all cultures are complex—I explore social complexity as it is linked with sociopolitical and economic inequality, recognizing that differences related primarily to age, gender, and aptitude may remain important. Both vertical (access to resources) and horizontal (individuals of equal rank but different professions) differentiation have an impact on complexity. For the Early Formative period, I focus on *relative* inequality (as opposed to absolute), where the hierarchical position of each person within a society can be defined along a dimension relative to all other individuals in society

(McGuire 1983:102). Regularization of inequalities and pervasive access restrictions lead to the formation of classes and formal social stratification (Fried 1967).

The differences between ranked and stratified societies center on different principles of status differentiation and are not always directly correlated with the political organizations of chiefdom and state (Sanders 1992). Ranked societies, in addition to limited status positions, feature ranking of lineages relative to each other. While ranked societies generally feature achieved status (determined by accomplishments in one's lifetime), they may also exhibit ascribed status, where one's status is determined by birth. One can have hours of fun determining if politicians, celebrities, or even friends can be best characterized by achieved or ascribed status—the two can obviously coexist. Ranked societies differ from stratified societies primarily in access to basic resources. In stratified societies, members have different access rights to subsistence resources, such as land and water; some members of the community become dependent on others (Fried 1967). In ranked societies, there may be different access to exotic or "prestige" goods, but all members of the community have access to basic resources. I define social inequality as differential access to goods, services, and knowledge within society; the introduction and systemization of these forces distinguish early complex societies from more egalitarian ones.

There are, of course, many ways of looking at social complexity. In a political approach informed by practice theory (see the text that follows), the goals of all social actors are the focus, as both prospective leaders and their followers benefit from the initial increase in social differentiation. Generosity of early aggrandizers, not coercion, has been suggested as critical in attracting followers, and as part of the reason why they surrender some of their own power (Clark and Blake 1994). Social inequality develops as a strategy within the parameters defined by the system, not as a response. In fact, the emergence of social inequality may be an unexpected result of certain individuals' pursuit of aggrandizement. Inequality is ultimately merely one expression of social complexity; it is not inevitable.

Of States and Stamp Collecting:
Levels of Early Formative Complexity

This volume focuses on the development of early social complexity, and displays a perhaps alarming lack of concern with trying to classify political organizations, generally divided into a variety of chiefdom types or states (see Haas 1982 for a useful summary). Some characterize the state as containing three to four levels of decision-making and administrative responsibilities (Wright and Johnson 1975). Following other researchers (see McGuire 1983), I have found "either/or" categories to be most useful for general discussion of larger issues, but should not be the focus of research. Attempts to pigeonhole societies as chiefdoms or states turn archeologists into "stamp collectors"—collectors of different societal types (Kluckhohn 1940). I prefer to focus on social transformation—the emergence of sociopolitical institutions and complexity in society—rather than categorization.

The formation of complex societies, particularly states, is traditionally viewed through two different perspectives: conflict theory and integration theory. Both theories form part of a rich body of literature in the social sciences. Karl Marx (1976), for example, formalized conflict theory, and integration theory is expressed in the writings of Emile Durkheim (1938). In conflict theory, epitomized in the work of Morton Fried (1967), the administrative institutions of states serve as a coercive mechanism to resolve intrasocietal conflict arising out of economic stratification. Integration theory, exemplified by Elman Service (1975), contradicts this view, positing the initial development of governing institutions as an integrative mechanism to coordinate and regulate the different parts of a complex society. Neither theory applies to all early states documented throughout the world.

Over the years, proponents of both perspectives have also offered monocausal explanations, focusing on one phenomenon such as control of hydraulic technology and projects (Wittfogel 1957). Monocausal theories lack explanatory power beyond perhaps one case, and even then the prestate priority of that feature can rarely be demonstrated. Although cross-cultural approaches have highlighted some interesting similarities, each has followed its own distinct trajectory, affected by both coercive and integrative elements. Here, I focus on one aspect—interaction—that may have played a role (along with other factors) in the development of social complexity in the Mixteca Alta.

Exchange and Interregional Interaction: An Overview

Societies rarely remain isolated, organic wholes, without contacts with external groups. Even prior to the formation of regularized exchange networks, material or information invariably comes into the group from the outside world. It has been a common failing of anthropology to view each society as an integrated and bounded system, separate and unique from other systems (Wolf 1982:4). Although it is more convenient to view the traits of a culture or site as unique and internally developed, interaction with external groups can have a range of impacts on social developments. This interaction can be both interregional (between regions) and intraregional (within the same region). Based on their research in Iran, Wright and Johnson (1975) cite intraregional rather than interregional trade and exchange as the major vehicle for the rise of the state, necessitating an effective integrative mechanism.

Interregional interaction can take many forms, from warfare to exchange. The term *exchange* is employed for both material goods, and for the communication of information and ideas; it is the primary form of interaction discussed in this study. Trade is just one form of exchange, defined as "the peaceful movement of goods among two or more societies" (Schortman and Urban 1987:49). The material goods left behind through exchange form an important part of the archaeological record and allow documentation of interaction. The nature and impact of the interaction, however, remain a matter of interpretation.

Exchange cannot be separated from the rest of society; it relates to other economic and noneconomic processes within society. In his pioneering study, Marcel Mauss (1954) identified gift-giving as a social act rather than just an economic one. Similarly, Bronislaw Malinowski (1922), in his research on the Trobiand *kula* system, saw the importance of this "trade" as more than economic. Rather than producing material profit, gift-giving forms a ceremonial exchange defining social relations and obligations between various participating ethnic groups.

Prestige Goods

In addition to subsistence goods, another type of material may be exchanged—prestige goods. The relation between prestige and other goods in society is quite complex. Prestige goods encompass items of rare or exotic raw materials not generally available and/or crafted by full- or part-time specialists with a high degree of skill or labor involved. In ancient Panama, elites exchanged small objects crafted from gold. These goods expressed sacrality due to the relative scarcity of the material and the specialized crafting, metaphors for sacredness and power (Helms 1979:75). In ancient Mesoamerica, a variety of material would fall into the category of prestige goods—such as greenstone/jade, portable sculpture, and shell—depending on the time and place. Unfortunately for archaeologists, only a small fraction of these materials are actually durable enough to be preserved.

In addition to exotic raw materials, technological innovations may also serve as prestige goods. For example, it has been argued that the first pottery in the Soconusco region (along coastal Chiapas) of Mesoamerica functioned for display purposes rather than cooking. Some scholars assert that these elaborately crafted ceramics, or the technology to manufacture them, served as prestige goods (Clark and Blake 1994). The exchange of prestige goods among elites in different regions often entails the circulation of a shared system of symbolism and iconography, which may have little impact on the vast majority of local material culture. These items may symbolize the kind of sacred knowledge or leadership role in community rituals that serves as an important noneconomic power base.

Studying Interaction: Evolution and Diffusion

Many of the concepts encompassed in looking at the impact of interaction on societies form part of a fundamental debate in anthropology that extends back to the conflict regarding the nature of the origin of human societies—the divide between evolutionists and diffusionists. Late 19th-century evolutionary anthropologists viewed culture change as internally driven, directional, and preordained, with the anthropologists' own society at the apogee of human development. Anthropologists developed ethnocentric sequences of cultural progress, which tracked the path of social development from savagery to civilization (Morgan 1877). Such scholars viewed contacts between societies as largely irrelevant; the individuals making these contacts were not important in the larger scheme of progress.

A response to evolutionism that arose in the early 20th century—diffusionism questioned the idea that all societies pass through the same stages. Rather than focusing on universal human culture, diffusionists concentrated on the development of individual societies, cataloging distinctive traits in order to understand their spread, and assuming that humans prefer to borrow rather than invent (Boas 1940). Many saw diffusion in a more limited scope, occurring primarily between contiguous areas, with an allowance for independent invention in isolated areas (Lowie 1917). One legacy of the diffusionist school is the concept of "culture area." In this sense, Mesoamerica is a culture area, loosely bound by exchanged and diffused ideas and luxury goods (Blanton and Feinman 1984:674).

Just like disco and any fashion trend preceded by the word *retro*, theories and models long out of favor in anthropology eventually come back into style (although they are generally modified by *neo* or *new*). Neoevolutionism gained special prominence during the so-called New Archaeology of the 1960s and 1970s. Much of this neoevolutionism was founded on the works of Julian Steward (1955), who proposed an essentially evolutionist and functionalist cultural ecological framework: Cultures adapt people to the environment. In this view, cultures in comparable environments would adapt in similar ways. The functionalist, inward-looking view of New Archaeology drew archaeologists away from issues of cultural contact. An outgrowth of this was the popularity of a so-called systems perspective (Flannery 1972). Based on a biological analogy, systems theory considered societies as living systems that tend toward equilibrium. In this perspective, trade is a subsystem linked with others within a society composed of functionally interrelated wholes. Its proponents saw systems theory as a corrective to rampant diffusionism, especially in Oaxaca where outside influences had been used to explain a variety of cultural phenomena (Bernal 1967).

Numerous problems have been noted with systems theory and ecosystem approaches (see Johnson 1999). By focusing on an entire population, such approaches obscure visibility of gender, class, and faction and neglect dynamics of change through internal negotiations; competition and factions within systems are overlooked (Brumfiel 1992). System approaches view political institutions as adaptive, failing to account both for change and active power building. Also, individual agents in systems theory appear as unthinking automatons. Furthermore, the complexity of the interactions and impacts with external agents often remains overlooked. In the following text, I briefly introduce two concepts that complement each other and provide a more holistic model.

WORLD SYSTEMS THEORY

There is a tremendous difference between world systems theory as first proposed by Immanuel Wallerstein (1974) and as deployed by archaeologists (Blanton and Feinman 1984; Hall 1999; Schneider 1977). Wallerstein developed world systems theory to analyze the transformations resulting from the emergence of capitalism in Europe during the late 15th and early 16th centuries and the process of European colonial expansion. In this Eurocentric model, the rise of capitalism generated a distinctive new form of cross-cultural interaction—a "world system"—larger than any political unit. Wallerstein applies the concept only to capitalist society, where he sees linkages as exploitative and primarily economic.

Three units comprise world systems: cores, semiperipheral areas, and peripheral areas (Wallerstein 1974:57, 100–102). Cores, characterized by strong political organization, accumulate surplus and extract raw materials from peripheries; they manufacture and trade items requiring skilled labor and technology. A semiperiphery may act as a "middle man" in trade between cores and peripheries, and serve as a buffer zone between them. Peripheries, characterized by weak political organization, are seen as providing the raw materials and unskilled laborers for the cores, while consuming products manufactured by the core. As formulated by Wallerstein, cores and peripheries have a hierarchical relationship; the interaction among them stimulates growth.

As is their wont, archaeologists have substantially modified Wallerstein's model to operationalize it for non-Western states and prestates. Relationships should not assumed to be formally exploitive on the part of the core. The interconnective linkages and relationships are of primary importance, including those mutually advantageous to both parties (Kristiansen 1987:82; Rowlands 1987:5). The primary focus on the core in Wallerstein's model overlooks the periphery's impact on the core, as well as the periphery's numerous responses to the core. Such relationships may be negotiated by the periphery to be advantageous on the local level. Rather than defining a periphery as dependent on the core, the relationship is better viewed as organic and interdependent (Kohl 1987). The impact of the core does not inevitably lead to the periphery's underdevelopment.

While Wallerstein rejects prestige goods exchange as a form of interaction with implications for social development, prestige goods have been especially important to archaeologists examining prestate societies, with some arguing that cores dominate peripheries through prestige goods networks, not subsistence goods (Brumfiel and Earle 1987:6; Frankenstein and Rowlands 1978:80–81). A more realistic view is that prestige goods systems exist in a variety of sociopolitical contexts, and that the relationships between the participants can range from simple differentiation to domination. The multivalent meanings of prestige goods, endowed with symbolic and ideological value, may be manipulated in rituals; materialization of ideology makes it possible to both control and extend influence. From this perspective, ideology constitutes one source of power within society (DeMarrais et al. 1996; Joyce and Winter 1996). The origin of an ideology or a symbol's meaning may be especially important, and the power of such symbols may increase with the distance associated with them (Helms 1979).

A World Systems Perspective

Rather than following world systems theory, which specifically implies and defines the nature of economic interdependencies, I employ a world systems *perspective* (Hall 1999). In my view, this is a paradigm or framework, not a theory, for viewing the interaction of autonomous groups linked into a larger system with certain expectancies. In many cases, such a framework may prove inappropriate for a given context. The inapplicability of the framework to a given case may also prove to be revealing. The interactions examined go beyond the economic, and the framework does not assume all polities are of a similar size or level of sociopolitical development.

I see such a perspective as useful because of its spatial nature, forcing archaeologists to transcend numerous boundaries in order to examine different levels or scales, and see a larger system in which their unit of analysis operates. While not defining *a priori* the exact nature of interaction, and not assuming a hierarchical relationship, it focuses on units of analysis as open systems, constantly engaged on some level with other entities. This dynamic perspective explores tensions and changes in relationships. I consider this perspective useful if it encourages a consideration of the complexity and dynamics of interregional interaction, exploration of the relationships underlying it, and attention to those interactions that preceded it. I do not see this as an inherently evolutionary perspective (*contra* Peregrine 1996).

One strength, or weakness, of such a perspective is its flexibility in dealing with scale. As long as this is carefully specified, a world systems perspective can analyze relationships between adjacent valleys, regions, or even emerging cores competing in different subvalleys within the same region. Unfortunately, it is often difficult to define boundaries of the system's components (Jeske 1999). Boundaries between social units are rarely sharply delineated, and can be delimited in ways not coterminus with a single community, such as flow of subsistence goods, information, prestige goods, and/or political interaction (Hall 1999). This perspective also hides the behavior of individual agents. This problem, at least, can be partially resolved by incorporating practice theory into this perspective.

PRACTICE THEORY: PUTTING PEOPLE IN THE WORLD

Alternate strategies for social transformation focus on forces beyond the solely economic, following cultural anthropologists' observations that many people outside of contemporary Western society talk more about religion and politics than modes of production (see Leach 1965). The early Spanish missionaries documented the extremely religious nature of the Mesoamerican people in the 16th century; to focus only on economics ignores important components of these societies (Coe 1981). Clearly economics is integrated with other spheres of action. An emphasis on the symbolic nature of interregional interactions and prestige goods involved, informed by practice theory, may provide a more balanced perspective.

A practice perspective (also referred to as praxis or action theory, although with some differences in application) explores the relationships of human actors within larger systems. Individuals are social actors, with self-interested goals and strategies; they make decisions in relation to multiple factors and other agents (see Barth 1966; Giddens 1979; Ortner 1984). Social actors are players in history, rather than primarily pawns played by it (Gailey and Patterson 1987:6–10). In the case of social complexity, one engine for change is self-interested competition among ambitious actors, often with exotic prestige goods that are important for enhancing and manipulating social roles (Clark and Blake 1994:17; Helms 1979).

Practice theorists focus on social identities and behavioral strategies, rather than details of individual lives (some attempts at practice theory are essentially reworkings of "Great Man" theories that celebrate the accomplishments of important historical individuals). Action is largely in terms of pragmatic choice and decision making as well as active strategizing or practice (Bourdieu 1977). Neither random nor unrestrained, actions occur within a structural context, constrained by both the biophysical and sociocultural environment. The system both determines and is affected by action, as human social activities continually recreate the system (Giddens 1984; Ortner 1984). Actors have a number of different social identities for particular situations; different identities can be used amongst local clients as well as in contacts between spatially dispersed groups involved in interregional interaction (Schortman 1989:54).

Interregional Interaction and Impact on Social Complexity

A world systems perspective informed by practice theory can show how agents and communities articulate with a larger system. An ethnographic study of Irish and Greek farming communities' responses to closer relationships with the European Union revealed both strategic and active roles farmers play in making production decisions limited by this world system (Shutes 1999). A practice-oriented perspective examines how prestige goods articulate through goal-oriented behavior of political actors constrained and enhanced by involvement in a larger system (Schortman and Urban 1996:107–108). The impact of prestige goods varies depending on time, place, and situation. While archaeologists often deploy stylistic analysis to prove the presence of exotic prestige goods and interregional interaction, I explore a more robust method—compositional sourcing—in Chapter 6.

When a small segment of the population accumulates nonlocal goods through interregional interaction, their near exclusive access to these exotic goods allows them to compete more effectively for prestige within the community; they can exchange the prestige goods for subsistence products, or use them to pay social debts, or to reward loyal followers. Prestige goods can be used in social reproduction, or display and legitimization. Agents remove prestige goods from circulation through burial or caches, further increasing their rarity. In the process of becoming mediators of exchange through control over foreign goods, local "elites" consolidate and extend their power within society, increasing preexisting tendencies toward class differentiation (Paynter 1981). The increase in social complexity that may intersect with interregional interaction forms an important component in the development of early chiefdoms or states.

FORMATIVE MESOAMERICA: OLMECS AND ZAPOTECS

In order to explore the major issues of this research, the larger context of Early Formative Mesoamerica must be understood. I review the two groups most likely to have interacted with the Mixtecs of Etlatongo. The Olmecs of the Mexican Gulf Coast played a highly variable role throughout parts of Formative Mesoamerica. Similarly, the Zapotecs in the adjacent Valley of Oaxaca developed a chiefdom centered at San José Mogote. Contact between Zapotecs and Mixtecs has been documented during the Late Formative and Early Classic periods (see Chapter 7), but earlier interaction remains unclear. I analyze the nature of possible interaction through a world systems perspective. Chapter 2 focuses on Etlatongo and the Mixteca Alta.

The Olmec

Until the recent discovery of the chiefdoms of the Mokaya people along the coast of Chiapas, archaeologists considered the Olmec of the Gulf Coast of Mexico to be the earliest complex society in Mesoamerica. Despite this important new research, the Olmec society that crystallized approximately 1200 B.C. at San Lorenzo, some 300 years after the early Mokaya chiefdoms, remains at a fundamentally different level of complexity. While this book is *not* about the Gulf Coast Olmec—a story that has been told many times and awaits additional revision (see Grove 1997)—I explore the nature of Olmec civilization, as their role in interregional interaction and influence in regional politics are essential to this volume. I follow the majority of scholars by using the term *Olmec* to refer to the Gulf Coast archaeological culture, and *Olmec-style* as a suite of attributes expressed on artifacts and art that may or may not be connected to the archaeological Olmec.

Due to the spread of stylistically similar artifacts, the Olmec are often seen as a horizon—in fact, two chronologically successive horizons (see Coe 1977; Grove 1993). Problems abound with applying the horizon concept to the Olmec, as the distribution of Olmec-style materials is not consistent across Mesoamerica, nor is there evidence of a rapid spread, *contra* the definition of an archaeological horizon (Willey and Phillips 1958:33). For convenience, I employ these horizons, but primarily as chronological markers. Different manifestations of material culture mark both horizons. The first Olmec horizon, the San Lorenzo horizon from approximately 1200 to 850 B.C., features distinctively carved ceramic vessels and white-slipped baby-face figurines. Data from a ritual site, El Manatí, at a spring located close to San Lorenzo, suggest that the Olmec civilization may actually have started hundreds of years earlier (Ortiz and Carmen Rodríguez 1994). Regional ceramic sequences contemporaneous with the San Lorenzo horizon are presented in Table 1.2. Named after a later

DIGGING DEEPER—WHAT IS MESOAMERICA?

Anthropologists created the concept of Mesoamerica, not geographers. It includes southern Mexico (beginning north of Mexico City), all of Guatemala and Belize, and the western portions of Honduras and El Salvador (Figure 1.1). It encompasses a region where people have shared cultural features for millennia. Although this is not the place for an exhaustive list (see Coe and Koontz 2002), such cultural features—while varying somewhat through time and space—include: both a sacred calendar of 260 days and an approximate solar calendar of 365 days; reliance on agriculture, particularly corn, beans, squash, and chilies; monumental architecture; blood sacrifice and ball games as part of ceremonies; and extensive knowledge of writing, mathematics, and astronomy. The legacy of Mesoamerica continues today, where people still speak these languages and employ innovations created by their ancestors.

Archaeologists traditionally divide Mesoamerican prehistory (or history prior to the arrival of the Spanish, as most Mesoamerican cultures could write or otherwise preserve their history through oral tradition and narratives) into four major periods (see Table 1.1).

At the beginning of the Archaic period (not included in Table 1.1), people lived as hunters and gatherers; by 1800–1500 B.C., the end of this period, farmers lived in villages. (Unless otherwise noted, dates in this book are uncalibrated; calibrated dates will be indicated by "cal.") The subsequent Formative period (subdivided into Early, Middle, and Late) is the focus of this book. During this period, villages throughout Mesoamerica experienced growth and different degrees of increasing social complexity. The first chiefdom probably arose among the Mokaya of coastal Chiapas early in the Formative period, while an even more complex society, the Olmec, developed along the Gulf Coast of Mexico by 1200 B.C.

The appearance of large urban centers across Mesoamerica marks the Classic period, with initial dates shifting depending on which region of Mesoamerica is the focus. In the Valley of Oaxaca, Monte Albán became a state. During the Classic period, states waxed and waned throughout Mexico and the Maya region. More fragmented political structures, with some exceptions, characterize the Postclassic period. The Aztecs dominated the final century of the

Gulf Coast center, the subsequent La Venta horizon endures from 850 to 500 B.C. Stylistically, this horizon is associated with whiteware vessels with double-line break designs, distinctive jade sculptures, and bas-relief carvings with narrative scenes that appear both at La Venta and at sites with possible contact (Grove 1984). The La Venta horizon will not be further considered.

The "Olmec heartland" lies along the Gulf Coast in the Mexican states of Veracruz and Tabasco (Figure 1.1). This region features great agricultural productivity, with much regional variation. The high agricultural productivity of the lands near San Lorenzo serves as the basis for several theories about the rise of the Olmec (Coe and Diehl 1980; Stark 2000). The region is poor, however, in mineral resources; sources for obsidian, iron-ore, good chert, and serpentine and jade (prized by the Olmec) are not located near Olmec centers. The major source of basalt, the stone employed in most of the carved monuments, lies in the Tuxtla Mountains, 50 miles away from San Lorenzo.

Postclassic period, representing a brief (and truncated) fluorescence of a Central Mexico–based empire. The Spanish invaders imposed a colonial regime throughout most of Central America. Despite devastation by massive epidemics and genocide, the indigenous population survived this onslaught with some pre-Hispanic elements intact or blended in a kind of synchronism with those of the Spanish.

Archaeologists devise regional chronologies primarily based on ceramics. Alfonso Caso and his colleagues created the chronology for Oaxaca (Table 1.1) based on ceramics excavated from the Zapotec center of Monte Albán (Caso, Bernal, and Acosta 1967). Stylistic parallels were critical in defining the contemporaneous sequence in the Mixteca Alta (Spores 1972). Founded by 500 B.C. approximately in the center of the three subvalleys that form the Valley of Oaxaca, Monte Albán rises on a hill some 1,300 feet (or 400 meters) above the valley floor. As Monte Albán became a city of 10,000 to 20,000 people, evidence of both the calendar and writing appear. A program of low-relief carved stones, known as the *danzantes* (dancers) because of their contorted limbs, was installed (Figure 1.3). Rather than illustrating ancient salsa dancers, some of these slabs probably represent warriors, sacrificed captives, city founders, and other important ancestors (Urcid 1998).

A state emerged in the subsequent period (Monte Albán II), with Monte Albán at the top of a complicated administrative settlement hierarchy within the Valley of Oaxaca. The city grew, centered around a main plaza (Figure 1.4) constructed through massive modification of the hilltop. Houses generally lay on artificial terraces extending from the hill slopes. While it has been argued that the Monte Albán II state was aggressive and expansionist, the impact of Monte Albán on adjacent regions remains a source of lively debate (Zeitlin and Joyce 1999). Ultimately during Monte Albán III, this city covered approximately 7 square kilometers and was occupied by 30,000 people. The importance of Monte Albán in terms of ceramics will be evident in the definition of a new ceramic phase in the Mixteca Alta—the Yucuita phase—approximately contemporaneous with early Monte Albán I (see Chapter 7).

The Olmec Problem

Although many Olmec problems exist, most scholars focus on the Olmec's level of sociopolitical complexity and the Olmec's impact on other contemporaneous regions (see Diehl and Coe 1995; Sharer and Grove 1989). Much of the problem relates to the initial definition of the Olmec. Long before the location of the archaeological Olmec had been identified through efforts such as Matthew Stirling's 1942 excavations at La Venta, museum curators had recognized objects in the Olmec style from sites throughout Mesoamerica. Objects without context that resembled those recovered from the La Venta excavations, and later at San Lorenzo, were lumped together as Olmec (Blomster 1998b; Grove 1997). Thus, an implicit and *a priori* connection developed between Olmec-style artifacts and the Olmec culture. Scholars sowed the seeds of the Olmec problem, which have blossomed into a contentious debate.

Figure 1.3 Alternating rows of large vertical slabs and small horizontally oriented ones (the photograph includes two of each type still in situ), the low relief sculptures (referred to as the danzantes) exhibit themes of warfare and ancestors. Early occupants of Monte Albán created these sculptures.

Figure 1.4 The Main Plaza of Monte Albán took shape around the same time as the formation of the Zapotec state centered at this hilltop site. This view, taken from the top of the South Platform, shows the expansive Main Plaza, with Mound J in the foreground and the North Platform in the background.

TABLE 1.2   EARLY FORMATIVE CERAMIC
CHRONOLOGIES FROM ACROSS MESOAMERICA*

Nochixtlán Valley	Valley of Oaxaca	Laguna Zope (Isthmus)	San Lorenzo (Gulf Coast)	Tlapacoya (Basin of Mexico)	Soconusco (Chiapas Coast)
Middle Cruz	San José	Golfo	San Lorenzo	Ayotla	Cuadros Cherla
Early Cruz	Tierras Largas	Lagunita	Chicarras Bajío Ojochi	Nevada	Ocós Locona
					Barra
	Espiridión				

*Shading represents the San Lorenzo horizon. Roughly similar ceramic phases are correlated based primarily on shared ceramic attributes, with fine-tuning provided by radiocarbon dates. Adapted from Blomster 1998a:Table 2.2; Flannery and Marcus 1994:Figure 1.2; Clark and Pye 2000.

Olmec art differs from contemporaneous and later Mesoamerican art styles in formal qualities of shape, line, and space, and has an iconographic content absent from the limited imagery created earlier (Coe 1965:747). In fact, little iconography and no monumental art exist prior to the San Lorenzo Olmec. A curvilinear naturalism, "realistic" in the depiction of human, animal, and imaginary creatures, distinguishes Olmec art (Figure 1.5). This style appears on a variety of media. Olmec iconography on pottery represents highly stylized and abstract versions of themes more fully expressed in monumental sculpture. Scattered throughout Mesoamerica, fragments of ceramic vessels and figurines bearing Olmec-style designs constitute the material evidence at the heart of this debate.

The debate over the impact of the Olmec has become increasingly polarized into two perspectives. The nuclear-linear or so-called mother-culture school views the Olmec as a precocious group in terms of social complexity, synthesizing and generating cultural traits essential to all later Mesoamerican societies (Clark and Pye 2000). In both the Gulf Coast heartland and other regions, stylistic and iconographic expressions of the Olmec style appear on ceramic vessels, figurines, and stone carvings. Many objects referred to as "Olmec style" actually are not; this category needs to be cleansed of much excess baggage (Blomster 2002).

The lattice development model or so-called sister-culture school views the Gulf Coast Olmec as just one of many Formative groups utilizing a shared symbol set with other regions of Mesoamerica, without any priority in developing these symbols or attainment of a greater level of social complexity (Flannery and Marcus 1994). An important component of this debate is the level of sociopolitical complexity of the Olmec (thus the reason why definitions of types of social organization are so important—and problematic). While some mother-culture advocates identify it as a state, the sister-culture proponents—most of whom work outside the Gulf Coast—interpret the Olmec as a chiefdom. Minimally, the Olmec comprised several independent, non-egalitarian societies with an agriculturally based subsistence system, monumental construction projects, intrasocietal differentiation, complex religion, long-distance exchange, and a distinctive art style (Diehl 1989:18–19). These two conflicting views will be assessed by a brief summary of the first Olmec center—San Lorenzo.

Figure 1.5 The most recently discovered colossal head at the Olmec center of San Lorenzo, Veracruz. Excavated by Ann Cyphers, Head 10 stands 1.8 meters (5.9 feet) high. Weighing many tons, the ten San Lorenzo heads depict leaders of this important site.

The San Lorenzo Olmec: Big Heads

San Lorenzo, the earliest Olmec center, is located along the Coatzacoalcos River in modern Veracruz state. The riverine system surrounding the site provided important resources as well as a vital communication/transportation network. The central portion of San Lorenzo sits atop a salt dome, a plateau that rises 150 feet above the surrounding lowlands, extending nearly a mile north to south (Figure 1.6). The ancient inhabitants dramatically altered this plateau, and the result has been characterized as one of the largest works of early monumental architecture in Mesoamerica, involving massive amounts of human labor (Coe and Diehl 1980; Cyphers 1997). Evidence of occupation of the site goes back several hundred years before the emergence of full-blown Olmec civilization around 1200 B.C.

A recent survey of both the site and surrounding area demonstrates the enormous size of San Lorenzo (Cyphers 1996). San Lorenzo may have covered more than 690 ha (hectares), while the majority of contemporaneous villages across Mesoamerica were 5 ha or less, with exceptional villages in the 20–70 ha range. San Lorenzo, as a regional center, sat atop a complicated administrative hierarchy of different site types (Symonds 2000). Organized to efficiently exploit its hinterland, San Lorenzo delegated some of its administrative and ritual functions to lesser centers at strategic loci along waterways. Monumental art found at key nodes along rivers and at secondary centers graphically represents the integration and control over this region

© 2003, J. Blomster

Figure 1.6 The San Lorenzo plateau, featuring the site's center constructed on a modified salt dome, requiring enormous labor. The Red Palace is located on this massive platform.

exercised by San Lorenzo. The Olmec at San Lorenzo had achieved a high degree of sociopolitical complexity; the amount of both internal and regional control has led some Gulf Coast archaeologists to identify San Lorenzo as an incipient state (Symonds 2000).

Colossal stone heads epitomize the Olmec, and San Lorenzo has yielded the most heads (ten) of any Olmec site. The heads vary in size, with some measuring over 10 feet in height and weighing many tons (Figure 1.5). Each head has different facial features and headdresses, and probably depicts a specific person—an Olmec ruler. Features in the headdress, such as the probable depiction of ilmenite beads in Head 10's headdress (see Figure 1.5), may show lineage or family affiliation. That individuals were able to express their power through these monumental sculptures is suggestive of status differentiation, as does the control of labor involved in bringing the basalt to San Lorenzo. While some consider the Olmec a chiefdom, no known chiefdom matches the degree of public labor and specialized skill of the Olmec (Stark 2000:35). Other diagnostic artifacts of the San Lorenzo Olmec are distinct ceramic styles—called Calzadas Carved, Limón Incised, and Xochiltepec White (see Chapter 6)—as well as solid and hollow figurines that replicate on a small scale the physiognomy on monumental art (Blomster 2002).

An additional line of evidence suggestive of true social stratification at San Lorenzo is the so-called Red Palace (Cyphers 1996). While leaders at other sites lived in houses not fundamentally different from the reed and mud houses of everybody else in the village, Olmec elites lived in a large structure with plastered and painted walls, large basalt column roof supports, a stone aqueduct, and step coverings. Further, crafts under elite control were concentrated along the Red Palace, where Ann Cyphers has exposed a basalt workshop. No contemporaneous structures comparable to the Red Palace have been documented in Mesoamerica.

The Olmec and Their Neighbors

While agriculturally productive, the Olmec heartland lacks many minerals and raw materials, providing one economic motivation for Olmec interregional interaction. Material in the Olmec style in a variety of media extends south to El Salvador. For evidence of San Lorenzo horizon interaction, I focus on the presence of Calzadas Carved or Limón Incised pottery and Olmec-style figurines and other portable art.

No one characterization typifies Olmec interaction; it varies with each region. For example, in the Soconusco region of Chiapas, the Mokaya appear to have been radically transformed by their Olmec contact—a process referred to as "olmeciza-tion" (Clark and Pye 2000). Archaeologists document the movement of Olmec people, objects, and knowledge into this region, beginning in the Cherla phase (Table 1.2), a time of rapid change in both ceramics and clay figurines. It appears that the Mokaya adopted Olmec ways as part of an effort of the elite to solidify their legitimacy through foreign contacts. In the subsequent Cuadros phase, the actual presence of Gulf Coast Olmec has been postulated (Clark and Pye 2000:234). The figurine assemblage becomes almost exclusively seated Olmec images, Calzadas Carved pottery appears, and pottery from San Lorenzo arrived in the region (Neff and Glascock 2002). Politically, a major reorganization of the local chiefdoms occurred. Villagers largely abandoned previously important centers, such as Paso de la Amada, and settled in a large chiefdom centered at San Carlos. The change in the material record is clear and dramatic, indicative of the strong impact of this interregional interaction.

The Early Formative Valley of Oaxaca

Much of what is known about the Formative occupation of the Oaxaca Valley results from the efforts of the University of Michigan project "The Prehistory and Human Ecology of the Valley of Oaxaca." Through research at ancient villages such as Tierras Largas, near the center of the valley (Winter 1972), and San José Mogote, in the Etla or northwest branch (Flannery and Marcus 1994), the foundations of entire houses and public structures have been documented; these will be discussed in more depth in Chapter 4.

Elements of the San Lorenzo horizon appear during the San José phase in the Oaxaca Valley (Table 1.2). In the preceding Tierras Largas phase, 19 sites have been identified; all but one average 1 to 3 ha in size, with perhaps 4 to 12 families. One village, San José Mogote, was already more than twice as large as the others (Marcus and Flannery 1996:78). With houses being virtually identical, the communities appear to have been roughly egalitarian. At San José Mogote, however, evidence for public structures and achieved status in burials has been documented (Marcus and Flannery 1996:84).

During the San José phase, differences between San José Mogote and other villages increased dramatically. The central part of San José Mogote expanded to 20 ha (70 ha including outlying barrios), with a possible population of 1,000 (Marcus and Flannery 1996:106). Some archaeologists believe a chiefdom developed at the site, which sat atop a three-tiered settlement hierarchy (including small hamlets with no specialized architecture; some scholars who only count the sites with possible public architecture would call this a two-tiered hierarchy). Villagers devoted approximately 2 ha of San José Mogote to small public buildings (Flannery and Marcus

1983:54). Two carved stones, each under a foot in length, come from one of these public structures. Social inequality lay along a continuum, with some houses some-what more elaborate than others, and with some differences in burials goods. Archaeologists discovered evidence of craft specialization, including shell and iron-ore mirror production (Wheeler Pires-Ferreira 1978:83–85). Olmec-style objects appear in the Valley of Oaxaca during this time.

Oaxaca and the Olmec: From Emulation to Peer Polity

Scattered Olmec-style objects have long been associated with the state of Oaxaca, such as a large jadeite "ax" sculpture in the American Museum of Natural History with an unspecified Oaxaca provenience (Covarrubias 1946:Pl.5). Ignacio Bernal (1971) labeled Oaxaca as "Colonial Olmec" because it sent luxury products to the Olmec heartland—a periphery in world systems terminology. Thirty years later, the pendulum has now swung the other way; the Olmecs are seen as having absolutely no impact on ancient Zapotec society (Flannery and Marcus 1994).

The appearance of Olmec-style materials during the San José phase coincides with settlement changes in the Valley of Oaxaca. The dramatic growth of San José Mogote into a nucleated center occurred while some other early villages in the Oaxaca Valley decreased in population (possibly abandoned) during the San Lorenzo horizon (Winter 1994:136). A whole suite of utilitarian and ceremonial items, some of them with Gulf Coast linkages, appears for the first time in Oaxaca during the San Lorenzo horizon. The ceramic changes include new forms, slips, and decorations, including Olmec-style designs (see Chapter 6). Solid ceramic figurines, probably employed in domestic rituals, had previously depicted primarily females. During the San José phase, figurines frequently represent males, while female figurines become increasingly stylized (the identification of male and female is a biological one, based almost entirely on secondary sexual characteristics, as artisans rarely depicted geni-talia). Some male figurines feature Olmec-style faces, with cylindrical heads and heavy jowls, with a white/buff slip. Other materials with a possible ceremonial importance were introduced as well, including conch-shell trumpets and turtle-shell drums, both of which may be from the Gulf Coast (Flannery 1976c:335). Prismatic obsidian blades and stingray spines, employed in autosacrificial bloodletting rituals, also appear (Marcus and Flannery 1996:62). Overall, exchange increased dramati-cally during the San José phase.

Initially, scholars interpreted the appearance of Olmec-style symbols in Oaxaca in a functionalist vein, with exchange and exotic symbols having an "adaptive value." It was in the interest of the Oaxacan elite to participate in this relationship and emulate the behavior of these distant elite (Flannery 1968). This perspective, which recognized limited Olmec priority in some traits, has been referred to as the emulation model. More recently, the Olmec-style symbols often referred to as "were-jaguars" and "fire-serpents" have been reinterpreted as distinct expressions of ancient Zapotec beliefs. Due to differential distribution of these motifs both within and between sites, Joyce Marcus (1989:169) suggests they represent two separate descent groups. I critique this interpretation in Chapter 6.

Once Olmec priority behind such symbols was dismissed, the emulation model was substantially revised into a "peer-polity" model (Flannery and Marcus 1994:385–390). The revision concludes that the Gulf Coast Olmec and the Valley of

Oaxaca Zapotec operated at the same level of sociopolitical development during the San Lorenzo horizon. Contemporaneous groups shared Olmec-style designs; since no one region contains the full spectrum of motifs, no one region originated the style. Ultimately, the Valley of Oaxaca data have been employed to support a sister-culture approach. I critique this view in Chapter 8.

Of Cores and Peripheries in Formative Mesoamerica

The issue of whether the Olmec constitutes a chiefdom or state level of sociopolitical development has become largely typological, a problematic situation due to both various definitions of *state* and *chiefdom* as well as associated archaeological correlates. I prefer to compare sociopolitical complexity of contemporaneous San Lorenzo horizon groups rather than being sucked into this typological quagmire. One definition provided for the Olmec (Diehl and Coe 1995:11)—a hierarchical society dominated by a small elite with political territories, long-distance trade in exotic goods, and a distinctive (probably the first) known art style and symbol system—by itself is insufficient to identify the Olmec as a state, which is usually defined based on administrative hierarchies (Wright and Johnson 1975). Recent discoveries of both a well-organized settlement hierarchy and extensive internal organization support the interpretation of San Lorenzo at least as an incipient state, and as having been at a different level of sociopolitical complexity than any contemporaneous site.

The primary goal of this review has been to determine if a "core" can be identified for contemporaneous San Lorenzo horizon communities in the Gulf Coast and Oaxaca. In terms of a world systems perspective, San Lorenzo can be seen as a core within the Gulf Coast, although more data from contemporaneous Gulf Coast sites are needed to determine how far this influence extended, within the possible core, on both a political and ideological level (see Arnold 2000). In economic terms, data are needed to determine if this was an extractive relationship, with San Lorenzo obtaining raw materials from the Gulf Coast hinterlands and exporting finished or labor-intensive goods. Ultimately, even a loose definition of a core may not characterize the Olmec—a topic that is considered in Chapter 8.

The data derived from the Etlatongo excavations can be used to assess if the San Lorenzo Olmec can be considered a core on a larger, macroregional level. I examine both style and physical properties of ceramics from the Mixteca Alta and Valley of Oaxaca to determine if materials moved between the Gulf Coast and Oaxaca, as well as between the Nochixtlán and Oaxaca valleys (Chapter 6). The Early Formative Mixteca Alta has often been consigned to the status of a "periphery" in the sense that it "lagged behind" the Valley of Oaxaca in terms of social complexity and interregional interaction (Drennan 1983:50; Marcus 1989:194). Considering that the San José Mogote chiefdom at best only controlled part of the northwest Valley of Oaxaca, it is clear from the outset that political domination is not likely. The Nochixtlán and Oaxaca valleys will be compared in terms of both social complexity and interregional interaction to determine the nature of their relationship, and the larger impact of macroregional processes in these valleys. Ultimately, locations in contact with the Olmec may have been much more than "peripheries." An assessment of this model appears in Chapter 8.

2/Designing Research for the Nochixtlán Valley
Or Why I Went to the Mixteca Alta

Undoubtedly, the most frequent questions posed by both students and colleagues regarding the Etlatongo investigations focus on the selection of that site for research: Why Etlatongo? How did you decide where to excavate at the site? Such questions form a frequent refrain. Having provided a general overview of Mesoamerican civilization, particularly of the Early Formative period, I now turn to a more detailed consideration of the landscape and culture of the Mixteca Alta. By summarizing what was known about this region prior to the 1992 fieldwork, I will demonstrate what this site in particular offered that would allow investigation of the issues presented in Chapter 1.

The fieldwork schedule at Etlatongo differed from the norm. Many academic archaeologists conduct projects piecemeal, with a month or two of fieldwork a year completed over a long span of time. The academic calendar dictates such a schedule. I conducted the Etlatongo fieldwork as a graduate student, and thus was free of the vexing restraints of a semester system. A single six-month field season at the Etlatongo site in 1992 produced all the data presented in this volume. Analysis of the materials recovered during archaeological fieldwork invariably consumes more time than the actual excavations; it is estimated that one day of fieldwork generates five days of laboratory work and analysis. In the case of Etlatongo, there have been four major seasons of laboratory work: 1992, 1993, 1998, and 2002. The need for additional analyses of all classes of material recovered in the field still looms over the principal investigator's head. While artifact analysis lacks the sense of adventure and excitement associated in most people's mind with the actual process of "digging," the interpretations presented throughout this volume would not be possible without this analysis.

THE MIXTECA ALTA AND THE NOCHIXTLÁN VALLEY

The Mixteca Alta is actually one of three cultural and geographic subregions occupied today by ethnically Mixtec people. Combined, Mixtecs occupy 50,000 square kilometers. The other two subregions, the Mixteca Baja and Mixteca de la Costa, are both lower in elevation than the Mixteca Alta and have been less intensively investigated archaeologically (Figure 1.2). Early Spanish colonists named all three regions, which are separated from each other by rugged mountains. The Mixteca Baja lies to the north and west of the Alta, between 1,600 to 1,700 meters above sea level, while elevations in the Mixteca de la Costa, which extends south to the Pacific Ocean, range from sea level to 750 meters above sea level.

The Spanish Conquest and centuries of colonization by Spanish-speaking people have had a heavy impact on all three Mixtec regions. The effects on Mixtec language and culture have been catastrophic. The Spanish forced many villagers into planned communities, often not far from the original Mixtec village. Early Catholic priests made a concerted effort to exterminate all vestiges of native religion, and large cathedrals were built in major towns throughout the Mixteca Alta (see Figure 2.1). As in many other parts of Latin America, this cultural holocaust only partially succeeded, with elements of ancient belief and ritual often maintained and combined with elements of the introduced Christian beliefs. The Mixtec language itself has been under constant assault and is no longer commonly spoken, at least in front of strangers, in many of the major towns, such as Nochixtlán, in this region. Continuing efforts by Mixtecs to preserve this rich heritage and language highlight their resistance on many levels to a vast array of hegemonic forces.

Land and Resources

The Mixteca Alta is located in the Mesa del Sur, the southeast extension of the Sierra Madre del Sur, and harbors human occupations at elevations ranging from 1,650 to 2,500 meters above sea level. Mountains, some rising over 3,000 meters above sea level, surround the Mixteca Alta. The Mixteca Alta incorporates approximately 6,000 square kilometers in the drainages of the Upper Balsas and Atoyac-Verde rivers. Approximately 80% of the Mixteca Alta is comprised of mountains; only 20% consists of narrow, irregular valleys (Smith 1976:24). This landscape includes abundant microenvironmental diversity.

As the largest valley in the Mixteca Alta, the Nochixtlán Valley encompasses 250 square kilometers of generally flat land. This valley would have been one of two important routes into the Valley of Oaxaca from the northeast. From the Puebla Valley, one would go through the Nochixtlán Valley to enter the Etla arm of the Valley of Oaxaca. Important minerals that could have been exploited in the Nochixtlán Valley include: salt, basalt, limestone, processed lime, chert, gold, and mica (Spores 1984:12). Gold, the most famous export associated with Mixtec craftspeople, was exported from the Mixteca Alta only during the Postclassic period, the final fluorescence of Mesoamerican cultures prior to the arrival of the Spaniards (see Chapter 1).

Farming has been practiced in the Nochixtlán Valley for three millennia. This is the only valley within a 50-kilometer radius that can support continual year-round cultivation. Because of the high altitude, however, temperatures may limit the year-round planting of frost-sensitive crops such as maize (Kirkby 1972:54). Another deterrent to agriculture is the dramatic erosion and soil degradation, both natural and anthropogenic (due to human impact), which this valley has experienced for millennia (Joyce and Mueller 1997). Although in the pre-Hispanic past the Mixtec combatted the erosion with a unique terrace system, referred to as *lama-bordo,* erosion continues to circumscribe the area available for agriculture (Figure 2.2). Recent

Figure 2.1 The 16-century Spanish church at Teposcolula. The size of this structure appears out of proportion to the current size of this village; these churches were placed at the locations of important pre-Hispanic centers, many of which have seen precipitous population declines. On the left of the photograph is an "open chapel," used by Spanish friars for the conversion of the indigenous population. The entrance to the attached convent is on the right side of the photograph.

efforts to reinstate some of these ancient Mixtec erosion control devices offer hope for the future.

Dramatic rainy and dry seasons mark the agricultural cycle in the Nochixtlán Valley. The rainy season usually lasts from May to October. While it generally rains once a day during the rainy season in the Valley of Oaxaca, Nochixtlán Valley rain is not as regular. Several days of torrential rains may be followed by overcast days, with episodic drizzling, as well as weeks devoid of any rain. During the recording of the final stratigraphic profiles at Etlatongo in July and August of 1992, however, two to three weeks passed without rain, and villagers in Etlatongo noted the rainy seasons of 1996 and 1997 were both unusually dry. Thus, harvests are not always assured. In parts of the Nochixtlán Valley, villagers practice extensive irrigation.

The current flora and fauna of the Nochixtlán Valley bear little resemblance to those available in ancient times. An oak-pine forest once covered the valley, the clearing of which probably began after the first permanent settlements were established (Smith 1976:10). Clearing and more intensive agriculture associated with Mixtec urban centers exacerbated the pronounced erosion visible in Figure 2.2. Farming and the gathering of firewood have had a dramatic impact on the vegetation of the valley. While the Nochixtlán Valley formerly contained a variety of wild fauna, including deer, turkey, dove, quail, rabbit, fox, squirrel, coyote, and small felines,

© 2003, J. Blomster

Figure 2.2 View of the Nochixtlán Valley looking south from the Classic period hilltop site of Yucuñudahui. The small spur in the center foreground of the photograph exhibits the dramatic erosion so prevalent in this region.

extensive overhunting of the Nochixtlán Valley has led to the scarcity or extinction of most native faunal species. The virtual elimination of many species in the Nochixtlán Valley is more pronounced than in any other portion of the Mixteca. During the close to seven months of survey and excavation at Etlatongo, I spotted no wild animals larger than small rodents or songbirds, except for a dead skunk, in the portion of the site closest to the modern town. A few wily rabbits and other small mammals still occupy portions of a hill included within the boundaries of both the modern town and the site of Etlatongo.

The Nochixtlán Valley lies primarily in a geologic formation referred to as the Yanhuitlán Beds, composed of red to purple calcareous shales. This material, high in calcium carbonate, was uncovered as "bedrock" or "sterile" at the base of the majority of units during the 1992 field season at Etlatongo. The Yanhuitlán Beds form fertile soils, but because of their softness, they are very susceptible to erosion and natural forces. Cretaceous limestones dominate the ridges to the northwest and northeast of the valley, while the conglomerate Jaltepec Beds are located to the south and east; these provide suitable clays for pottery manufacture (Kirkby 1972:5–13).

The site of Etlatongo is located in the Nochixtlán Valley north of the confluence of the Yucuita and Yanhuitlán rivers (Figure 2.3); these two rivers are part of the upper Río Verde basin. The modern town of San Mateo Etlatongo is situated an additional kilometer to the west of the site. This land remains some of the most fertile and productive in the Mixteca Alta. Most of what I define as the site of Etlatongo is under constant cultivation by residents of modern San Mateo Etlatongo, composed primarily of a Spanish-speaking *mestizo* population. A com-

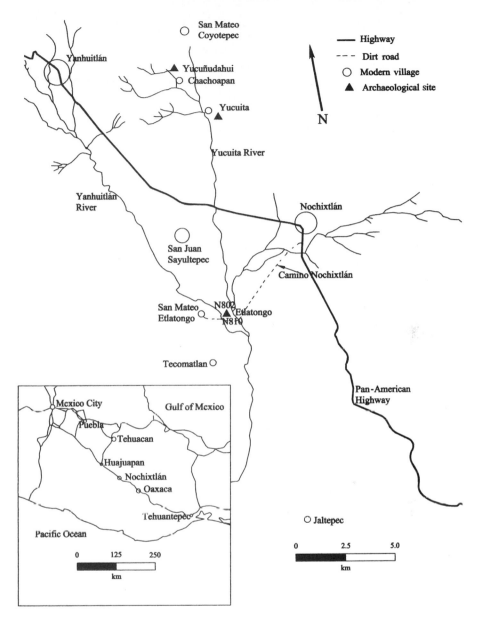

Figure 2.3 Map showing the location of the site and modern town of Etlatongo within the Nochixtlán Valley. The circles representing modern towns are approximately proportionate in size to the towns' populations. Inset map shows major towns, cities, and transportation routes through southern Mexico. A recent "superhighway" (not included on either map) has been built through this area. Adapted from Blomster 1998a; Spores 1972. © 2003, J. Blomster.

bination of migration to the United States and Mexico City for work, increasing interaction with other, primarily Spanish-speaking communities, and various political and economic tactics by both federal and state governments collaborate in the declining proportion of Mixtec speakers throughout parts of the Nochixtlán Valley.

RESEARCH IN THE MIXTECA ALTA

Any archaeological project begins with extensive background research into the area to be investigated, including geologic and environmental variables. A major component of this research involves the examination of previous projects in the area. The contributions of archaeological and ethnohistorical (utilizing colonial maps and documents) research provide windows into the lives and societies of the ancient occupants of the Mixteca Alta. The rich oral traditions of contemporary Mixtec communities also yield insights that can provide analogies with both colonial and pre-Hispanic communities of this region. As with modern towns and cities throughout the world, 16th-century Mixtec and Zapotec towns often had border disputes. Of importance to anthropologists, arguments supporting each side were presented to Spanish officials, often accompanied by maps of a town's boundaries. Previous archaeological projects also provide critical data. Unfortunately, archaeological investigations in the Mixteca have not been as numerous as or on the scale of those in the nearby Valley of Oaxaca; we know far less about ancient Mixtecs compared with contemporaneous Zapotecs. Similarly, early colonial documents for Oaxaca are far less abundant than those for Central Mexico cultures such as the Aztecs.

Nonetheless, important ethnohistorical documents have survived to the present day. These were written primarily by Spanish missionaries and officials, and contain valuable data about pre-Columbian life in the Mixteca Alta. Fray Francisco de Alvarado published the first dictionary of the Mixtec language in 1593; this manuscript provides tantalizing clues to the Mixtec perception of self, culture, and society. The Mixtecs themselves produced documents, either prior to the Conquest or in association with colonial officials in the years after the Spanish occupation of Oaxaca. These documents include maps (*lienzos*), often utilized as evidence in the border disputes previously mentioned, and painted picture books known as codices.

Archaeology of the Mixteca Alta

In a sense, Mixtec archaeology remains in its infancy, despite a history of sporadic investigation stretching back over 60 years. The Nochixtlán Valley has received the most attention by investigators within the Mixteca Alta, although research at sites such as Huamelulpan and its associated valley is contributing to an understanding of other portions of this region (Crohn 1998; Gaxiola González 1984; Winter 1989). Through the considerable research of Mexican, European, and North American scientists, a framework has been developed for the cultural history of this region, upon which the next stage of research is being built. The laudable efforts of both archaeologists and ethnohistorians have firmly established the Mixtec in their own historical tradition within larger Mesoamerican culture (e.g., Jansen and Pérez Jiménez 2000; Spores 1984).

Much of what supposedly typifies pre-Hispanic Mixtec culture is based on the final era of Mesoamerican civilization, the Postclassic period. The Postclassic Mixtec have become known primarily for their codices—painted pictorial manuscripts on bark paper (*ámatal,* in Nahuatl, the Aztec language) or animal skin (usually deer hide)—which depict genealogies and histories of the rulers of Mixtec kingdoms, as well as information regarding the calendar and various deities. Individuals are named by a combination of their names and the calendar day on which they were born, such as 8 Deer in Figure 2.4a, plus often an iconic "nick-name" (for 8 Deer, this was Jaguar Claw, the symbol for which can also be seen in Figure 2.4a). Unlike Maya and Zapotec writing, Mixtec scribes related events in these codices primarily through illustrations, with glyphs reserved for dates, names of people, and places. Because Mixtec is a tonal language, scribes engaged in phonetic substitutions in writing place names—a kind of rebus or "puzzle" writing (Troike 1990). Scholars have calculated that these codices depict a time span of 600 years (Rabin 1981).

These manuscripts paint a rich tapestry of Mixtec life and history, illustrating marriages, alliances, and murders. The machinations of Mixtec caciques would give even contemporary politicians pause. The great Mixtec leader 8 Deer was a warlord/politician associated with the town of Tilantongo (close to Monte Negro in a small side valley of the Nochixtlán Valley). In Figure 2.4a, a priest pierces 8 Deer's nose, probably in the late 11th century, at a place that may have symbolically represented the great Postclassic Central Mexican city of Tula, or simply a generic name for a place invested with great sacred power and authority. By this action and the affiliation with such a legendary place, 8 Deer attempted to legitimize his claims to power and enhance the prestige of his lineage. Through outright conquest and intermarriage, 8 Deer controlled numerous Mixtec communities before being killed by a rival.

Famed as the creators of the Tomb 7 treasures at the Valley of Oaxaca city of Monte Albán, the Mixtecs were known throughout Postclassic Mesoamerica as master artisans due to their skill in crafts such as gold-working. The Aztecs appreciated, and appropriated, the skill of Mixtec goldsmiths. Due partially to the richness of Postclassic culture in terms of material objects and documents, Mixtec scholarship often focuses on this period.

The antecedents of this complex, intrigue-filled Postclassic Mixtec society of small city-states (or *cacicazgos*) prior to the arrival of the Spanish are of interest here. One approach to examining the development of the earliest Mixtec settlements is to travel back in time to the initial stages in the formation of a discreet Mixtec language, reconstructed primarily through glottochronology (see the "Digging Deeper" section in this chapter). This development would not have begun prior to the split of the Mixtec language from Zapotec, a divergence that has been hypothesized as starting as early as 3700 B.C., but was probably quite advanced by the final major divergence, from the Trique language, between 1300 and 500 B.C. (Marcus 1983:6; Winter et al. 1984:79–83).

Ancestors: Nochixtlán Valley Archaeology and Mixtec Interaction

Interaction and intergroup contact has always been a theme in the study of Mixtec culture. For years, the Mixtec were thought to have been an invading or intrusive force that overwhelmed the Postclassic Zapotecs in the Valley of Oaxaca, spreading their material culture and influence throughout this region in the final years before the Conquest—a view that is now being reassessed (Winter 1989:94). The Mixteca Alta prior to this pre-Conquest fluorescence, however, has often been characterized as a "cultural backwater," with the Mixtecs being either the passive receivers of interaction or inhabitants of a region too remote to allow them to be active participants (Paddock 1966:176). Life in the Mixteca was assumed to be a combination of

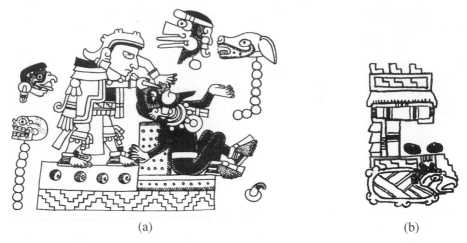

(a)   (b)

Figure 2.4 Two views from Mixtec codices: (a) a scene from the Codex Zouche-Nuttall,
illustrating the nose-piercing ceremony of 8 Deer, an important Mixtec leader. His name,
depicted by a deer head and eight dots, can be seen directly above him. His nickname,
Jaguar Claw, can be seen below his feet. (b) the place glyph for Etlatongo, taken from the
Codex Selden. A temple, illustrated in profile, exhibits stairs leading up to the main surface,
where two black beans rest. Adapted from Codex Nuttall 1975:52; Smith 1988: Figure 1b.
© 2003, J. Blomster.

provincial Teotihuacan (the largest city of Classic Mesoamerica, located in Central
Mexico) and Monte Albán ways. In world systems terminology, the early Mixtec
existed on the periphery of Mesoamerican cores.

This portrayal of Mixtec culture can be traced to the first site in the Mixteca Alta
to be systematically excavated over a series of field seasons—Monte Negro (Caso
1938, 1942; Acosta and Romero 1992). Alfonso Caso, famed for his many seasons of
fieldwork at Monte Albán, directed excavations during the late 1930s at this Late
Formative site. Perhaps due to Caso's emphasis on Monte Albán, the site of Monte
Negro was interpreted in a way so it did not contribute to a distinctive Mixtec cultural
trajectory. Rather, the importance of this site was viewed in relation to the emergence
of the Zapotec state in the Valley of Oaxaca. Caso interpreted Monte Negro, a site with
public architecture, as an early version of Monte Albán—a sort of experiment or trial
run leading up to the establishment of Monte Albán and the social complexity represented by its foundation in the Valley of Oaxaca. More recently, Monte Negro has been
interpreted as a Monte Albán outpost, as part of the hypothesized expansion of that
Zapotec state (Flannery 1983). In both interpretations, developing Mixtec sociopolitical complexity is largely ignored. The Mixtecs constituted either an earlier, primitive
stage of development "leading" to the Monte Albán complex, or were incorporated
into it as a frontier. This view of the Mixteca Alta as a periphery of larger, more complex centers—particularly those in the Valley of Oaxaca—has been projected back by
many scholars to the Early Formative as well (Drennan 1983; Marcus 1989).

Focusing on the Nochixtlán Valley, only episodic archaeological research
occurred after the work of Caso and his colleagues in the 1930s at both Monte
Negro and the Classic period site of Yucuñudahui (see Spores 2001 for a useful
overview). While the pioneering Eulalia de Guzmán informally surveyed much of

---

DIGGING DEEPER: WHAT IS GLOTTOCHRONOLOGY?

Glottochronology is a technique of linguistic comparison; it has been utilized to examine the divergence of distinct languages from an earlier, ancestral language (Fernández de Miranda, Swadesh, and Weitlaner 1960). For example, the ancient hunter-gatherer ancestors of the Zapotecs and Mixtecs once spoke a common language, an ancestral Proto-Otomanguean language (the name of the language family to which both of these modern language groups belong). Theoretically, the order of separation of given languages can be examined back through time, primarily through the investigation of cognate, or similar, words retained in related languages. A basic principle is that those languages with the most similarities have been separated most recently. Both temporal and geographic components must be considered. The greatest similarity is generally seen between neighboring dialects in a region; differences usually increase with geographic distance. These similarities can be traced back in time, recognizing that language change follows specific patterns (Marcus 1983:5). Both the degree and duration of separation must be assessed. The linguist Morris Swadesh (1967) composed a "basic vocabulary" word list and examined retention rates among historically known languages. Dates of separation of languages are given only in terms of "minimum" centuries for separation before the present. This technique is also useful for identifying "loan" words, which are words that are introduced into a language from elsewhere.

---

the area in the 1930s, the first systematic large-scale investigation of the Nochixtlán Valley did not occur until the 1960s. Survey of the Nochixtlán Valley, directed by Ronald Spores of Vanderbilt University, began in June of 1966 and continued until July 1971. This survey was the first to systematically document all prehistoric, historic, and modern communities in the region. It was a diachronic study guided by the direct historical approach, which assumes substantial continuity between past and present communities. The project explored evolving patterns of community organization and intercommunity relations between the Nochixtlán Valley and other regions of Mesoamerica (Spores 1972:2). The Vanderbilt project documented 176 sites in the Nochixtlán Valley, and created the basic chronological sequence that remains in use, albeit with revisions (see Table 1.1). In addition to the pedestrian reconnaissance, there was also limited archaeological testing.

Spores identified 18 sites with Cruz phase occupations. (As noted in Chapter 1, the Cruz is an occupational phase defined by ceramics roughly equivalent to the Early and Middle Formative periods.) Eight of these sites have been interpreted as intensive occupations; approximately half a dozen of these were Early and Middle Cruz hamlets and villages, dating from 1500 to 800 B.C. (Spores 1972:169, 1984:18–19). Cruz phase sites are generally small and are located in three different positions in the landscape: on lower ends of piedmont spurs reaching toward river's edge; stream confluences; and low rises/hill-piedmonts in the central portion of the Valley. The survey identified Etlatongo, the site upon which this volume focuses, as an important early village.

Yucuita and the Early Cruz

The scattered Early Cruz hamlets of the Mixteca Alta probably approximated the size of those better documented through excavation in the Valley of Oaxaca—roughly 1 to 3 hectares in size and occupied by 4 to 12 families (Marcus and Flannery 1996:78; Spores 1972). In both regions, one village exceeds the standard hamlet size, suggestive of a two-tier site hierarchy (with small, undifferentiated hamlets as the lower tier). The concept of site hierarchy refers to relative size as well as connections between communities in a region; some villages had economic, political, or religious functions that had an impact on smaller sites. Ideally, different sizes and types of sites can be defined based on surveys and excavation. By examining architecture and associated artifacts, archaeologists correlate differing power and administrative structures between villages. Larger villages in such a hierarchy, with a larger suite of public space, often controlled access to exotic goods and public ritual. Just as one early village in the Valley of Oaxaca, San José Mogote, appears to have been twice as large as any other contemporaneous settlement in the valley, one Early Cruz village in the Nochixtlán Valley—Yucuita—was also substantially larger than any hamlet in the region. Yucuita, situated in a fertile pocket of the northern Nochixtlán Valley, is located approximately 10 kilometers north of Etlatongo (Figure 2.3).

Yucuita has received extensive archaeological investigations, beginning with two excavation units placed by the prolific Caso in 1937. As a result, Yucuita has provided the majority of Early Formative data for the Mixteca Alta prior to the 1992 Etlatongo excavations. These data come from the survey and excavations of Spores (1972, 1974), the intensive survey of the Yucuita sector of the Nochixtlán Valley by Patricia Plunket (1983), and the long-term project in the Mixteca Alta under the auspices of the Regional Center of Oaxaca, Archaeology Section (a division of the Mexican National Institute of Anthropology and History, or INAH), initiated in 1974 by Marcus Winter (1982), who conducted excavations at Yucuita from 1976 to 1980, as well as more recently. Nelly Robles García (1988) excavated a series of Late Formative houses at Yucuita (see Chapter 7).

The Early Cruz phase occupation of Yucuita was surprisingly large compared to contemporaneous Tierras Largas phase hamlets in the Valley of Oaxaca. It appears the early village covered at least 10 to 20 hectares and probably consisted of 40 households containing approximately 200 people (Winter 1994:133). Higher estimates, ranging from 90 to 120 households, have also been suggested, although these figures are based primarily on surface survey (Plunket 1990; Winter 1982). During the Early Cruz at Yucuita, villagers engaged in some limited contact with people in the Tehuacán and Oaxaca valleys, based on pottery similarities. Obsidian, a volcanic glass manufactured into various tools, also would have entered the site through interregional exchange (Winter 1984, 1994). During this time, the Yucuita sector of the Nochixtlán Valley featured eleven hamlets and one large community at Yucuita; this large village may have been divided into two sections and contained 81% of the population of the sector (Plunket 1983:343). Thus, by the Early Cruz phase, there appears to be two site types present in the Nochixtlán Valley.

A dramatic shift in population occurred in the transition from the Early to Middle Cruz phase, when the mean population estimate for Yucuita significantly declines (Plunket 1983:341). Archaeologists found a few Middle Cruz sherds (fragments of broken pottery vessels; American archaeologists often reserve "shard" for glass fragments) in one feature at Yucuita in the 1970s, and additional material appeared at a separate location at the site in 1993, indicating at least two Middle Cruz households at the site (Winter 1996, personal communication). The large Early Cruz village of Yucuita was reduced to a small Middle Cruz hamlet, possibly of two to ten households. The saga of Yucuita, however, does not end in the Middle Cruz. The ancient village experienced a substantial population increase during the Late Cruz and into the Ramos phase (see Figure 2.5), so by 200 B.C., Yucuita had become a center of approximately 3,000 people (Winter 1982:12).

Etlatongo: More than a Hill of Beans

I am often asked how I found the site of Etlatongo—how I knew where to look for a location that could address my research issues. In fact, I had nothing to do with its discovery. Although I do not want to make the original Vanderbilt recorders of the site feel old, I was less than a year old when that survey project of the Nochixtlán Valley began. As will become clear, however, the 1992 Etlatongo Project benefited greatly from the previous research at the site. This research first indicated this would be an appropriate site at which to address questions regarding Early Formative interaction and social complexity, and secondly informed the creation of the research strategy for the 1992 Etlatongo Project.

Large sites such as Etlatongo, occupied for many centuries, are not difficult to find in southern Mexico. Due to both the density and duration of occupation, features and artifacts reflective of ancient village life abound on the surface. These remains have not been covered with large layers of natural materials, such as from flooding or volcanic episodes. Many of these sites, or at least portions of them, have been occupied nearly continuously. This situation contrasts with other parts of the world, such as the northeastern United States where a camp (or even larger sites) occupied 2,000 or 3,000 years ago may be buried by close to 3 meters of naturally deposited debris since the site was abandoned (Kreber 1997). Large sites such as Etlatongo have remnants of platform mounds still present on the surface. Indeed, it is often difficult to travel any distance within the modern state of Oaxaca and not encounter an archaeological site. Parts of the Mixteca Alta that currently appear sparsely populated were once covered with sites ranging from small hamlets to thriving cities.

Although first documented in the field as part of the Vanderbilt project, there had already been speculation that Etlatongo was an important Postclassic Mixtec center due to the appearance of its place glyph in Late Postclassic/Early Conquest period codices. A place glyph (see Figure 2.4b) symbolically represents a city or smaller locale such as a ceremonial center (Byland and Pohl 1994). In some cases, place glyphs have been correlated with modern villages and/or archaeological sites, due to either prominent topographic features incorporated into the place sign or Mixtec names for places that reflect the symbols chosen for them in the codices. The Codex Mendoza, a copy of an Aztec tribute list with Spanish glosses, is especially useful, as place signs are indicated along with the Nahuatl (Aztec language) name of the village. This document allows the identification of the Postclassic Aztec names for villages throughout Oaxaca; in many cases, the names may represent a Nahuatl translation of what the villages were actually called by their inhabitants on the eve of the Spanish Conquest. It remains unclear how far back such data can be stretched to identify earlier communities within Oaxaca.

© 2003, J. Blomster

Figure 2.5 A large platform construction, initiated in the Late Formative period, at the site of Yucuita. A staircase provides access to important structures that lay atop this massive platform.

The Etlatongo place glyph, originally thought to mean "hill or place of beans" (Smith 1973:92), is a direct glyphic representation of the Nahuatl name for this site (Figure 2.4b). Many villages in Oaxaca have Nahuatl names because of the presence of the Aztecs in this region, although the nature of the Aztec presence and the extent of their control in Oaxaca varied. The Etlatongo glyph shows several black beans arranged in what has traditionally been interpreted as a "hill" or "place" glyph. This glyph has been reinterpreted (Smith 1988) as "temple of the beans," as part of a process of determining if these place signs refer to a topographic location or an architectural feature. This place sign occurs in both the Codex Selden and the Codex Muro.

The Vanderbilt survey documented two sites, separated by less than half a kilometer of land, near the modern town of San Mateo Etlatongo (Spores 1972:150–153). Spores labeled one site (N802 in his project's sequence) as the "Cerro [hill] de Etlatongo," located on the hill 2 kilometers north from the center of the town (Figure 2.6). This hilltop site was estimated to encompass 2 square kilometers, including mound systems with exposed stonewalls and plaster floors. The site was interpreted primarily as a Classic (Las Flores phase) and Postclassic (Natividad) occupation; it appears to have been the Postclassic town of Etlatongo, one of seven kingdoms during the Natividad phase in the Nochixtlán Valley.

Spores identified the second site (N810) nearly 500 meters to the south of the hill's base, labeling it the South System, or "Etlatongo entre los rios [Etlatongo between the rivers]," reflecting the fact that the Yanhuitlán River bounds it to the west and the Yucuita River to the east (see Figure 2.3). Spores documented heavy

© 2003, J. Blomster

Figure 2.6 Looking north to the Etlatongo hill, taken from the southeastern edge of Area 3, close to the dirt road leading to the site from the Pan-American Highway. Even from this distance (over one kilometer!) Mound 4-1 is visible atop the hill, on the right side of the photograph. The 1992 project demonstrated that all of the land between the road and hill constitutes part of the Etlatongo site.

concentrations of ceramics from the Formative and Early Classic periods, although the survey did not distinguish between Early and Late Cruz materials. In addition to the presence of mounds, a massive earth and stone platform was identified adjacent to the Yanhuitlán River—probably one of the largest single construction projects undertaken in Formative Mesoamerica. Based on field observations of this mound, Spores (1972:173) interpreted it as "a hydraulic construction . . . submerged under more than eight meters of later Ramos phase constructions."

Limited archaeological testing by Roberto Zárate Morán eventually followed the Vanderbilt project in 1980 as part of the larger project in the Mixteca Alta initiated by the Regional Center of Oaxaca/INAH mentioned earlier. Excavating only in the so-called South System, he established seven 1 × 1 meter units on the south side of a modern road bisecting a massive mound at the site. The construction of roads through large mounds appears to be, unfortunately, a common phenomenon throughout Mexico. Employing the road cut as the north of the four walls of each unit, Zárate Morán placed test pits according to features and artifacts visible in the profile exposed by the road.

The units extended just beyond three meters in depth, and Zárate Morán defined four basic strata for all seven units. He interpreted the strata as representing Cruz and Ramos deposits; two of the strata yielded a series of radiocarbon dates. Based on these data, the deepest deposits were interpreted as being occupied during the Early and Middle Cruz periods, from 1390 to 850 B.C., although no primary deposits of Early Cruz material were reported (Zárate Morán 1987:111). Although the units were nestled too close together to provide much horizontal coverage of the site, this research exposed stratified Formative remains and recovered scattered ceramic sherds with Olmec-style designs. The characteristics of six of the published ceramics from the 1980 excavations resemble the San Lorenzo horizon traits described in Chapter 1.

Unfortunately, five of these six sherds are listed as found "out of context," thus limiting possible interpretation based on provenience. The concept of context, which is critical in archaeology, refers to an artifact's vertical and horizontal location and its association with a cultural feature, such as a house floor or platform fill. An artifact discovered in what is called a primary context, defined as the original deposition of an artifact (an example would be an artifact still in place where first dropped on the floor of a house), is more meaningful than one that was redeposited and used as platform fill and/or disturbed by recent agricultural activities. Ultimately, these out-of-context sherds provide tantalizing but limited information.

Why Etlatongo?

The available information led to the selection of the Nochixtlán Valley and specifically Etlatongo for several reasons. Depiction of the Mixteca Alta as peripheral to Early Formative sociopolitical developments seemed to contradict the evidence already available, and quickly drew my attention. Despite what appeared to be a large Early Cruz village at Yucuita, the perceived lack of exotic materials and foreign symbols, partly a reflection of a much smaller database than that available for the Valley of Oaxaca, had fostered the impression that elements of social complexity remained largely undeveloped in the Early Formative Mixteca Alta. While not explicitly discussed in terms of a world systems perspective (see Chapter 1), scholars had portrayed the Nochixtlán Valley as "lagging" behind and not taking part in (or being peripheral to) the sociopolitical transformations experienced in the Valley of Oaxaca (Drennan 1983:50). Scholars also had consigned the region as peripheral to the interaction and movement of Olmec-style objects characteristic of the San Lorenzo horizon (Marcus 1989:194). Despite Zárate Morán's discovery of several Olmec-style designs on ceramic sherds at Etlatongo, as well as Olmec-style jadeite pieces from an undocumented site in the Mixteca Alta (Clark 1994b:129), some scholars continued to characterize this region by the absence of Olmec-style motifs and interaction networks. As I looked for a site to satisfy my research interests, my attention turned to Etlatongo. The fact that this issue had not been specifically addressed in the Mixteca, except by negative evidence, warranted closer examination.

The presence of a fairly large Early Cruz village at Yucuita suggested that an initial site hierarchy had developed as early in the Nochixtlán Valley as in the Valley of Oaxaca. The precipitous decline in population during the Middle Cruz at Yucuita seemed difficult to explain by examining solely the Yucuita data. Where did this population go? Perhaps the answer lay elsewhere in the Nochixtlán Valley. Both Spores's survey and Zárate Morán's excavations indicated Etlatongo might have had a larger Middle Cruz population than Yucuita. Was this village, in fact, comparable in size to Early Cruz Yucuita? If so, this could indicate complex social and political processes underlying the ascendancy of this village over Yucuita.

The published Olmec-style sherds from Etlatongo lacked the quantity, variety, and context necessary for understanding the broader patterns and systems of interregional interaction and development of social complexity. Their presence, however, suggested that other samples could be found, perhaps some associated with features or other discrete contexts at the site. Thus, Etlatongo seemed to have the potential for examining issues of both social complexity in the rise of a large village and interregional interaction.

RESEARCH DESIGN: GREAT EXPECTATIONS

Now that the reader is familiar with both the issues to be explored and the data available from the Mixteca Alta that attracted my attention, the question of the selection of Etlatongo has been answered. It is time to turn to the research design. How does one approach a site about which very little is known, and where later occupations may have covered materials from the earliest settlement? While there are many approaches to the past depending on both the goals of the investigator and the audience, the answer to this question for an anthropologist involves some form of archaeological testing.

Archaeological Data: Sherds, Stratigraphy, and Beer Bottles

Archaeological excavation must be designed to facilitate the understanding of anthropological issues. The research must have larger relevance, rather than being nothing more than a glorified treasure hunt or an activity in which the staging of the fieldwork is conducted as some hoary archaeological tradition—a ritual performance in which the excavations become the goal or focus rather than simply a research technique. The fieldwork must address specific issues that provide a focus for the research; otherwise, the investigator falls prey to a promiscuous collecting of data, in which the deluge of information threatens to or actually does—overwhelm the unwary researcher. These larger issues have been discussed earlier.

Unfortunately, the nature of the archaeological beast ensures a veritable Pandora's box of disturbed stratigraphy. Recently deposited glass beer bottles are encountered, recorded, and processed along with the data directly pertaining to the issues being investigated. Fieldwork invariably produces a plethora of both relevant and extraneous information. This is especially the case with a multicomponent site such as Etlatongo, located near a modern town. Because the archaeological record cannot be replaced once it is excavated (archaeologists are, after all, the only anthropologists who kill their informants), all data exposed during fieldwork must be properly recorded. Thus, the research strategy is crucial; its design must address specific issues while allowing for enough flexibility to navigate situations that develop in the field, and must incorporate procedures for responsibly documenting all material encountered. Even the staunchest supporters of an "explicitly scientific" or "positivist" approach in archaeology recognize the need to reconfigure both methodology and hypotheses while in the field to more accurately reflect the kinds of data that are being recovered (Watson, LeBlanc, and Redman 1971:14). By explicating both the original research strategy and the subsequent redesign of this strategy, I hope to show how the research design, rather than being a static entity, evolved and adapted to the situations specific to the fieldwork. At every stage of the 1992 Etlatongo Project, the research design was informed and directed by an increasing amount of information.

Any project must start with clearly defined research objectives or hypotheses that will be tested and supported or rejected by data collected during the investigations.

It is not possible to ever completely confirm a hypothesis, but it is possible to select what appears to be the most compelling hypothesis for the data currently available. Few archaeologists would claim their interpretations represent exactly what happened in the past. An invigorating debate in archaeology questions whether archaeologists simply impose their present onto the past and whether there is an "objective" past (Hodder 1986; Johnson 1999). There appears to be some consensus that a more reflexive archaeology may allow researchers to be more aware of their biases and to critically examine many of their assumptions—both conscious and unconscious.

In forming hypotheses for the Etlatongo project, the important contributions made by the research of both Spores and Zárate Morán at the site were crucial. As detailed previously, Spores had documented two separate sites near the modern town of Etlatongo, one of which exhibited only Classic and Postclassic occupations, while the other contained primarily Formative (Cruz and Ramos phases) remains. The 1980 test pits reinforced the presence of Middle Cruz materials in this southern sector.

Spores noted the extreme depth of deposits at the southern sector, cautioning that to excavate Early Cruz material at Etlatongo would probably "necessitate the removal of eight meters of deposit" (Spores 1972:174). This alarming prophecy derived from observation of the mound by the Yanhuitlán River, which is primarily post–Middle Cruz in construction, and therefore largely outside of the 1992 Etlatongo Project parameters. Zárate Morán's excavations appeared to have yielded Middle Cruz remains extending not much below 3 meters in depth. Unfortunately, this is still a considerable volume of material to be excavated, especially when the strata above the Cruz deposits contain features and surfaces representing later occupations that must be documented. In the Valley of Oaxaca, researchers have benefited from working at sites with shallow deposits (often less than half a meter) covering Early Formative remains, and have employed large excavation units that focus on horizontal exposure. This type of horizontal excavation—robotage—allows for the investigation of entire houses, surfaces, and associated features. From what had been recorded about Cruz deposits at Etlatongo, they appeared largely buried under extensive later occupations. As will be seen in the text that follows, this contributed to the emphasis incorporated into the 1992 research design on sondage, or deep vertical test pits, rather than a reliance primarily on robotage.

Research Objectives

Three main objectives of the research design guided the 1992 excavations at Etlatongo:

1. Explore the development of intrasite social complexity at Etlatongo during the Formative period. This objective encompassed demographic growth and change in sociopolitical complexity primarily during the Early and Middle Cruz phases at Etlatongo.
2. Determine the participation of Etlatongo in Early Formative interaction, the changes in this interaction through time, and its impact on developing sociopolitical complexity at Etlatongo. Applying a world systems perspective, the research would determine if Etlatongo and the Nochixtlán Valley could best be characterized as a core or a periphery (or neither). In terms of interregional interaction, the focus was on possible interaction between Etlatongo and the

nearby Valley of Oaxaca, as well as between Etlatongo and the Olmec of the Gulf Coast of Veracruz.

3. Understand the site chronology and occupational boundaries at Etlatongo, and how they changed through time.

Due to the unexplored nature of the majority of the site, the Etlatongo Project assumed responsibility for documenting the full sequence of habitation and its extent at both sites recorded by Spores, defining the approximate boundaries of the site for each time period.

From the first two objectives, a hypothesis emerged: The initiation or increase in interregional interaction had an impact on the nascent development and trajectory of Early Formative sociopolitical complexity at Etlatongo. This was a time marked by exchange networks that connected distant parts of Mesoamerica. One of the items exchanged during this time period is obsidian, a volcanic glass with great potential for source derivation due to the well-defined and discrete nature of Mesoamerican sources. Ceramics constitute an additional line of data often used to assess intersite relationships, although often through stylistic grounds rather than compositional analysis. Ceramics and obsidian obtained from the 1992 excavations would be subjected to instrumental neutron activation analysis to assess production and exchange at the site. This procedure will be explained in Chapter 6.

The Objectives Operationalized

I operationalized the three research objectives for testing in the field—the fieldwork was designed in a way to most effectively provide data for them. Planning fieldwork involves making decisions on both where and how to explore based on available time and budget considerations. Archaeologists must determine if the project is more amenable to survey (pedestrian surface examination) versus subsurface (excavation) testing, realizing that both methods have advantages and problems. There is also a basic division between the techniques defined earlier as sondage and robotage (see Chapters 4 and 5). In order to estimate the site's boundaries throughout the phases of the Formative period and beyond (the first and third objectives), an approach that archaeologically sampled the extent of the Formative period and later occupation at Etlatongo was necessary. Such a strategy involves a combination of surface survey and a program of subterranean sampling through sondage or small test units (Figure 2.7). This approach samples different portions of the site, striving for broad coverage, which is best achieved through numerous test units—each circumscribed in dimensions to provide more units across the landscape (as opposed to larger but fewer units). The goal of the test units was to reach bedrock or sterile soils (material deposited by natural forces prior to human occupation).

The two primary objectives of assessing social complexity and interaction warranted a research strategy that included robotage, in order to find cultural materials associated with meaningful stratigraphic levels and features (see Figure 2.8). This would provide an actual cultural context for artifacts, rather than having them be isolated finds in small test units, the strata of which are often difficult to interpret without broader horizontal exposure. Thus, the research design featured an alliance between sondage and robotage. Sondage would determine the nature and extent of the Formative period occupation at the site, while the horizontal excavations would explore feature and artifact associations.

© 2003, J. Blomster

Figure 2.7 An example of sondage. A small but deep test unit excavated to bedrock in Area 3 at Etlatongo. The photograph emphasizes the decreasing visibility with great vertical depth; the base of the unit is not visible. Note the thick plaster floor approximately 1 meter below modern ground surface.

DRAFTING THE RESEARCH STRATEGY

The research objectives had been established, and the site to test them had been selected. Based on the considerations enumerated previously, the research design that guided the archaeological fieldwork at Etlatongo included strategies for surveying, mapping, sampling through archaeological testing, and excavating on a larger scale, with each stage of the project informing the subsequent one. The first stage of the fieldwork clearly required an intensive pedestrian surface survey of the sites. The survey would both determine approximate size and boundaries for the two Etlatongo sites and allow division of the sites into research strata for archaeological sampling.

Survey and Mapping of Etlatongo

Numerous researchers rhapsodize over the efficacy of surface surveys, promoting the technique as capable of providing direct correlations of artifact types on the surface with those in the subsurface matrix (Redman and Watson 1970:289). The deep deposits encountered at Etlatongo contradict this dictum. In fact, the artifacts recovered in the first test unit at Etlatongo did not correspond with those on the surface (see Chapter 4). Throughout the project, surface survey results elicited skepticism rather than reification without archaeological verification.

Figure 2.8 An example of robotage. A broader, horizontal area at Etlatongo (Excavation Area 2) is in the process of excavation, exposing numerous contemporaneous (and noncontemporaneous) features. A wall, associated with the occupation being documented in the northeast corner of the unit (where the arrow pointing north is located), pertains to an occupation later than that represented by the exposed postholes in the southwest corner. Earlier occupations lay beneath both of those exposed in the photograph. Scale is 30 cm long.

Surveys have been a valuable tool in identifying archaeological sites throughout Mesoamerica. There have been extensive regional surface surveys in both the Valley of Oaxaca and the Nochixtlán Valley (Blanton et al. 1982; Spores 1972). Surveys identify and order sites on a regional level. The Vanderbilt survey documented sites throughout the Nochixtlán Valley and allowed the research at Etlatongo to be placed in a larger context than would be possible without it. Although these surveys have been instrumental in the identification of sites, too often chronologies and population estimates derived from surveys have been taken as "truth," when in fact they are hypotheses waiting to be tested archaeologically. Elaborate visions of diachronic valley politics, based primarily on surface surveys, have been offered for various regions of Oaxaca. As will be discussed in Chapter 3, this practice is both hazardous and misleading without support from excavations. As documented in numerous test units at Etlatongo, surface surveys of multioccupational sites can be relied upon only for the most basic of information. The earliest occupations often remain invisible from the surface, having been covered by later components.

Additionally, the composition of a surface survey can change over time in the same field, depending on the amount and depth of plowing. As noted earlier, the majority of the land at Etlatongo is under cultivation; plowing of a field raises artifacts from lower levels to the exposed ground surface, while often burying or sub-stantially moving those previously visible on the surface. If surveys were conducted every time a field was plowed at Etlatongo, there would be considerable variability in the assemblage of materials on the surface.

The surface survey conducted in 1992 did not focus on the collection of cultural materials from the ground. The goal of the survey centered on identification of occu-pational periods at Etlatongo, and not statistical analysis of artifact collections. A sta-tistically significant surface collection—where a percentage of grid squares are selected and all materials on the surface within a square collected—lay beyond the objectives and temporal duration of the project. The sampling of the Valley of Oaxaca site of San José Mogote through surface collections provides a cautionary tale as to the amount of data that can be generated. While the area sampled was less than 1/500th of the site, it still produced 25,000 sherds; most of this material was examined in the field (Flannery 1976b:58). Due to the incredibly dense concentra-tions of ceramics sherds throughout Etlatongo, I partially emulated this technique during the 1992 site survey by conducting a random pickup of artifacts rather than an intensive systematic collection of artifacts. Ceramics were generally identified *in situ* on the surface, with their temporal affiliation and location noted. A small surface sample of diagnostic and unusual ceramics was saved, and a systematic collection of all surface sherds was performed in conjunction with the excavation of each test unit.

The research design stipulated that systematic topographical mapping of the site would commence once the boundaries of the site had been demarcated through the surface survey. The map—in addition to helping with the obvious necessities of locating the research in space, establishing site size, and generating a grid through-out the site—would serve to delimit subtler constructed features and affirm relation-ships between architectural mounds and mound groups.

Archaeological Sampling

Looking over the expanse of a largely unknown site, the archaeologist must decide where to begin excavation and must choose some type of sampling strategy. In choosing a "sample," the archaeologist explicitly selects only a certain portion of a site or region to investigate in the field. Sampling techniques have been developed and tested on both the site and regional level (see Plog 1976a; Winter 1976). In this case, the focus is on sampling a site rather than a region.

The concept of sampling contradicts a common misconception about archae-ological fieldwork. Thanks largely to movies, the public's perception is that archaeological fieldwork entails the complete excavation of a site. As with other archaeological myths and fantasies involving such things as bullwhips and enchanted talismans, this is not the case. Casual visitors to an excavation in progress generally yawn in response to watching the slow, careful excavation of a small portion of a site, so unlike the massive reconstructed sites they may have viewed elsewhere.

Why do archaeologists choose not to excavate an entire site? Actually, in most cases complete excavation is not an option. The logistics of completely excavating even a small site in Mesoamerica would be staggering. Using controlled excavations, it would not be possible to completely explore a site such as Etlatongo in one per-son's lifetime, not to mention the additional lifetimes it would take to adequately analyze all cultural material and publish the results, which is part of the responsibilities of any archaeologist.

Additionally, archaeology is inherently destructive. Archaeological sites are a nonrenewable resource that is being rapidly destroyed by forces ranging from looters to development projects. Thus, rather than being yet another destructive force, the archaeologist wants to preserve part of a site. Since it is anticipated that research questions will change and data recovery methods will improve in the future, probably to the point where many features and surfaces can be detected without disturbing the soil, archaeologists attempt to destroy only as much of the site as needed.

The exact placement of the test units may seem mysterious to some. Many people assume the archaeologist has some strange sixth sense, or magical intuition, that guides placement of the units. During the 1992 fieldwork, even my field assistants suspected that I had some communion with the ancients, as every test unit yielded prehistoric materials. The reality is that at a site such as Etlatongo, it would be nearly impossible to place a unit within the boundaries of the site and not encounter cultural materials. The occupation was so continual and intense that the ancient inhabitants affected nearly all of this area. The decision of where to excavate and the choice of how to sample the site are made long before the archaeologist even enters the field.

Decisions regarding the type and size of sample are made in consideration of both research goals and also more practical issues of funding and time. Ideally, the sample should be large enough to be representative or statistically significant of the total site. Unfortunately, when large, multicomponent sites such as Etlatongo are investigated, the possibility of excavating a statistically significant portion of the site quickly diminishes without a budget many times that of the 1992 Etlatongo Project and a virtual army of archaeologists. Due to the great depths of cultural materials at this site, the amount of time necessary to complete even a small excavation unit precluded excavating a statistically significant portion of the site. The goal was to sample the site with the time and resources available, as the first stage in a longer-term plan of research at Etlatongo. Thus, the decision concerning how to sample the site was critical.

A Stratified Random Sample at Etlatongo

The selection of a particular sampling strategy—in this case, a stratified random sample—requires a decision between two competing models of sampling: probabilistic (or random) versus judgmental. The paucity of data relating to the subsurface remains emerged as central in selecting an appropriate strategy, and suggested a strategy based on probing the site randomly. I use the term *random* more as a synonym for "simple random sampling" (Cowgill 1975), rather than "unbiased," recognizing that any level of analysis requires decision making. Even the choice of a random sample (an oxymoron in itself) is a cultural behavior (Hole 1980:231).

Theoretically, a probabilistic or random sample ensures more replicable testing, based on the principle that all potential units share an equal chance of selection for excavation, which facilitates comparisons with other random samples, both intrasite and intersite. Units can also be placed at consistent intervals; when the location of the first unit is selected randomly, this is referred to as a systematic random sample. One advantage of random samples is that statistics can be applied to determine the probability the materials excavated through the sample are representative of the entire site. A larger sample will have to be excavated at Etlatongo before statistics can be appropriately applied, for reasons noted previously.

I have explained the "random" part of my stratified random sample, but what about the "stratified" part? The term *stratified* refers to the partitioning of the site. Based on the results of the survey, the site (or sampling universe) was to be stratified into smaller zones, namely research areas (or simply "area," but with a capital "A," e.g., Area 1). The division of the site into areas is merely a heuristic device to assist in the placement of test units. In selecting strata, I chose to partition Etlatongo based on purposive selection, "in which some characteristic of the population, such as the distribution of environmental zones, is used as the basis of stratification" (Plog 1976a:139). I divided the site into strata based on a combination of cultural and topographic markers, reasoning that partitioning a site this large into strata would ensure wider aerial coverage of randomly placed test units and would facilitate different levels of comparison within the site. I envisioned an explicitly stratified sample in order to avoid the clustering of test units in one small section of the site—an infamous byproduct of random sampling. In data tested in the Valley of Oaxaca, employing a stratified random sample was much more efficient than using a simple random sample (Plog 1976a:150–151).

Since the test units would serve to explore the boundaries of the site for each chronological period rather than artifact and feature associations (the domain of the subsequent phase of robotage), I elected to sample Etlatongo through 1 × 1 meter units, reasoning that anything larger than this would provide scant additional temporal data at a tremendous increase in labor costs. Experiments conducted in survey strategy support employing smaller units, and data from different sampling techniques in the Valley of Oaxaca indicate that smaller sampling units are more efficient than larger ones (Plog 1976a:157). Hence, I reasoned that at Etlatongo, 1 × 1 meter units would provide much greater aerial coverage across the site.

Initially I established the number of 1 × 1 meter test units to be excavated at 12, due to calculations of time and labor required to excavate down to sterile soil. With the goal of equal allocation of test units to each research area, this amount would also be easily divisible by the number of areas (which could be 2, 3, 4, or 6). This part of the plan could have worked out well if not for complications discussed later. Based on the surface reconnaissance, I defined four research areas; each was scheduled to receive three test units. To facilitate the timely investigation of these test units, they would be excavated by arbitrary 20-centimeter layers, with the exception of cultural features such as floors and storage pits, which would be excavated as discrete entities. Excavation procedures are detailed in Chapter 4.

In contrast to the archaeological testing, the location of robotage units—the final stage of the fieldwork—would be completely judgmental, based on the identification of Early Formative occupations of the site by the sampling program. I had hoped (in vain, as it turned out) that the surface survey and test units would reveal undisturbed areas with scant post–Middle Cruz overburden. In an ideal world, these undisturbed Middle Cruz deposits would contain middens, features, and surfaces from either residential and/or public contexts. As opposed to the test units, the two large areas would be excavated by natural—or more accurately, cultural—strata, in order to optimize the amount of associated data per stratum. Based on calculations involving time, labor, and the size of Formative houses and features as defined in the Valley of Oaxaca, I proposed investigating two large "excavation areas," each not to exceed 7 × 7 meters.

Changes in Research Design

Ideally, the research design outlined in the previous text would have been followed without any deviations. The reality of archaeological fieldwork at a site without significant prior investigation, however, contains a great many unknowns that are unearthed during excavation. The challenge is to adapt the existing strategy to meet new situations while maintaining the general goals of the project. As noted, an ongoing dialogue between the researcher and the data is part of any "scientific" method (Watson, LeBlanc, and Redman 1971:14); the relationship between research design and fieldwork must be dynamic. Now that the ideal plan has been presented, I will expose what really happened, and show how the design was adapted to meet conditions encountered in the field.

The first problem that developed was the realization that the site was much larger than anticipated. The land separating the two Etlatongo sites identified by the Vanderbilt survey was documented through the 1992 surface survey to have been occupied, thus drastically changing the overall size of the site (see Chapter 3). Based on both survey and excavation, I now calculate the total size of Etlatongo as 208.2 hectares. Following previous conclusions that the hilltop site was separate from the rest of the lower Etlatongo site, it was thought that after sampling that hilltop site to ensure no Formative materials were present, the remainder of the fieldwork would focus on the lower Etlatongo site. While there had never been the illusion that 12 test pits would constitute a statistically significant sample of the sites, the connection between the northern and southern sites and the increase in overall site size reinforced the necessity for further archaeological sampling.

The other major problem was the occupational depth at Etlatongo. Several test units extended below 5 meters from the surface, resulting in an enormous expenditure of labor and time to excavate. Further, we never encountered Middle Cruz remains without several meters of overburden from later occupations. I envied those doing excavations in the Valley of Oaxaca, where Formative houses were found less than half a meter below modern ground surface. The site size and occupational depth at Etlatongo necessitated two changes in the core premise of the sampling program—the reliance on probabilistic sampling as well as the number and allocation of test units. As other investigators have noted, "deep-site excavation strategies do not allow for probabilistic sampling . . ." (Brown 1975:58). It seemed clear that even by stratifying the site into four areas, probabilistic sampling within each area would prove too rigid and inflexible to adapt to the field conditions. The survey identified portions of the site that necessitated at least one test unit, usually to determine such a basic issue as whether a topographic anomaly was natural or artificial. Similarly, several large, clearly artificial features emerged as locations to avoid; 8 to 10 vertical meters of fill would have to be excavated if the probabilistic sample dictated that a test unit be placed on the apex of one of these mounds.

Thus, the first change in research design was instituted in response to the extreme depth of the Middle Cruz occupations, and the often invisible nature of these deposits on the surface. The only way to accurately assess the size of the Middle Cruz occupation of the site was to increase the number of test units in order to provide a more representative sample of cultural deposits across the site. To remain within the budget and time frame of the project, the amount of sondage was augmented while the size of each robotage excavation was diminished to less than 7 × 7 meters. This was a difficult decision to make, but in retrospect the correct one. The size of the

Middle Cruz occupation of the site reconstructed in Chapter 3 would be significantly reduced if it were not for the additional test units that sampled Area 3.

Furthermore, to facilitate understanding of as much of the site as possible, I adjusted the research strategy to combine elements of random and purposive selection. In order both to avoid concentrations of test units in one portion of an area and to sample (or avoid) certain portions of an area, a given research area was further stratified into smaller subregions that would receive (or be excluded from receiving) at least one test unit, while the exact coordinates of the test unit continued to be selected randomly. Once an area had been subdivided and the general direction of the test unit established, the process of selecting coordinates for the majority of test units would begin. First, a random distance and angle (but within the target range) from the nearest mapped point would be programmed into a calculator. Then, the calculator would compute coordinates located on the site grid for the projected unit. Thus, while the general region of the test unit was judgmentally selected, the exact coordinates of the test unit remained random. This also could have been accomplished with a table of random numbers generated for each subdivision of an area, with each number representing a possible test unit within a defined universe of possible units based on size of the subdivision.

There was one final change in research strategy. In the process of abandoning the reliance on a strict random sample, the tenet of equal allocation of test units per each of the four research areas also proved impractical. By the time all areas had been sampled archaeologically by at least one test unit, it became clear that some areas had greater potential to answer the primary research questions of Middle Cruz social complexity and interregional interaction than others. The surface survey results and the data yielded by the first test unit in Area 4 (the Etlatongo hill) did not recover any evidence of pre-Ramos materials. The project's goals would not be advanced by excavating an equal amount of test units in Area 4 as in the other three areas, all of which did yield abundant Formative remains. Thus, I focused on defining the extent of Cruz materials in Areas 1 through 3, concentrating test units in these areas at the expense of equal coverage of Area 4. In addition, the amount of test units each area received remained flexible, adapting to incoming data as the excavations progressed.

By sharing all the details of the research design, from background information to changes in strategy in the field, I give the reader the opportunity to arrive at his or her own decisions on what could be done differently given similar circumstances, time, and resources. A great deal can be learned from challenges encountered in the field, which can inform future research designs. I have presented my experience in the hope of aiding future archaeologists in deciding what to do, and what not to do, when designing fieldwork.

The revamped research design resulted in a total of twenty-two 1×1 meter test units excavated over a period of six months. Several of these units were in fact 1×1 meter extensions of previous units, designed to further explore a feature or surface. Thus, a small percentage of these test units was selected judgmentally; I exclude nonrandom units from any comparisons between randomly selected ones. Additionally, a 1×2 meter salvage unit (Unit 23) and two larger units referred to as excavation areas were excavated. As a result of the 1992 excavations, a total surface area of 74.5 square meters was explored archaeologically at Etlatongo. The almost insignificant portion of the site excavated emphasizes the preliminary nature of the conclusions I draw about ancient life at Etlatongo.

3/Community and Change
Etlatongo through Time

A basic goal of both past and ongoing research centers on understanding the occupation of Etlatongo through time. The site exhibits occupations from numerous time periods. As part of the 1992 research, I deemed it critical to understand approximate village size for each chronological period, and how occupation of Etlatongo changed through time. Survey and excavation established probable site boundaries for major chronological periods; this generated maps for the different temporal occupations of Etlatongo. An often-ignored problem involves the correspondence between site boundaries devised by archaeologists and the community as envisioned by ancient inhabitants—a split between what anthropologists refer to as etic (the observer's perspective) and emic (the informant's perspective). In this chapter I explore this issue, after first discussing some other basic issues related to site survey and mapping. Based on data derived from both surface survey and excavation, I conclude this chapter by guiding the reader on a tour of Etlatongo.

SITE SURVEY AND MAPPING AT ETLATONGO

In addition to excavation, two procedures proved essential in establishing different temporal occupations at Etlatongo: a surface survey and production of a site map.

The 1992 Site Survey—In the "Zone"

A site survey initiated the 1992 field season at Etlatongo. The survey consisted of two related procedures, beginning with a systematic pedestrian reconnaissance over the site itself prior to the excavations. As outlined in Chapter 2, the goals of this phase of the survey focused on defining the site boundaries for each time period and dividing the site into discrete research areas or "strata" for the purpose of assigning each an equal share of test units. In conjunction with the mapping of Etlatongo, the second phase of the survey refined boundaries, explored problem areas, and involved nonsystematic collection of limited samples of diagnostic material.

In addition to the creation of site boundaries, the survey explored the supposedly uninhabited zone (referred to simply as "the zone") between the two separate

Etlatongo sites, N802 and N810 (Spores 1972). Researchers thought these sites, separated by an expanse of land, represented very different temporal and distinct occupations. As the earlier of the two occupations, Site N810 had been interpreted as largely abandoned by the Classic and Postclassic periods, at which time the occupation of N802 began (see Chapter 2).

Systematic surface survey performed in 1992 over this "zone" encountered a plethora of cultural features and artifacts. Recently plowed fields revealed dense artifact concentrations throughout, while a road cut yielded abundant evidence of cultural activity, including a series of plaster floors. The 1992 survey demonstrated no break in occupation between the two hypothesized sites. Rather than demarcating two sites, this zone provides an occupied connection between the southern and northern portions of the site, with artifact assemblages having more in common with the southern portion of the site (N810) than the site on the hill. As noted in Chapter 2, this discovery had a significant impact on the research design, as the hill site could not simply be written off as a separate and later site, but was connected to N810. All of the land surveyed in 1992 would have been occupied during the Postclassic period (see following text). Rather than two sites, I define Etlatongo as one site of 208.2 hectares (514.2 acres or 2.08 square kilometers), with occupations encompassing over 2,500 years.

The Etlatongo Map Project

In conjunction with the site survey, I initiated a program of mapping at Etlatongo, which far outlasted the pedestrian survey in duration. The initial plan was to complete a detailed topographic map of Site N810, the Formative period component of the site that would be the focus of the excavations, as well as to document the architectural features atop the Etlatongo hill. The mapping of N810 would establish the site size and allow for the generation of a grid over the site, from which units could be randomly selected within strata (see Chapter 2). A bevy of problems appeared in the field, including delays in the arrival of crew and mapping equipment. This resulted in excavation commencing prior to map completion, although an idea of site size, and associated range of possible units, had been established. The realization that the two "separate" Etlatongo sites formed one massive Postclassic site indeed proved daunting. Initially armed only with a vintage Nikon H-5 transit, the prospect of mapping such a vast space of great topographic diversity caused considerable consternation. This problem was resolved through the fortuitous intercession of Damon Peeler, whose interest in mapping had inspired him to purchase a laser transit. While not a total station or EDMI (electronic distance measuring instrument), which would have measured both horizontal and vertical distances and allowed in-field storage and processing of data, the far greater distances accurately measured by this transit—which actually emits a laser beam intercepted by a crewmember holding the appropriate device ("prism") above the point to be recorded—enabled us to map the vast expanse of the Etlatongo hill.

When not utilizing the laser transit, I employed a three-person mapping crew; one person manned the transit and recorded data, another stretched the measuring tape for horizontal distance, while the third supervised the stadium rod for elevations. I established the datum point at the highest spot in the southern part of the site on the summit of Mound 1-1, with the elevation established arbitrarily at 100

DIGGING DEEPER: TO COLLECT OR NOT TO COLLECT?

Careful readers of Chapter 2 already know that I did not systematically collect surface artifacts. Informed by the results of a surface survey at a comparable site in the Valley of Oaxaca, visions of thousands of bags of sherds, with only a surface context, danced through my head. Since the focus of my research lay under the ground and I knew that sherds from better contexts would be forthcoming, I analyzed most surface sherds where they lay on the ground. I did, however, collect extremely diagnostic or partially complete objects to allow for more detailed study by myself and other scholars. There was a practical component to this decision: If I didn't collect largely intact objects and record their contexts, local pothunters would collect them, thus removing them forever from analysis. In fact, some of the only pieces of jade and/or greenstone available for analysis from Etlatongo are those collected from the surface.

I reflected on the wisdom of this decision recently while participating in a surface collection in eastern Pennsylvania. We prepared to survey an area by establishing a series of 10-meter squares; the goal was to collect everything on the surface—mostly stone tools and production debris—in each square. After several days of artifact collection, we noted a distinct lack of tools, especially projectile points, in the southern portion of the study area. Filled with the excitement that can only be derived from pattern recognition, a cold blast of reality struck. I discovered that at times when the research team was not surveying the surface, a local collector "walked the fields" of the project area and snagged for his own personal collection all intact projectile points. The fact that he employed our grid system to enhance his own efficiency provided little consolation, and points to another problem with surface surveys that are not completed in one event.

meters; these elevations can be related to those on topographic maps of the region which place the Etlatongo hill summit at approximately 2,100 meters above sea level. We attempted to make the datum point as permanent as possible by placing it near well-established modern features. We established a "false origin" for the datum point's horizontal coordinates, assigning them arbitrary numbers based on the location of this point relative to the overall unmapped site. Magnetic north served as the basis for the north-south orientation of the site grid, established by the transit's compass from the datum point; a declination adjustment must be made for true north.

We established initial station points (used for mapping and establishing test units) at 45-degree intervals from the datum point, with all subsequent station points based on these initial ones. The mapping crew labeled each station point, noting the date of placement and relation to landmarks. Initially, measurements radiated out from each station point in standard 30-degree intervals, with points measured at every 5 meters for each radius. Experimentation proved that the most efficient technique involved adapting the number of measurements to the terrain, with fewer measurements necessary in expansive flat areas. In order to obtain distance measurements of the actual ground surface rather than a straight line parallel to the surface, as is often performed by holding a taut tape above the ground, we opted to place the tape on the ground surface itself, and employed a calculator program to correct for slope. This was extremely labor-intensive and became a nightly ritual for the mapping crew; the process would have been greatly facilitated by an EDMI!

The mapping crew scoured every meter of Etlatongo, braving vicious dogs, nopal cacti, and other spiny plants. In the three months of the Etlatongo Mapping Project, they recorded approximately 6,000 points. Specific elevations from features and excavation units can be tied into the overall elevation system of the site, and the coordinates of all major landmarks, from roads to houses to electrical power poles, have been recorded as reference points. We ultimately entered the data into SURFER, a computerized mapping program, to produce a topographic site map (see Figure 3.1), as well as more detailed maps of each research area.

SITE BOUNDARIES:
CONCEPTUAL ISSUES AND COMMUNITIES

The practice of establishing site boundaries poses numerous conceptual quandaries, especially at a multicomponent site such as Etlatongo. Any boundaries established are, by the nature of the data, the projection of the archaeologist; they are artificial and do not reflect the community as conceived by the ancient occupants. Conclusions regarding boundary definition center on the presence or absence of artifacts on modern ground surface, which generally has been highly disturbed. The ceramics exposed in plowed fields for the archaeologist's viewing pleasure change with every harvest. The boundaries I establish for the site derive from observations specific to the 1992 field season. While less than precise, defining limits for the site was a necessary methodological part of the research. In sampling, it is imperative to have an idea of the total size of the universe to be explored.

Sites as Communities: The Quest for Correspondence

Archaeologists typically study sites or regions rather than communities—the level of social organization most relevant and important to the people at the center of the analysis. Communities lie between individual houses and regions, and as a concept entail both a social component (familial and corporate ties; economic linkages) and a territorial aspect. Members of a community generally exhibit regular interaction and share access to resources (Murdock 1949; Varien 1999a). Communities can be defined through social reproduction, agricultural production, and self-identification (Kolb and Snead 1997:609–611). This last element, the "imagined community," remains especially important to the ancient people yet the hardest to access archaeologically. Communities may not correspond with spatial boundaries, which create problems if archaeologists equate what they define as sites with communities. Political manifestations of regional affiliation can be partly accessed by studying settlement systems and relations with other regions, but the element of shared identity remains difficult to define. Much variety exists in the application of the concept; even when dealing with contemporary people, we hear talk of entities such as "Internet communities"—people who often never have any face-to-face contact.

Community identification is dynamic and socially constructed; from a practice perspective, community identities are socially negotiated and contingent upon

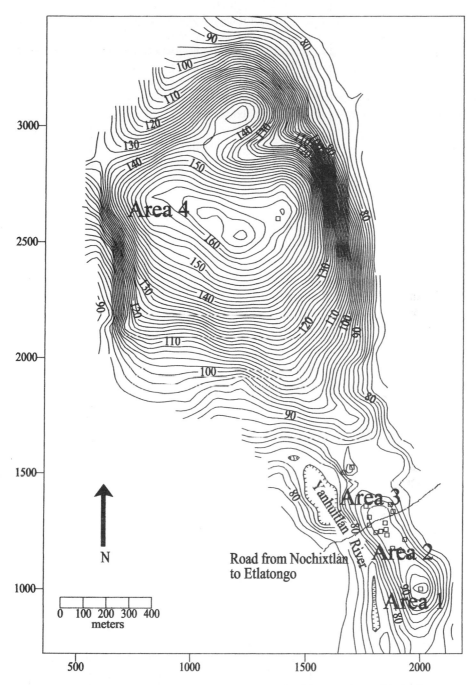

Figure 3.1 Topographic map showing the boundaries of Etlatongo, along with the four research areas (in bold) that divide the site. The small squares represent the locations of the 1992 test units; they are not to scale. Contour interval is 2 meters; the arrow points to magnetic north. © 2003, J. Blomster.

human agency (see Chapter 1). Community identity may be both plural and contested—not everyone within the community shares its ideals and identity. Disparate groups may subscribe to a common "community" identity in order to serve a common goal, such as the pan-Pueblo consciousness developed in parts of the 17th-century southwestern United States as resistance to Spanish intrusions (Preucel 2000).

Archaeologists usually focus on a village as a collection of artifact concentrations, features, and structures, equating the architectural village with a community. Archaeologists must take a more inclusive view, and consider other factors, such as outlying lands and possibly satellite hamlets, which constitute a community. The roles of individuals who live great distances from their community vary; those who no longer live in the physical community ultimately may not have a significant impact on daily community constitution. While it may not be possible to draw community boundaries on a map, archaeologists can cite differences between what they have bounded as a physical village and as a larger community. As archaeologists, we can conceive communities that extend beyond the concentration of ceramic sherds and architectural remains. The term *community* may also be applied to multiple archaeological sites organized as a community by examining spatial patterning and settlement types. Usually, archaeologists define large sites with focal architecture as the "center" of the community, with smaller sites organized around them (see Smith 1993:98).

Ethnographic research in the Valley of Oaxaca reveals the difficulties inherent in boundary definition of archaeological sites as physical communities (Dennis 1987). Two towns studied in the Valley of Oaxaca segregate themselves from each other based on straight lines, invisible but known intimately by the villagers. These lines run between physical boundary markers, which include locally named natural or artificial features. Archaeologists would have little access to the meanings and existence of such markers; these lands would remain beyond their site boundaries. Villagers have used violence and bloodshed, dating from prehistoric times, to defend their community boundaries, which encompass fields, grazing lands, and forested hills (used for gathering firewood), from the encroachments of neighboring communities. The community envisioned by these Zapotec informants includes both the humanly created village and the natural land surrounding it. In this system, each village resembles a separate republic, where cultural differences (such as dialect, dress, marriage ceremonies) and physical community limits function as boundary-maintaining mechanisms (Dennis 1987).

Similar phenomena have been seen in the Mixteca Alta, as observed in the boundary construction of two communities to the west of Etlatongo, Jaltepec and Tilantongo. A natural feature, a limestone ridge, demarcates much of the 10-kilometer north-south boundary line. At Classic period sites lying between these communities, villagers erected piles of stones to delimit the boundary (Pohl et al. 1997:207). Powerful spiritual forces associated with the well-being of the particular community inhabit many of the features (such as mountains, lakes, and canyons) that delineate boundaries on the Mixtec landscape. Early colonial documents emphasize the importance of the land surrounding villages in the Nochixtlán Valley; individual fields were often named and control of them contested by the adjacent village and larger regional center (Spores 1984). Only some of these phenomena remain within the archaeologist's grasp.

The Contemporary Etlatongo Community

The modern village of San Mateo Etlatongo currently contains about 100 families. Of some satisfaction to archaeologists, when I asked people in San Mateo Etlatongo for population estimates, they would cite approximately 100 families, and then make the same conversion as archaeologists (assuming five people per family) to calculate a population of 500 people. As is the case with many contemporary towns in the Mixteca Alta, San Mateo Etlatongo occupies different land than the archaeological site. For administrative purposes, the Spanish Colonial regime forcibly resettled many indigenous towns some distance away from the pre-Hispanic village. The earlier town often remains within sight of the resettled community. Following what is probably an ancient pattern, three small satellite hamlets or ranches (*rancherias*) are associated with San Mateo Etlatongo: San Antonio, La Luz, and Los Angeles.

In addition to growing staple crops such as maize and beans, farmers at Etlatongo also grow crops, particularly alfalfa, either for trade in the Nochixtlán market or as feed for their animals. Land not utilized for crops undergoes extensive grazing, particularly by goats, although sheep are raised as well. Cattle are less common, found only in a few compounds and the *rancherias* on the periphery of town. Some residents still maintain oxen as draft animals, while others have turned to mechanical apparatus to plow their fields. Permanent cement irrigation canals have recently been installed throughout parts of the site, ensuring year-round planting of the majority of the land. The continuous farming of this land in the present alters the past that lies beneath.

Any definition villagers provide of what they consider as the Etlatongo "community" includes the land they farm. In 1992, these lands formed part of the *ejido* system of land tenure, where villagers have usufruct rights to individual tracts but ultimately the land belongs to the village as a whole. Villagers readily identified who had rights to which parcel of land, and employed landmarks—often not readily visible to outsiders—to differentiate between plots. Villagers usually included residents of the *rancherias* in their definition of the community, as well as a few residents living in isolated homesteads in the general vicinity of town. Absent members of the community, often working in Mexico City or the United States, generally retain active community identification, depending on the frequency of their visits. The celebration of the town's fiesta serves as a focal point for returning villagers. Absent villagers never remain truly isolated from their village; friends and relatives often share their accommodations while they are away from San Mateo Etlatongo.

Just as the current inhabitants of San Mateo Etlatongo have very strong ideas of community boundaries, so undoubtedly did their predecessors. The nature of archaeological evidence generally precludes including agricultural fields within site boundaries. For now, my solution is to present the Etlatongo boundaries as simply defining the ancient physical village, informed by the knowledge that I exclude both physical properties of the ancient community (such as fields) and the imagined community. Improving archaeological technology, such as soil analyses (which can detect human activity leaving organic residues, due to concentrations of phosphorus, nitrogen, calcium and carbon in the soil), may enable the determination of which tracts of land served as agricultural fields in the past.

Many members of the modern community have a strong interest in the ancient Etlatongo community. Visitors frequented the site, allowing me to provide them with at least one perspective—that of an archaeologist—on the past of this region. It is important that archaeologists endeavor to promote understanding of their research throughout the modern communities in which they work, expressing another aspect of the rich history and tradition of regions such as the Nochixtlán Valley. I talked with several teachers, for example, and in the future hope to encourage organized tours by school groups. Learning, of course, goes both ways. Modern villagers also have a great deal of information they can share with the archaeologist (see the text that follows). Through time, archaeologists themselves become part of the local oral tradition, as various projects and individuals are conflated. On a recent visit to San Mateo Etlatongo, I was especially pleased to see the 1992 project featured in local textbooks.

Etlatongo Site Boundaries

Working with the caveats just presented, the survey served to establish site boundaries for Etlatongo. I employ extant topographical and artificial features to define both site boundaries and divisions between areas where possible, preferring both the easy recognition on the ground of actual landmarks and the ability of others to find these boundary markers.

As the map of Etlatongo illustrates (Figure 3.1), the site's north-south dimensions greatly exceed its east-west dimensions. The Etlatongo hill dominates the site and immediate vicinity. Due to the inclusion of the hill within the site boundaries, elevations at the site range just over 100 meters—a range traversed on a daily basis during the excavations of a test unit on the hilltop.

The Yanhuitlán and Yucuita rivers converge south of what I define as the southern boundary of the site, and the Yanhuitlán River also serves to bound the western part of Etlatongo. The extremely fertile land south of where I bound the site may have occupations covered by alluvium, or may have served the ancient inhabitants of Etlatongo in the same way as villagers use it today—as excellent farmland. The Yucuita River fails to provide an eastern boundary for the site; artifact concentrations falter well before it. I define the eastern boundary through a series of modern impositions on the site—roads and irrigation canals. Much of the land lying between the eastern boundaries of the site and the river may have also been used as fields in pre-Hispanic time, and would have been part of the community.

The Yanhuitlán and Yucuita rivers probably served as natural barriers, if not actual boundaries, for parts of the site in ancient times. Although erosion has increased in recent times, the Yanhuitlán River prevents easy crossing of the riverbed during the rainy season without a bridge or submergible vehicle. The dramatic break in artifact concentrations west of the Yanhuitlán River supports the interpretation of this river as a natural boundary to the ancient physical community. Scattered artifacts have been observed in the contemporary town of San Mateo Etlatongo, which may be situated atop a possible pre-Hispanic site at the base of the piedmont slope (although the Nochixtlán Valley survey did not identify a pre-Hispanic site here).

Access roads and ravines define the northeast and northwest boundaries of the site, as these features lay in a zone of greatly reduced artifact concentrations. The boundaries follow artifact concentrations; we discontinued surface survey after significant falloffs in these concentrations. Only additional intensive surface survey, combined with random test units, of the land adjacent to but outside of the 1992 site boundaries will determine the inclusiveness of what is defined here as "Etlatongo."

THE SITE SURVEY: RESEARCH AREAS AND OCCUPATIONS

In addition to boundary definition and investigation of the zone lying between Sites N802 and N810, the survey resulted in a division of Etlatongo into four research areas (see Chapter 2). These areas serve as organizational contrivances to summarize the surface features observed during the site survey. I attempted to correlate areas with discrete chronological phases based on surface artifacts—an effort doomed to failure due to the expansive multioccupational nature of the site (Table 1.1 summarizes all phases). When possible, I employed prominent landmarks or features to bound these areas; for example, nearby power poles served to mark the change in chronological occupations represented in surface materials between Areas 1 and 2. Arbitrary but well-marked divisions were selected so future investigations can reestablish the area boundaries for additional sampling. The specifics of area boundary definition have been presented elsewhere (Blomster 1998a). The areas run in ascending order from south to north, which is how our journey through the site shall be organized.

A Word on Platforms and Mounds

Mounds are defined as topographic rises; without investigation, a mound's origin remains unknown. Mounds may be largely natural or entirely man-made. They often represent an accumulation of structures and surfaces from different occupations. Many of them may have served as platforms, but until documented, the mound designation remains. I label them in two ways. When confined to one research area, a mound has two numbers—the first number refers to the area, and the second to the sequential number within the area (such as Mound 1-1). Structure designation at Etlatongo also follows this convention. I refer to mounds that expand across research areas by letters (such as Mound A, the massive structure first documented by Spores).

I use the term *platform,* on the other hand, to refer specifically to an architectural feature built to support and elevate another structure. Platforms can be relatively small, constructed as a base for one occupation of a house, or massive, built as the base for an elevated public structure. The use of this term clearly identifies a platform as a man-made construction, an identity established by archaeological testing. This distinction has also been applied in Early Formative Soconusco, with platforms defined as forming a raised surface of 0.5 meter or more (Lesure 1997:220). Numerous structure-supporting platforms, including smaller ones than in Soconusco, have been documented in the Valley of Oaxaca (see Chapter 4).

Research Area 1

Area 1 occupies the southernmost portion of the site of Etlatongo (Figure 3.1). This area lies outside the maps of both Spores (1972) and Zárate Morán (1987), but was included in the 1992 survey primarily due to a large mound visible from the main road to town. The land south of the mound, leading to the confluence of the rivers, exhibits the least dense surface artifact concentration in Area 1. Alluvium (from river flooding) probably covers occupations, highlighting an obvious problem with surface surveys. We probably underestimated the size of this part of the site; test units would demonstrate if the site extends beyond the boundaries we imposed. To the northwest of Mound 1-1, the slopes merge with the constantly farmed fields of Area 2.

Mound 1-1 rises 20 meters from the valley floor, and ascends nearly 10 meters above the fields immediately adjacent to it to the north (see Chapter 4, Figure 4.2). We examined Mound 1-1 during the survey to determine if it represents a purely geological feature or a constructed and humanly modified part of the landscape. Despite bedrock outcrops that protrude in places less than a meter from the apex of the mound, it seemed apparent from the surface inspection that Mound 1-1 was occupied—and drastically modified—in pre-Hispanic times. The distinctive shape of Mound 1-1 features a broad, flat surface on its apex, with a horizontal diameter substantially larger than the vertical ascent. Prehistoric plaster floor fragments provided less-than-subtle clues that the shape is not due solely to current use of the mound as a threshing floor.

The extant portion of Mound 1-1 encountered in the field in 1992 is suggestive of an accumulation of numerous occupations that probably served as platforms for a superstructure; this structure would have been substantially elevated above the surrounding land. Due to modern use of Mound 1-1, we encountered few artifacts other than small, worn sherds on its apex; sherds, however, covered the slopes of this mound. These sherds represented primarily Ramos phase occupations. Due to the surface remains, I interpreted Area 1 as representing primarily Late Formative occupations. The first test unit excavated in Area 1 (see Chapter 4) demolished this interpretation, and reinforced the dubious nature of chronological interpretations based solely on surface surveys. I return to how test units inform our understanding of Area 1 later in this chapter.

Local informants provided critical data that contradicted the Ramos surface remains atop Mound 1-1. Owners of a large house south of Mound 1-1 showed me a collection of pre-Hispanic material from a broad range of time periods encountered during their use of Area 1 (Figure 3.2). Members of this family claimed to know where to find "intact" objects, and seemed infinitely amused by my ability to find "only" sherds and figurine fragments. Archaeologists often undervalue the knowledge of local informants, but I quickly realized that people who lived on the site, or farmed it on a daily basis, knew much more about the soils and what lay under the surface of Area 1 than I did. One member of the family served as one of my most valued field assistants.

Research Area 2

Area 2 comprises most of what Spores (1972) designated as N810, Etlatongo between the rivers, and includes additional land to the east and southeast. Geologically, Area 2 centers on a broad plane lying between the rivers, further from and less affected by the sloping riverbed than the southern portion of Area 1. Due to both its geophysical situation and intensive farming, this land forms a remarkably level surface. Nearly all of the significant elevation changes occur toward the rivers lying to the east and west. Upon further inspection, it appears that a large part of this extensive plane rises artificially from the surrounding land, representing a series of intensive occupations forming a large mound (Mound X), with the effects of con-

Figure 3.2 Sample of largely intact pre-Hispanic materials collected by the family that farms much of the land encompassing Mound 1-1 and Unit 1. The photograph shows ceramic urns, rattles, and whistles.

secutive occupations culminating in the surface present today. The survey suggested the hypothesis, to be tested by excavations, that portions of this feature may have been elevated, similar to a Near Eastern tell—an accumulation of numerous structures and related occupational debris, with the abandoned structures underlying successive ones. It remained unclear if ancient villagers employed this previous debris as a platform to place structures, or if the flat nature visible on the surface merely represented many discrete occupations homogenized by the passage of time.

The main road to San Mateo Etlatongo slices through Mound X, and served as the location for the 1980 test units discussed in Chapter 2. This road serves as the boundary between Areas 2 and 3, a very artificial but permanent dividing line. During the survey, we observed examples of most ceramic phases on the surface, although the proportion of materials changed after each fresh plowing. Indeed, it became a favorite activity to examine one section of the field immediately after plowing to determine how it differed from previous observations. As noted in Chapter 2, this encouraged speculation about how this part of the site would be characterized by only one surface reconnaissance over its surface. We observed Middle Cruz materials scattered throughout much of Area 2.

Compared with Spores's survey, the amount of Postclassic material observed during the 1992 research in Area 2 surprised us. These ceramics generally accounted for the highest quantity of surface material, and we frequently encountered concentrations of ladles and distinctive bi- and polychrome (multicolored) Natividad ceramics. In terms of total artifacts, we observed a higher concentration of surface sherds in Area 2 compared to Area 1. While not systematically collecting materials, we

quantified and documented surface materials by collecting surface materials for each
test unit (see Chapter 2). Area 2 surface collections averaged 35.7 sherds per test unit
surface, while Area 1 averaged 23.5 sherds.

Research Area 3

I bounded the region north of the road slicing through Mound X to the base of the
Etlatongo hill as Area 3 (Figure 3.3). Much of this region lay outside the area referred
to as Site N810, although it does include the massive construction adjacent to the
Yanhuitlán River (Mound A) first documented by Spores (1972). Based on surface
materials, Area 3 initially appeared distinct from Area 2 due to the higher percentage
of Ramos sherds in Area 3, and the less frequent appearance of Natividad (Postclassic)
material. The large accumulation of habitation debris, Mound X, continues 70 meters
north into Area 3. Mound X terminates dramatically in Area 3, with a 4-meter descent
from it to the elevation of the majority of this area. In retrospect, this may have been a
better boundary between Areas 2 and 3, although it remains unclear how much of this
truncation reflects ancient behavior versus modern alteration.

MOUND A   Mound A, a large artificial platform partially exposed through
Yanhuitlán River-induced erosion, bounds the western portion of Area 3 (Figure 3.4).
This massive feature rises to an elevation averaging 8 to 9 meters above the
Yanhuitlán River bed. Throughout the eroded profile of Mound A, stone and adobe
walls have been exposed; these walls range from roughly constructed efforts to well-
made walls with many courses of similarly sized dressed stones and adobe blocks.
Villagers report caches of vessels and figurines—probably from burials—from this
feature. A magnetite mirror fragment originates from this part of Etlatongo (Winter
1992, personal communication). Mound A may continue along the western boundary
of Area 2 under Mound X. The ancient villagers extensively modified this portion of
this site; at least some of the structures incorporated into Mound A represent a large
platform, probably to elevate this portion of the site above the riverbed. This massive
construction effort began, based on both surface and subterranean materials, in the
Late Cruz phase.

MOUND 3-1 AND POSSIBLE ASSOCIATED MOUNDS   The majority of Area 3 lies to the
east and above the exposed profile of Mound A, and may lie on associated constructions. Most of Area 3 consists of a large flat plazalike area surrounded to the east
(Mound 3-3) and south (Mound 3-2) by two low, highly eroded protuberances—
labeled here as potential mounds—ascending slightly above the "plaza" surface
(Figure 3.3). Only fragments of a possible large northern mound remain visible. The
eastern feature (Mound 3-3) remains more visible, but has been highly affected by a
house on its summit, and its eastern half has been largely obliterated by an access
road. The most intact and visible of these features is Mound 3-1, highly symmetrical
and located 40 to 50 meters east of the section of Mound A exposed by erosion.
Mound 3-1 rises nearly 4.5 meters above and west of the "plaza," and has a maximum length from east to west of approximately 35 meters. Mound 3-1 appears as an
almost perfect circle on the topographic map of Area 3 (Figure 3.3).

The great height of Mound 3-1 relative to its narrow width generated debate
regarding its origins. These dimensions and proportions differed greatly from

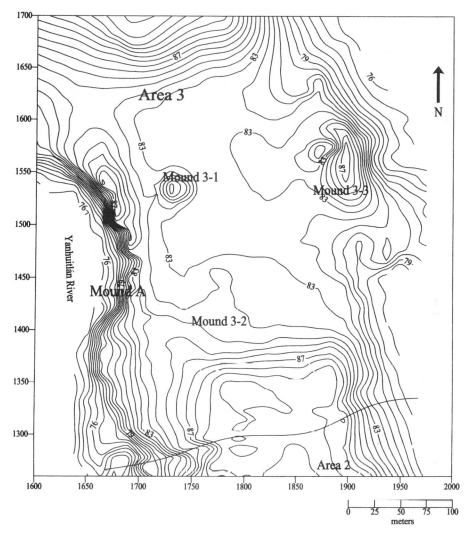

Figure 3.3 Topographic map of Area 3, showing relationships among mounds arranged around an open plaza. The massive Mound A appears to the left, adjacent to the Yanhuitlán River. Numbers on the left and bottom of the map represent the grid utilized during the 1992 research. Contour interval is 0.75 meters; arrow points to magnetic north.
© 2003, J. Blomster.

other constructs encountered at Etlatongo, and many of the villagers credited its extreme artificial roundness to recent field clearing, through which the debris scraped off the land surface was unceremoniously dumped onto this pile. The amount of loose plants and topsoil packed with roots on the mound's surface gave some credence to such claims. The survey identified this feature as a problem to be resolved through a test unit, which ultimately documented its pre-Hispanic origin. This was the only feature identified as a mound during the survey that evinced no signs of looting.

Figure 3.4 Mound A, the huge platform exposed by the Yanhuitlán River, with remnants of numerous construction episodes visible. Part of an exposed wall is visible in the top right of the photograph.

Research Area 4

Area 4 encompasses all of what Spores (1972) identified as N802, Etlatongo on the hill. At its highest elevation, the hill rises nearly 100 meters above the level of the valley floor below. This area exhibits the densest concentrations of Classic material at Etlatongo; Postclassic materials also abound. In addition, documented Yucuita and Ramos phase materials in Area 4. Ramos sherds appeared most frequently on the southern slopes of the Etlatongo hill—the portion adjacent to Area 3. This suggests that the Ramos materials found in Area 4 represent an expansion of Etlatongo's population up the hill slopes from the lower site center during the Late Formative/Early Classic period. Scattered Ramos sherds also lay atop the hill.

The systematic surface survey and mapping of Area 4 provides most of the data pertaining to this portion of the site contributed by the 1992 Etlatongo Project. We detected no pre-Yucuita materials through either the surface survey or test unit; thus, in the redesign of fieldwork, we lavished no additional excavations on Area 4 (Chapter 2). Area 4 encompasses more land than Areas 1 to 3 combined (see Figure 3.1). In fact, the apex alone of the Etlatongo hill (Figure 3.5)—an area of 410,000 square meters—is larger than the other three areas combined. One small, isolated hill to the west also exhibited scattered remains of a Classic/Postclassic occupation, but I exclude it from the boundaries of Etlatongo, as a zone without surface artifacts lies between it and Area 4. This small hilltop site probably represents an associated but isolated fortification or some other type of extension related to Classic period Etlatongo.

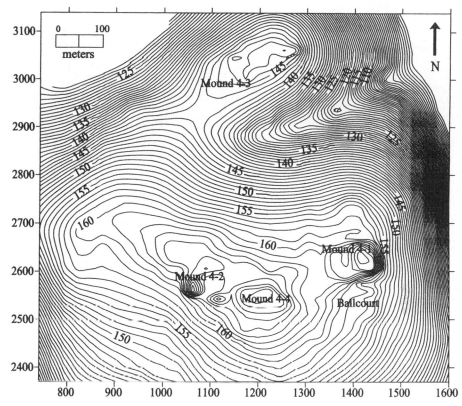

Figure 3.5 Topographic map of the apex of Area 4, showing a concentration of mounds and a ballcourt to the south, separated from an isolated mound group (Mound 4-3) to the north by a steep ravine. Contour interval is 1 meter; arrow points to magnetic north.
© 2003, J. Blomster.

SLOPES AND TERRACES   Terraces, mostly pre-Hispanic, proliferate on the heavily farmed slopes of Area 4. The exact form and construction of these terraces could not be determined due to both farming and erosion. I suspect many of the pre-Hispanic terraces served a dual function; expansion of agricultural fields and erosion control, as well as some occupational use. The dense artifact concentrations and thick plaster floor fragments exposed by recent plowing at some portions of these slopes are indicative of such occupations (Figure 3.6). I also observed subterranean features and roof stones from looted burials on these terraces.

These terraces appear analogous to those examined by Richard Blanton on the slopes of Monte Albán in the Valley of Oaxaca (see Chapter 1), but less systematically arranged and on a smaller scale. Blanton (1978:7–8) notes that the "bulk" of the documented 2,073 terraces at Monte Albán appear residential; others lacked any evidence of occupational debris, and probably served as agricultural terraces. A project focused on archaeologically testing and documenting the Etlatongo terraces would further illuminate how the ancient villagers utilized them.

© 2003, J. Blomster

Figure 3.6 Exposed plaster floor close to the apex of Area 4, just one example of the many occupations that probably covered the slopes of this hill. Mound 4-1 rises in the background.

THE ETLATONGO HILL SUMMIT   The summit of the Etlatongo hill contains mound systems, intact pre-Hispanic stone walls, plazas, and even a previously undocumented ballcourt. Several features observed by Spores (1972), such as steps and specific mounds, have been destroyed in the 20-plus years between the two studies, victims of the intense farming practiced on the hill summit. Unlike other parts of the site, much of the farming of the hill incorporates machines, which devastate surface features.

The survey and mapping revealed three major mound groups, two of which (Mounds 4-1 and 4-2) bound an expansive flat surface—a possible plaza—on the hill's summit (Figure 3.7). An additional mound (Mound 4-3), separated from the other two systems by a large ravine, lies in the northeastern face of the hill summit. All three mounds feature large craters excavated in their centers by looters. In the case of Mound 4-1, this abyss extends to its base, with the crater separating the mound into two "peaks." Residents of Etlatongo maintain that a random group of French pothunters looted these mounds; Spores (1992, personal communication) heard that a local family from Nochixtlán devastated these mounds in the 1960s.

The northernmost mound system, Mound 4-3, appears associated with other smaller constructed features to the southwest (Figure 3.5). These two features, probably connected, rise 1.5 meters above the surrounding land, and with Mound 4-3 form a larger aggregation similar to what Winter (1989:45–46) defines in the Valley of Oaxaca as a TPA (temple, patio, altar) complex. This ritual-ceremonial precinct consists of a temple (in this case, Mound 4-3) with an associated enclosed patio containing an "altar" or square building in its center. The temple encloses the patio on one side and a lower mound (probably two eroded features southwest of Mound 4-

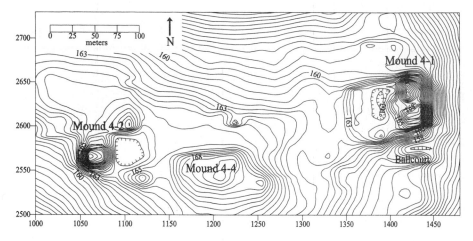

Figure 3.7 Topographic map showing the relationship between Mounds 4-1 and 4-2. A flat expanse of land—a possible plaza—lies between these mound groups, bounded to the south by Mound 4-4. The small contour interval, 0.5 meter, exaggerates the apparent irregularities in this plaza surface. The mound group represented by Mound 4-2 especially shows a well-preserved large central mound, flanked by two smaller mounds, with a small sunken patio in front of the main mound. Only vestiges of these features remain with the heavily damaged Mound 4-1. Arrow points to magnetic north. © 2003, J. Blomster.

3) on the side opposite the temple. This architectural arrangement appears during the Classic period at Monte Albán (contemporaneous with the Las Flores phase in the Nochixtlán Valley) and apparently spread to other sites both in the Valley and beyond (Winter 1989). Excavation of Mound 4-3 would more fully determine if it corresponds to a TPA, yielding insights into architectural layouts and use of space at Classic period centers.

Two other mound systems, both substantially larger than Mound 4-3, lie on the southern portion of the hill's summit (Figure 3.7). Both mounds appear to have smaller constructions flanking them to the north and south, potentially forming a three-mound arrangement, which is characteristic of Classic Valley of Oaxaca sites. In both cases at Etlatongo, these flanking mounds—close to but not touching the central mound—remain difficult to define, having been greatly affected by farming. Overgrown and visible in the field as irregular bumps, they emerge more clearly on the maps. Examples documented in the Valley of Oaxaca exhibit three mounds roughly equivalent in size without the dramatic size difference between what I refer to as "flanking mounds" at Etlatongo (Winter 1989). Mounds 4-1 and 4-2 may represent a distinct Mixtec manifestation of a Valley of Oaxaca architectural arrangement, with a large central mound flanked by two substantially smaller mounds. At Etlatongo, each system is arranged so that the three mounds form a small patio between them. Mound 4-2 includes a sunken patio; a well-defined rectangular depression descends approximately 0.5 meter below the surrounding patio. Exposed plaster floor fragments remain on both mounds, and a substantial stone wall rises from the sides of Mound 4-2.

The mound systems face each other, with the central mounds aligned. A broad, flat expanse of land—approximately 225 meters from west to east—connects these two mound systems (Figure 3.7). I refer to this open space as a possible plaza. This flat plane resembles large plazas documented at other Mixteca Alta sites such as Huamelulpan and Yucuñudahui. The elevation of the Etlatongo plaza averages 83 meters above the level of the valley floor, with a change in elevation over an area of approximately 16,975 square meters of only 2 meters, most of which is extremely gradual.

These hilltop mounds still play important roles to contemporary Etlatongo villagers. They serve as excellent vantage points from which to watch animals graze, and on Mound 4-2, several wooden crosses continue as focal points for offerings, including candles, small ceramic objects, and stones.

A possible Classic/Postclassic palace lies to the south of Mound 4-1. Although highly eroded, we recorded this feature as a possible mound (Mound 4-5). I base this initial identification on both excavated and surveyed floor structures encountered in the Valley of Oaxaca and the Mixteca Alta (Winter 1992, personal communication). While on the surface possible partitions within the feature emerge, their orientation and arrangement with each other remain unclear. The possible internal arrangement of space, and the placement of this structure on the south edge of the "plaza," appears similar to the location of a probable "palace" at Monte Albán. The artifacts examined during the survey indicate that the possible Postclassic structure that remains on the surface probably overlies an earlier Classic structure.

THE ETLATONGO BALLCOURT   The surface reconnaissance revealed an architectural feature previously unrecorded at Etlatongo—a ballcourt (Figure 3.8). The ballcourt lies immediately to the south of and abuts Mound 4-1, located in the initial drop-off from the hill's apex 7 meters above. This position at Etlatongo—near and below an eastern corner of a plaza—is similar to that of the main ballcourt at Monte Albán, which lies on but just below the level of the Main Plaza near its northeast corner.

The Etlatongo ballcourt follows the conventional shape of these structures in Mesoamerica—a capital "I." The ballcourt is approximately 45 meters long by 15 meters wide, oriented approximately east to west (75 degrees east of magnetic north). Problems exist with these measurements, however, due to the destruction of the ballcourt's eastern portion. While the longer, sloping sides (the batters) of the ballcourt are readily visible, the "end zones" are highly eroded. The flat central playing area is used for farming. Based only on survey, this ballcourt represents a Classic period construction, due to its relation to the purported plaza and Mound 4-1. The ballcourt was built after or in conjunction with the construction of the plaza and Mound 4-1; it incorporates the southern embankment of the plaza/Mound 4-1 as its north axis or batter.

Many questions remain unanswered about how ancient Mesoamericans played the ball game. Clearly a ballcourt represented much more than mere sport and included a highly sanctified ritual aspect. These courts played important ritual/symbolic roles, as well as roles in sociopolitical and economic spheres. Among the Mixtec, some scholars suggest that some Postclassic ballcourts on the border of a community's territory, often along with a market, served as boundary markers and were places in which antagonistic communities could interact (Pohl et al. 1997). Not all contemporaneous sites have ballcourts. In fact, the presence of a ballcourt probably reflects that site's importance in the regional site hierarchy. Both Mixteca Alta sites noted for the presence of broad plazas, Huamelulpan and Yucuñudahui, also have ballcourts. Both sites have also been interpreted as being central sites in their

Figure 3.8 Looking southeast from the top of Mound 4-1 to the Etlatongo ballcourt, south of and adjacent to Mound 4-1. The long axes of the ballcourt are oriented approximately east to west.

respective subregions. Contemporaneity of these ballcourts remains to be established through excavations.

Although the complete layout of the Etlatongo hill summit will never be completely understood because of the continual disturbance of surface remains, the features that remain illustrate a layout similar to "urban centers" (Winter 1989:42) found throughout Oaxaca during the Classic period. The main public buildings lie on ridge tops and high points (i.e., the summit of the Etlatongo hill), and residential terraces cluster on the slopes.

SUMMARY OF SURVEY RESULTS

The 1992 Etlatongo surface survey documented that two supposedly separate sites share remnants of an extensive Postclassic occupation. Rather than the supposed uninhabited zone between them, occupation from the lower site expanded during the Late Formative period to include the hill and its southern slopes. I refer to this as one site, Etlatongo. I divided this site into four research areas, or strata. From the surface remains, Area 1 appeared to be primarily occupied during the Yucuita and Ramos phases, with fewer Las Flores and Natividad materials than the other three areas. Areas 2 and 3 exhibited similar surface materials as Area 1, but manifested a marked presence of Cruz materials (particularly Middle Cruz) throughout most of Area 2. The survey did not find any definite Early Cruz materials on the surface at Etlatongo. Also, we noted a great increase in the amount of Natividad remains in these two areas compared with Area 1. Area 4, the Etlatongo hill, contrasted with the other areas by exhibiting proportionately less Yucuita and Ramos material, while manifesting dense concentrations of ceramics from the Las Flores and Natividad phases. We encountered no Cruz materials in Area 4. Thus, from the survey results, people first inhabited Etlatongo during the Middle Cruz phase, with successive generations occupying the site throughout the remainder of the pre-Hispanic sequence. While the surface survey results exhibited less early material than anticipated, the data demonstrate that these first inhabitants occupied Area 2 and, to a lesser extent, Area 3.

Population and occupational density increased dramatically in the Yucuita and Ramos phases (Late Formative/Early Classic periods), reflected in the occupation of Areas 1, 2, and 3, and with some colonization of the southern slopes and apex of Area 4. The ceramic sequence is not sufficiently sensitive to chronological change to determine the contemporaneity of this occupation. Conceivably, different portions of Areas 1, 2, and 3 could have been occupied by successive generations, making the actual extent of the site occupied at any one time less widespread than that envisioned based on the survey data. The recent definition of a new ceramic phase—the Yucuita phase (see Chapter 7)—provides a new tool with which to further refine the chronology.

A major settlement change occurred late in the Ramos phase/early in the Las Flores phase, when many of the inhabitants, and apparently many public structures, shifted to the apex of the Etlatongo hill, Area 4. Population in the remaining portions of Etlatongo appears to have been more diffuse during the Las Flores phase than in the previous Ramos phase; much of the population probably lived on the slopes of the Etlatongo hill. Generally, the Las Flores phase is difficult to detect consistently in Areas 1 through 3. One reason centers on the lack of diagnostic ceramics for the Las Flores phase. Few ceramic types have been defined that occur only in the Las Flores phase; excavation of numerous Las Flores phase contexts would aid in resolving this problem. Finally, during the Natividad phase, a widespread and dense occupation covers the entire site of Etlatongo. Only on the apex and slopes of the Etlatongo hill are Postclassic remains not abundant.

MICROSETTLEMENT PATTERNING AND DIACHRONIC CHANGE AT ETLATONGO

On an intrasite level, the site survey data from Etlatongo support the changes in settlement pattern at the regional level in the Nochixtlán Valley observed by Spores (1972:171–192). I refer to this as microsettlement patterning (Blomster 1995). In a large site, such as Etlatongo, that encompasses different—and adjacent—topographic zones, it is possible to compare diachronic changes in site occupation and utilization with the regional settlement pattern proposed for the Nochixtlán Valley. By examining continuity and changes in village size and placement, it is possible to assess both the impact of similar variables on the village and on a valleywide level, as well as the degree of integration of the site into the regional system. Such an analysis has been performed for 12 centuries of a Nubian village, where significant changes in village composition and land utilization have been related to larger regional processes, both in the social and physical environments (Adams 1968). One problem with comparing 1992 data and Nochixtlán Valley patterns lies in the lack of chronological refinement for the period as first established by Spores (1972). In his definition of the Nochixtlán Valley ceramic sequence, Spores defined only four pre-Hispanic phases: Cruz, Ramos,

Las Flores, and Natividad, without the subphases and refinements that others, building on Spores's research, have contributed (see Table 1.1).

Summarized, Spores's pattern begins with the earliest Cruz villages located along the valley floor, primarily in fertile bottomlands and the tributary valleys adjacent to them. Later Cruz sites also lay on low *lomas* (slightly raised areas near alluvial bottomlands). Such locations served to decrease the risk of flooding to villagers. During the Ramos phase (i.e., both the Yucuita and Ramos phases utilized in this volume), in addition to continued utilization of Cruz locations, settlers incorporated land at somewhat higher elevations, with low *lomas* and the ends of high ridge spurs becoming preferred village locations. Ramos phase sites occur more frequently and appear generally larger than Cruz villages (Spores 1984).

A major settlement shift occurred in the Las Flores phase, when villagers abandoned the low-lying, unprotected areas on the valley floor, and instead selected hills and high ridge tops for their settlements. Villagers shifted their residences away from *lomas* and alluvial land that could be farmed; utilizing this land for farming rather than occupation is seen as a response to increased population (Spores 1972). Several sites first settled in the Las Flores phase, such as Yucuñudahui, are planned, complex centers on hill summits—Spores (1972, 1984) called them urban centers or civic ceremonial centers. The settlement pattern defined by Spores appears most diffuse in the Natividad phase. The high ridges and hills so distinctive of the Las Flores phase continue to be inhabited, but villagers also return to the low-lying areas they had largely abandoned in the previous phase. Sites occupied for the first time during the Natividad phase occur at lower elevations. This shift to lower, less defensible positions (often on good farmland) relates to demographic pressure; crowding on the high ridges and hills forced a downward shift in settlement placement (Spores 1972:190). The Natividad phase represents a time of maximum population density in the Nochixtlán Valley. Sociopolitical and economic strains were becoming increasingly severe by the time of the Spanish arrival (see Chapters 1 and 2).

The settlement pattern at Etlatongo discernible from the surface survey largely follows the model proposed by Spores. Data, however, from the test units and excavation areas greatly refine the understanding of Etlatongo's settlement history. Here I summarize the occupation for each of the four areas by phase, revising our tour of Etlatongo.

Early Cruz Phase

Previous excavations at Etlatongo in 1980 (Zárate Morán 1987) encountered no evidence of primary Early Cruz occupation at Etlatongo. The 1992 survey and excavations also failed to uncover primary Early Cruz deposits, although we uncovered stylistically related sherds and figurine fragments in early Middle Cruz contexts. This represents continuing utilization of such styles, if not actual earlier vessels, from the Early Cruz. Obviously, ceramic style change from the Early to Middle Cruz did not occur overnight; we should expect to see signs of a transition. Some sherds probably represent actual vessels constructed during the later Early Cruz phase that continued to be used in the Middle Cruz phase.

The most abundant materials from this late Early Cruz/early Middle Cruz transition originate from Area 2. Excavation Area 2 (EA-2) exposed possible Early Cruz vessel fragments and a figurine head in the earliest deposits from this 5 × 7 meter unit (see Chapter 5). A bell-shaped pit excavated into bedrock (Feature 29) included both ceramics from the early Middle Cruz phase and others diagnostic of the Early Cruz. Both a carbon date and ceramic types support an interpretation of this feature as associated with the early portion of the Middle Cruz phase, that is, pre–1000 B.C.

We encountered several Early Cruz figurine fragments in Area 1, in Middle Cruz deposits laden with figurines (see Chapter 4). These deposits are probably somewhat later than those in Feature 29 (see Chapter 6, Table 6.1). These Early Cruz figurine fragments occur in secondary refuse deposited during the Middle Cruz phase. Thus, while the 1992 excavations encountered fragments of Early Cruz materials at Etlatongo, no primary occupation—in the form of floors or features—corresponds solely with the Early Cruz phase. Primary deposits from this earliest ceramic phase probably exist at Etlatongo, but represent a small occupation. Additional archaeological testing will clarify this.

Middle Cruz Phase

Materials from the Middle Cruz phase cover much of the lower portion of the site and will be discussed in more depth in subsequent chapters. The 1992 excavations demonstrated that the Middle Cruz occupations extended much farther than observed only through surface survey. The pedestrian reconnaissance documented Middle Cruz materials mostly in Area 2, with some overlap into the southern portion of Area 3. In contrast, the excavations showed that the Middle Cruz occupation extended into most of Area 3 and also into Area 1, all the way to the southernmost unit excavated in 1992 (Unit 1). Based on a combination of data from the survey and the excavations, the Middle Cruz occupations can be projected to have encompassed an area of 26.2 hectares (see Figure 3.9, which differentiates high- and low-density areas of occupation). The great depth of Middle Cruz occupations was evident in excavations throughout Areas 1 through 3, where we identified Middle Cruz materials and primary occupations over 5 meters below modern ground surface. These Middle Cruz deposits, including features and floors, often extended 1 to 2 meters in depth.

Contradicting the surface survey, all Area 1 test units yielded Middle Cruz ceramics. Middle Cruz deposits appeared scattered throughout Areas 2 and 3; they were absent in some test units but present in others. Areas 1 through 3 contain extensive examples of Middle Cruz platform construction. The most abundant Middle Cruz remains came from EA-2 in Area 2; I date four occupations, two of which consisted of numerous resurfacing episodes, to the Middle Cruz (see Chapter 5). Three of these occupations occur on platforms ranging from 15 to 50 centimeters in height.

With little Early Cruz precedent, the Middle Cruz phase appears to have been a time of tremendous demographic growth at Etlatongo. Middle Cruz occupations rest directly over bedrock, with no intervening Early Cruz deposits; in all cases, they represent the earliest documented occupations at Etlatongo. These occupations were concentrated on low *lomas* and the bottomlands close to the Yucuita and Yanhuitlán rivers.

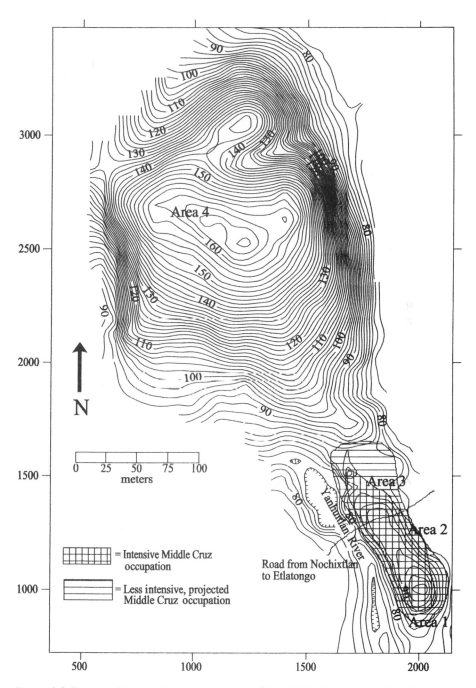

Figure 3.9 Topographic map showing the extent of the Middle Cruz occupation of Etlatongo, with areas of intensive and less intensive occupation indicated based on surface survey and excavations. Contour interval is 2 meters; arrow points to magnetic north.
© 2003, J. Blomster.

Late Cruz Phase

Defining the exact limits of the Late Cruz phase remains problematic at Etlatongo. While following the pattern proposed for the Nochixtlán Valley of general growth in settlement from the Middle Cruz to Ramos phase (Spores 1972), Late Cruz deposits do not always cover Middle Cruz occupations. Construction on several Middle Cruz platforms appears to have ceased in the Late Cruz phase, and some long-lasting Middle Cruz occupations appear to have been abandoned by the Late Cruz. There is often little continuity in utilization of space between these successive phases. In at least three units, Late Cruz deposits represent the earliest occupations encountered. We encountered Late Cruz materials throughout Areas 1 through 3, but not in Area 4. With additional information, a map of the Late Cruz occupation would slightly expand on that for the Middle Cruz (Figure 3.9).

The 1992 excavations exposed examples of Late Cruz large-scale construction efforts. In Area 3, explorations of Mound 3-1 revealed an intact wall over 3 meters in height. This structure clearly evinces construction and utilization during the Late Cruz phase. I interpret the wall's location, on the edge of this large mound, as representing an expansion of earlier structures—these may date to the Middle Cruz, and may provide crucial evidence in the transition from Middle to Late Cruz. While possibly having some Middle Cruz antecedents, Mound A—the massive deposit of walls and fill adjacent to the Yanhuitlán River—probably began to assume its initial form in the Late Cruz or early in the Yucuita phase. Thus, while some of the construction loci changed in the Late Cruz, it appears that approximately the same amount of the site was occupied, although there may have been some increase in occupation itself.

Yucuita and Ramos Phases

I discuss the Yucuita and Ramos phases together, as we did not distinguish the then unidentified Yucuita phase from the Ramos during the 1992 fieldwork. The Yucuita and Ramos phase occupations cover much of the lower portion of Etlatongo, and represent a clear increase in the amount of land used from the Late Cruz phase. Throughout Areas 1 through 3, Yucuita and Ramos remains usually covered earlier Cruz remains; few previously occupied portions of the site remained unoccupied during this time, and previously unoccupied portions received Yucuita and Ramos occupation.

Yucuita and Ramos occupations often expanded on earlier Cruz platforms, and at least one possible platform was first constructed during the Ramos phase. Activity in the southern portion of Area 3 may have been part of a program of redesigning space formerly dominated in the Cruz phase by Mound 3-1. Two possible public buildings in Area 2, both marked by large, faced stones set in mortar, also date to the Yucuita and Ramos phases. In addition, we exposed abundant examples of domestic space associated with the Yucuita and Ramos phases. Besides surfaces, features, and other small fragments of dwellings, we documented walls of two Yucuita phase houses. We also explored a dense concentration of Yucuita phase occupations in Area 2, where we documented a sequence of structures, features, and burials, interpreted as associated with generations of the same family (see Chapter 7).

A dramatic settlement change, dating more to the Ramos than the Yucuita phase, involves the initial colonization of portions of the Etlatongo hill (Area 4). On the southern slopes of this hill, we encountered dense concentrations of Ramos materials, including some nearly complete bowls probably from a disturbed burial. On the summit of the hill, a test unit documented two Ramos floors, one of which was elevated by a small deposit of platform fill. Ramos artifacts did not cover all portions of the Area 4 summit, which I have tried to reflect in the estimation of the Ramos occupation of Etlatongo. Only additional excavations in Area 4 will be able to further establish the amount of the hill that was occupied during this phase.

The expansion of Ramos occupation to the Etlatongo hill parallels the pattern that Spores (1972) proposed for the Nochixtlán Valley, when new villages occupied ridge spurs and *lomas* not adjacent to bottomlands for the first time. In addition to the new land colonized by villagers, the lower lands continued to be intensively occupied.

Las Flores Phase

The Las Flores phase evinces the most dramatic shift in site occupation at Etlatongo. Ancient Mixtecs intensively occupied Area 4, the Etlatongo hill, and constructed much of the public architecture—mounds, plazas, and a ballcourt—that is still visible. We excavated one test unit to the west of one of the major mounds in Area 4. These excavations revealed that a massive platform, created largely through boulders used as fill, elevated the southern portion of the hill more than 1.5 meters above the earlier Ramos occupations, creating the large flat "plaza" area observed during the survey between Mounds 4-1 and 4-2. The stratigraphic profile documents this massive construction project, with the plaza surface created through deployment of boulders capped by a 32-centimeter thick stucco floor (see Figure 3.10). From the brief window into this construction opened by the 1992 excavations, the creation of this plaza is comparable (albeit on a smaller scale) to the construction of the Main Plaza at Monte Albán, which involved removal of bedrock outcrops and filling of depressed areas to create a flat surface. Such projects represent a massive modification of the landscape.

In contrast to the Ramos occupation, Las Flores materials appear inconsistently scattered throughout Areas 1 through 3. No primary occupations dating to the Las Flores phase could be defined; we excavated no floors or features from this phase. We encountered Las Flores ceramics only in the upper strata in a few test units, as well as in both excavation areas. As noted, diagnostic ceramics for the Las Flores phase remain poorly understood, and thus the current Las Flores boundaries probably underestimate the size of this occupation. It appears, however, that villagers either abandoned much of the low-lying portion of Etlatongo or utilized this portion of the site differently, and much less intensively, than before. Because we excavated no Las Flores houses in Areas 1 through 3, the Classic period occupation of the lower portion of Etlatongo remains unclear, but probably was very limited. This Etlatongo shift in settlement matches what Spores (1972:183) observed for the Nochixtlán Valley as a whole, where he noted the initiation of new "urban" centers on hill summits during the Las Flores phase.

Natividad Phase

During the Natividad phase, a dense occupation covered the majority of Etlatongo. At different times during this phase, villagers occupied almost all of what I bound as Etlatongo (Figure 3.1). We encountered test units that yielded few Natividad materials. In particular, portions of Area 3, such as Mound 3-1, appear to have been less intensively occupied than other portions of Etlatongo during the Natividad

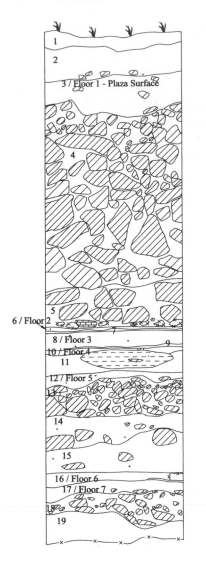

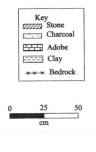

Key
Stone
Charcoal
Adobe
Clay
Bedrock

0   25   50
cm

Figure 3.10 Stratigraphic profile of the north wall of the Area 4 test unit, documenting massive construction activities employed to modify this landscape. The thick plaza surface represented by Floor 1 appears to be the final and grandest in a series of efforts to raise surface elevation through rock fill. Numbers refer to stratum and/or floor number. Grass indicates modern ground surface. © 2003, J. Blomster.

phase. The absence or scarcity of Natividad materials could also be due to post-abandonment destruction. Just as their presence over earlier deposits grants enhanced visibility to Postclassic surface materials, they also are the artifacts most likely to be destroyed and redeposited by modern site utilization.

In Area 2, Natividad occupations occurred in test units where no earlier materials had been documented; in such cases, Natividad occupations lay directly atop bedrock. These represent either the first occupation in that location, or these inhabitants removed traces of earlier occupations, although this latter interpretation appears unlikely. The spread of occupation to all portions of Etlatongo during the Natividad phase may represent the increase in population Spores (1972:190) suggested for this time. As observed for the Nochixtlán Valley, crowding on high ridges may have forced a significant portion of the population back down to the lower piedmont areas, where they constructed houses over valuable farmland.

Through the survey and excavations, we documented signs of this increased population. With few exceptions, Natividad materials remain the most highly represented on modern ground surface (although this can be partially attributed to their placement over earlier remains). Given that caveat, Natividad surface remains are staggering in their frequency. We observed numerous thick stucco floors, some with a painted surface, throughout cuts exposed in Area 2. During the Natividad phase, occupation at Etlatongo probably covered close to 208.2 hectares. Additional survey and excavation beyond the 1992 site boundaries may increase the total area of Natividad occupation at Etlatongo.

In conclusion, the large size of Etlatongo, its multioccupational nature, and the range of geographic diversity it encompasses make it an ideal site to which to apply Spores's (1972) model of the Nochixtlán Valley settlement pattern. The correspondence between site and region appears clear; Etlatongo represents a microcosm of Nochixtlán Valley settlement dynamics and reflects diachronic changes in that pattern. While archaeological sites are often considered discrete, self-contained entities, their settlement and demographic variability reflect their role in a larger system. By analyzing intrasite changes and comparing them to settlement and demographic norms on a regional level, the site's role and integration in a larger system can begin to be understood. Etlatongo appears extremely well integrated into the larger Nochixtlán Valley system, reflective of the site's important role in the settlement hierarchy beginning in the Middle Cruz phase. The consistency with which settlement changes within Etlatongo parallel larger valleywide processes, along with archaeological data, lead me to interpret Etlatongo's size and role in post-Cruz settlement hierarchies and politics as having been more expansive than has generally been accepted.

A Final Word on Surface Surveys

The results of the excavations paint a stark picture of the reliability of surface surveys at deep, multicomponent sites such as Etlatongo. As noted in Chapter 2, some researchers hypothesize that a clear relationship exists between surface materials and subsurface remains, at least to a certain depth (Redman and Watson 1970). Extreme site depth also has implications for the sampling strategy, with deep sites less amenable to probabilistic methods (Brown 1975). Researchers investigating a site in Central Mexico, with a component contemporaneous to the Middle Cruz at Etlatongo, noted that materials 25 centimeters or more below the surface may not be detected by a surface survey (Tolstoy and Fish 1975). Even when one ceramic phase can be isolated at a site, in the Mixteca Alta such a time span involves at least 300 years (see Table 1.1). The site as defined by the archaeologist represents a mass of refuse and features that have accumulated over many life spans. The boundaries defined reflect the site at its largest extension, a size it may never have achieved in a single human generation at the site. As proposed in Central Mexico (Tolstoy and Fish 1975), it also appears that surface surveys overrepresent the population of a site at any given moment in time. Thus, I urge caution in drawing conclusions from surface surveys not tested by excavations.

4/Middle Cruz Social Complexity and Village Life at Etlatongo

A Formative Primer and Sampler

With an understanding of the approximate size of Middle Cruz Etlatongo provided by the site survey and test units, a goal of the research centered on emerging social complexity. Did some villagers have access to more exotic goods and exhibit a different socioeconomic status than others? Chapter 6 grapples with the first half of this question by exploring interregional interaction. To examine the second half of the question, the fieldwork was designed to explore different types of houses and structures, to compare features and architecture of possible higher-status houses and public structures with those of a typical house. In this chapter, I report two test units that provide possible examples of a higher-status house and a public structure and/or space. In Chapter 5, I derive additional information on higher-status households from larger-scale horizontal excavations. The units explored in Chapters 4 and 5 have also been selected because artifacts from contexts within these excavations shall be analyzed in Chapter 6. Before discussing these excavations and establishing what constitutes a typical Early Formative household, I briefly outline some of the excavation strategies employed at Etlatongo.

UNIT SELECTION AND EXCAVATION METHODS

I selected exact coordinates of units randomly (see Chapter 2 for details). Once an area had been subdivided as part of the stratified random sample, I established the general direction of the test unit and programmed into a calculator a random distance and angle. Operations for each 1 × 1 meter test unit began with a total surface collection of all cultural materials. We excavated units through a combination of trowels and small picks, with larger picks and *barretas* (an elongated crowbar) employed to quickly excavate through areas of recent disturbance. Reserving excavating by "natural" stratigraphy for the larger excavation areas, I elected to excavate test units in arbitrary 20-centimeter levels (see the text that follows and "Digging Deeper" section in this chapter). This allows for comparability between test units, although arbitrary levels often did not match the strata defined for the profile of the soil

---

DIGGING DEEPER: THE JOYS OF STRAIGHT-SIDED UNITS

Throughout the fieldwork, field assistants often questioned why I emphasized keeping unit walls straight. As I hovered above them with a plumb bob, in order to prevent crooked or undulating walls, they probably assumed that archaeologists derive some kind of obsessive pleasure from indulging in such behavior. The reality remains far more prosaic. Essentially, archaeologists test a site with units of the same size in order to enhance comparability between units. This is why it was useful to excavate test units by 20-centimeter arbitrary levels, before we clearly understood the "natural" stratigraphy of the site. This allowed for comparability in terms of artifact quantities both within the site and between sites excavated in a similar manner. In order to maintain the viability of such comparisons, however, archaeologists must ensure that their units actually measure 1 × 1 meters. Straight-sided units with consistent, nonundulating walls also enhance photography and profile documentation because shadows (which form when bulges or cave-ins exist in the profile) are eliminated. Thus, the joys of straight-sided units are many.

---

stratigraphy drawn for each unit. We mitigated this problem somewhat by treating culturally constructed features differently during the excavations. We excavated all features and floors as discrete units, as well as the 5 centimeters above the floor, as this deposit generally contains material related to floor use. All objects on floor contact were documented by their three-dimensional locations. We labeled a unit as "complete" only when bedrock lay exposed at the unit's base.

Evaluation of the test unit stratigraphy allowed excavation of larger horizontal units by what is normally referred to as "natural" stratigraphy. Previous excavations at Etlatongo, in fact, had conveniently divided the stratigraphy of all units into four "natural" strata (Zárate Morán 1987). I quickly realized it is unrealistic to expect the same strata to appear over large distances at sites such as Etlatongo. In fact, rather than "natural" stratigraphy, I prefer to employ the concept of "cultural" stratigraphy. Villages such as Etlatongo exhibit enormous amounts of various activities. Villagers constantly constructed houses, dug storage pits, deposited trash as middens, and used fill—both natural and cultural—to construct platforms. In all of the excavations at Etlatongo, no unit exhibited "natural" stratigraphy (except for bedrock at the base of most units) in the sense that purely natural forces, such as erosion or flooding, were solely responsible for the soil deposition. Humans severely affect formation processes at villages such as Etlatongo, and thus it is unlikely that any stratum relating to specific human activities will extend for any great distance outside of the household in which it was initially deposited.

We screened all soil from the test units with standard 0.25-inch mesh, retaining all artifacts. We also collected soil samples from middens, burials, and inside intact vessels. These procedures continued during the excavation of two larger horizontal units, with one exception to be discussed in Chapter 5.

ARCHAEOLOGY AT EARLY MESOAMERICAN
VILLAGES: A FORMATIVE PRIMER

Since this chapter explores early social complexity in terms of differential social rank and public space, I outline here the basic features of an Early Formative village and "typical" house. As detailed in Chapter 1, relative social inequality characterizes Early Formative social organization. Social status varied along a continuum within a community. Dramatic status discontinuities do not appear to be present in the Mixteca Alta, a conclusion also reached for contemporaneous Valley of Oaxaca villages (see text that follows). Thus, a term such as *higher-status residence* more likely reflects Early Formative social organization at Etlatongo, rather than "elite" or simply "high status." Public space contrasts with private space, but does not automatically entail economic-based social differentiation. Many nonstratified groups have public space, sometimes a sacred place, which the group as a whole constructs and maintains (Adler and Wilshusen 1990).

Many researchers of the Formative period diligently segregate "public space" from "higher-status" contexts, a practice I gamely attempt to follow. There remains the possibility, however, that the two categories lack the clear distinction we attempt to impose. Structure 4 from Mound 6 at Paso de la Amada, along the Pacific Coast of Chiapas, exemplifies this problem. Elevated by a platform, this Early Formative structure resembles a rectangle with rounded ends. While some scholars refer to this structure as a chiefly residence (Clark and Pye 2000:231), others identify it as an area of ritual and public space (Marcus and Flannery 1996:90–91). Due to the presence of both domestic artifacts and materials related to ritual at Paso de la Amada mounds, a more parsimonious interpretation emphasizes the lack of segregation between domestic and ceremonial activity. Status differences that emerged may not have been tied to significant economic advantages but rather to control over sacred knowledge and practice (Lesure and Blake 2002). In early villages, such as those in both Chiapas and Oaxaca, considerable blurring may exist between etic (imposed by the archaeologist) categories such as "higher status" and "ceremonial." Cross-cultural comparisons of small, politically nonstratified communities reveal many instances where so-called ceremonial structures also served as the loci for domestic chores, while a ritual may have been performed in a structure utilized as the full-time residence of the chief (Adler 1989). Only larger communities had structures with a primary ritual use.

The lack of a complete "typical" Middle Cruz house plagues the Etlatongo data. During the excavations, test units exposed glimpses of "normal" occupations, but these often remained ephemeral and hard to define—a problem also experienced by excavators at Paso de la Amada (Lesure and Blake 2002). Possible examples of typical houses generally did not have the kind of integrity suggestive of a well-preserved structure and were not allocated additional excavations. Both past and present Etlatongo excavations, as well as investigations at the nearby Early Formative site of Yucuita, have failed to document the architecture and dimensions of a complete, typical Middle Cruz house. The situation improves for the Late Formative at both Etlatongo and Yucuita (Robles García 1988; see Chapter 7). In the Valley of Oaxaca, with the dual advantage of less overburden (often less than half a meter) and long-term field projects, excavators have exposed entire house floors representing a variety of statuses. At Etlatongo, Middle Cruz occupations invariably sat below 2 to 3 meters of overburden. I selected one Middle Cruz context for more extensive excavations (see Chapter 5) due to extensive preservation of architectural features. Because higher-status and public structures are generally better constructed than typical domestic houses, preservation issues conspire to bias the sample.

Because data for contemporaneous "average" house plans remain absent in the Nochixtlán Valley, I turn to the Valley of Oaxaca in order to present an overview of typical Early Formative households—self-sufficient units that served as the focus of domestic life. While the basic split between Mixtec and Zapotec languages originates around 3700 B.C., by the beginning of the Early Formative period (around 1500 B.C.), many cultural divergences were still being established. In the Late Formative, Mixtec and Zapotec settlements distinguish themselves from each other through architecture and ceramics; these differences remain less developed in the Early Formative. Furthermore, these architectural differences manifest themselves primarily in public and higher-status loci rather than in the domestic realm of the typical villagers. Through research at early villages such as Tierras Largas (Winter 1972), Hacienda Blanca (Ramírez Urrea 1993), and San José Mogote, in the northwest branch of the Valley of Oaxaca (Fernández Dávila and Gómez Serafín 1997; Flannery and Marcus 1994), entire houses and public structures have been documented. Because the Nochixtlán Valley lacks comparable contemporaneous data, I present the Valley of Oaxaca data, informed and amended by Etlatongo observations, as a Highland Formative village primer.

House Size, Construction, and Interior Space

Walls of rectangular Formative houses extend 3 to 4 meters wide by 5 to 6 meters long, for a total area of 15 to 24 square meters, while floors consist of sand or stamped earth (Flannery 1976a). At Etlatongo, villagers often modified exposed bedrock to serve as surfaces. Valley of Oaxaca floors often slope toward the center of the house through use. Some researchers suggest floor space may have been subdivided into male and female work areas (Flannery and Marcus 1994). At this stage in the Etlatongo research, it remains difficult to make such gender-related divisions. In both regions, villagers often resurfaced floors, placing a consistent layer of new material atop an earlier floor.

Valley of Oaxaca houses feature stones placed at wall bases to support the foundation and wooden posts in the corners; walls largely consist of wattle (reeds) and daub (mud). This appears to be the pattern at Etlatongo as well, although we rarely encountered foundation stones *in situ*—I interpret this as being primarily due to reuse (see text that follows). In contemporary Oaxacan villages, wattle and daub houses may last between 10 and 25 years (Flannery and Marcus 1994:25). To build a house, ancient villagers constructed thatched roofs over a pole frame; the holes (referred to as post holes) dug into the ground for these poles remain for archaeologists to find. Household units, encompassing an area of perhaps 300 square meters, including the house and associated features (see following text), appear to have been spaced 20 to 40 meters apart. This observation proves critical in Chapters 5 and 7. Villages did not grow "straight up"; an analogy has been made to a corkscrew, or clockface, where house sites were abandoned and occupation shifted to land adjacent to the abandoned structure, eventually returning to the original site, which often served as a midden until reoccupied (Flannery and Marcus 1994:36).

Exterior Space

A prepared exterior space often served as the focus for many household activities (Winter 1989:23). Though difficult to assess based on a 1 × 1 meter unit, it appears that exterior floors often formed a less level surface than interior ones. I employ two terms for exterior surfaces: *dooryard* and *apron* (also see Flannery and Marcus 1994:25–34). Both terms apply to outside activity areas, but the term *apron* explicitly denotes a prepared surface and is the primary type of exterior space I observed at Etlatongo. While dooryard areas may be compacted, either through use or intentionally leveled, a separate deposit of packed earth or plaster was not utilized, as with an apron. In the Valley of Oaxaca, aprons occur primarily outside public buildings; this distinction is not supported by the Etlatongo data, although the Middle Cruz sample remains too limited for conclusive comparisons.

Associated Features

A variety of features, in addition to the actual house, comprise an Early Formative household unit.

STORAGE FEATURES   Excavated into bedrock or other deposits, storage features abound at early villages. Found both inside and outside of the house, these pit features are generally bell-shaped, cylindrical, or bottle-shaped in cross section. Initially these primarily held the household's maize and other foods, and were sealed with flat rocks to inhibit insect growth through oxygen deprivation. Through time, the pits spoiled and villagers devised other uses for them, such as trash receptacles and often for burials.

EXTERIOR PIT OVENS   Outdoor ovens, generally for roasting maguey, have been documented in the Valley of Oaxaca. It appears that most of the cooking was done in ceramic braziers rather than interior hearths (Flannery and Marcus 1994). These have not been well documented at Etlatongo, although some suggestive possibilities occur in later contexts.

BURIALS   In Mesoamerican villages, individuals continued to be part of the family after their death. One tangible manifestation of this relationship lies in the close proximity of the deceased to their homes; they were buried either under or outside of and close to the house. A sequence of post–Middle Cruz burials will be explored in Chapter 7.

MIDDENS   Villagers generally deposited refuse in various trash concentrations, or middens, near the house (Flannery and Winter 1976:34–37). Such trash includes food remains, broken vessels, and ash from cooking fires. Middens are great friends to archaeologists, proving invaluable as many of the artifacts remain relatively undisturbed after their disposal, even though a considerable time span during which villagers added trash to the midden may be involved. Most of the possible middens encountered at Etlatongo correspond to what Valley of Oaxaca archaeologists refer to as household middens—small areas of refuse-dumping near the house. A larger midden type, a community midden, has also been described in the Valley of Oaxaca (Flannery and Marcus 1994:28–31), involving relocation of household refuse to a larger disposal site. While this distinction remains to be proven in the Mixteca, I report one possible midden (used as platform fill) that appears larger than that from one household.

PLATFORM FILL AND CULTURAL FILL   In order to construct a platform that would elevate a surface or structure, villagers often reused refuse, especially from middens, and other material as platform fill. In the Valley of Oaxaca, this has been linked to public structures; at Etlatongo, I believe platform fill may have elevated either public or higher-status structures. *Platform fill* implies intentional behavior, as opposed to the term *cultural fill*, which I use as a very general interpretation when a given stratum appears to have been deposited by human action, but not serving an obvious construction-related purpose.

Higher-Status Houses

From the sample of houses excavated in the Valley of Oaxaca, some are clearly more elaborate than others in terms of construction. The more elaborate houses have a stone foundation and walls whitewashed with plaster or clay (which increases the use-life of the house). These houses also show a more diversified assortment of artifacts, including more deer bone, spondylus and pearl oyster shell, stingray spines, and more pots with Olmec designs (Flannery and Marcus 1983:55, 63). Such houses may have a sheltered exterior work area associated with them, and may even show some craft specialization, such as a magnetite mirror workshop at San José Mogote. At Etlatongo, such structures may be set apart from other structures by a small platform. In the Valley of Oaxaca, these platforms have been associated only with public structures. At Etlatongo, platforms exist on different size scales, which may correlate with either higher-status or public space. Examples of both will be discussed from Etlatongo. Generally, higher-status structures appear to rest on smaller platforms than do public ones.

Public Structures

In the Valley of Oaxaca, public space has been interpreted as dating prior to the Middle Cruz phase at sites such as San José Mogote, where small public buildings, coated inside and out with lime plaster, have orientations that set them apart from other structures. Small platforms also differentiate these structures, often elevating the structure from 20 to as much as 40 centimeters above the surrounding land, with the interior floor recessed into the platform rather than being flush with its elevation (Flannery and Marcus 1994). More posts supported the walls of public structures, and floors received a lime plaster coating, with the exterior surrounded by a plaster apron. Several other types of public buildings have been documented in subsequent chronological portions of the Early Formative in the Valley of Oaxaca.

Figurines

Fragments of small, solid, clay figurines are ubiquitous at early villages (see Figure 4.1). Researchers have proposed many different functions for figurines, ranging from toys to objects involved in negotiations of gender roles. Summarizing the variety of interpretations is beyond the scope of this chapter. Here I note only that I support an

© 2003, J. Blomster

Figure 4.1 A sample of Middle Cruz figurine fragments recovered from within the same small portion of the Unit 1 midden. The varieties of figurines reflect different styles of depicting the human body, including fragments of both solid and hollow figurines.

interpretation whereby villagers deployed at least *some* solid figurines within the contexts of household rituals. Figurine fragments lie scattered throughout these villages, rather than confined to one type of structure or one part of a site. They appear in middens, house floors, platform fill, and in features. I report one context at Etlatongo that contained a disproportionately high number of figurines, but I emphasize that these were all fragments—it is unusual to find intact figurines. When found whole, it has been possible to reconstruct the ritual scenes created with some figurines. One group of figurines found at House 16, San José Mogote, has been interpreted as reflecting status differences, with three male figurines in positions of submission and one male figurine sitting above them in an authority position (Marcus and Flannery 1996:100). These figurines may reflect burial patterns and emerging status differences. It appears that all village inhabitants had access to solid figurines. Less common in both quantity and variety of contexts are hollow figurines. These match neither the distribution nor frequency of solid figurines, a theme to which I return later in this chapter.

UNIT 1: PUBLIC SPACE AT ETLATONGO

I placed Unit 1, the first test pit excavated in 1992, on Mound 1-1 (in the southern portion of Area 1) in order to determine if this mound represented the result of human or natural processes (see Figure 4.2). After stratifying Mound 1-1 as a subsection of

Figure 4.2 Mound 1-1 in Research Area 1, the location of the first test unit in 1992. View is of the southwest face of the mound, showing the dirt road leading to a threshing floor (still utilized) atop the mound.

Area 1, I entered numbers into the calculator that reflected the edge of this mound to generate the exact coordinates of Unit 1; I excluded numbers pertaining to the mound's center in order to avoid the deepest portion of it. The presence of several bedrock outcrops protruding from the slope below Unit 1 suggested the vertical depth of this unit would not be exceptional. Excavations proved both this observation and the dating of the Mound 1-1 occupation based on surface survey to be incorrect. Excavations extended to a depth of 3.38 meters below modern ground surface and generated 6,692 sherds.

The Initial Middle Cruz Occupations

Contrary to expectations based on surface survey, much of Unit 1 represents an intensive Middle Cruz occupation, primarily from the middle portion of this phase (see Chapter 6). A carbon sample collected from Stratum 8 proved to be too small to analyze as a radiocarbon date. Instead, the laboratory employed a technique more appropriate for such small samples—accelerator mass spectrometry (AMS). Unlike radiocarbon dating, which measures a small fraction of the carbon-14 (^{14}C) atoms emitted from the sample's decay, AMS counts the atoms present in the sample. This procedure yielded a date of 3010 B.P., plus or minus 50 years, or 1060 B.C. An additional approach to reporting dates focuses on a range, due to problems with the calibration curve between "radiocarbon years" and "real time." In this case, the range is substantially earlier than the uncalibrated date, but 1060 B.C. better reflects the ceramic assemblage than the midway point of the range, which is 1260 B.C. cal.

While the exact date remains elusive, at some point midway through the Middle Cruz phase, villagers selected this portion of the site for construction, presumably due to a raised bedrock outcrop. As revealed by the base of Unit 1, even prior to construction this location would have been higher than the majority of the southern portion of Etlatongo, further increasing the elevations of subsequent constructions. Villagers flattened this irregular-shaped outcrop, constructing Floor 4 (or Stratum 12), the earliest surface exposed in Unit 1 (see Figure 4.3). Essentially, this surface is modified bedrock, with protrusions flattened and with some clay-loam soil added in low spots to form a smooth surface. Due to the limited nature of the exposed surface, I cannot determine if Floor 4—and subsequent surfaces—represents the interior floor of a structure, an apron, or even a plaza surface. Considering the nature of subsequent deposits, I favor the latter.

Although some cultural material may have accumulated atop Floor 4 as part of its occupation, or immediately after, the consistency of Stratum 11 and the way it covered Floor 4 suggests it may have been intentionally deposited in one event as platform fill. I argue that villagers placed Stratum 11 over Floor 4 in order to raise the subsequent surface, Floor 3, above the surrounding land. Stratum 11 elevated the very thin (2 to 3 centimeters) Floor 3 approximately 25 centimeters above Floor 4. As noted earlier, Valley of Oaxaca platform fill elevated early public buildings from 20 to 40 centimeters. Stratum 11, generally with low artifact frequency, formed a level platform for Floor 3, a compact sandy clay-loam. Floor 3 would have been substantially elevated by both its location on the raised bedrock outcrop and the platform fill that raised it above Floor 4. Based on subsequent utilization of this space, I propose Floor 3, and possibly its predecessor (Floor 4), represents a Middle Cruz public space or area of higher status. Platforms may signal more formalized areas for activities. Additional exposure of this area would reveal whether this series of platforms and floors shared the same orientation through time.

Middens, Ritual Refuse, and the Floor 2 Platform

After Floor 3 ceased to be utilized as a surface, it served as a locus for midden deposits, which grew over time during the Middle Cruz phase. Through a combination of texture, color, and inclusions, I identify three different deposits that comprise a large Middle Cruz phase midden. Strata 9, 8, and 7 represent discrete refuse disposal episodes that all occurred in the Middle Cruz phase; they form a midden on a scale beyond that of a single Early Formative period household. Strata 7 through 9 probably represent a community midden, including materials from several households, placed here to ultimately elevate the subsequent surface (Floor 2) an additional 60 centimeters above surrounding land and structures. I interpret these midden deposits as serving, indirectly or directly, as platform fill. Villagers placed a compact, clayey, and more stable soil over part of Stratum 7, probably to cap and prepare it for laying a surface. Floor 2 may have been utilized longer than Floors 3 and 4; a white clay lens covering a portion of it may be evidence of remodeling, suggesting repair and/or resurfacing—an effort absent in Floors 3 and 4. Combined with earlier surfaces, Floor 2 towered over 1 meter above the surrounding land. I interpret this surface, and the structure associated with it, as separate from the remainder of the community—one of the initial steps in the creation of public buildings or space. A

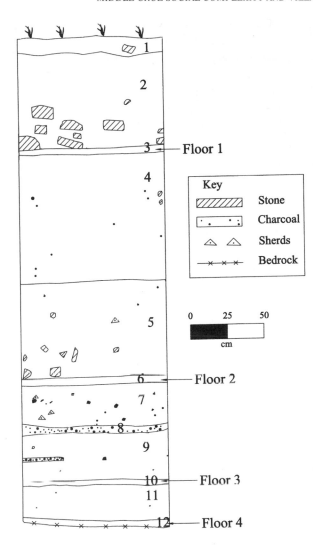

Figure 4.3 West strati-graphic profile of Unit 1, showing the succession of platform fill and construction episodes beginning in the Middle Cruz phase at Mound 1–1. © 2003, J. Blomster.

similar process of differentiation has been proposed in the Valley of Oaxaca (Flannery and Marcus 1994).

As typifies midden deposits, the strata below Floor 2 yielded high quantities of artifacts. Stratum 7 alone contained nearly 1,000 Middle Cruz ceramic fragments in an area with a volume of 0.20 cubic meters. Stratum 8 contained a high frequency of burned organic material, including the carbon sample discussed earlier. This stratum also yielded several waster fragments—poorly formed or fired clay objects destroyed during ceramic production. These wasters represent some of the best evidence for pottery production at Etlatongo. We also uncovered two archetypal Early Cruz figurine fragments in Stratum 8 (see Figure 4.4), indicating the inclusion of some earlier material in this secondary refuse. The Early Cruz figurine head exemplifies the type of eyes and more unique and individualized faces and hairstyles diagnostic of the Early Cruz, while a temporally associated body fragment features a neck designed to hold different, interchangeable heads.

Figure 4.4 An example of an Early Cruz figurine head from the Unit 1 midden deposit, found with primarily Middle Cruz materials. Both the style of the eyes and the hairdo associate this with the Early Cruz phase.

Not typical of midden deposits is the much greater proportional increase in fig-urine fragments compared with vessel fragments in Strata 7 and 8. Excavated in 20-centimeter levels, the level immediately above the midden deposits yielded no figurine fragments; this contrasts with 28 fragments found in the first 20-centimeter level of the midden (see Figure 4.1). Combined, Strata 7 and 8 (including the first 5 centimeters of Stratum 9) contained a total of 59 figurine fragments, weighing 1,903.0 grams. Figurines comprised between 2% and 3% of the total ceramic assem-blage from these midden levels; this compares with an average percentage of fig-urines from all 20-centimeter levels at Etlatongo, including middens, of 0.18%. I calculate figurine frequency from these midden deposits as over 10 times greater than anywhere else at Etlatongo. Figurines proved so abundant they oozed out of the pro-files. As the purpose of excavating 1 × 1 meter units is to provide comparability, methodological purity overcame the temptation to collect figurine fragments visible in the profile.

We recorded horizontal and vertical data for all figurines encountered *in situ.* Ultimately, it appears the ancient villagers included a heavy frequency of figurine fragments in these midden deposits, but did not place them in any order. I observed only that the majority of figurines occurred in a 25-centimeter vertical band within this midden (primarily Stratum 8), and the southwest corner exhibited a slightly higher figurine concentration. Due to the anomalous figurine frequency, I suggest these deposits represent refuse from specialized activities that occurred on or near Mound 1-1 during the Middle Cruz phase, and villagers subsequently redeposited them as midden/platform fill.

As noted, scholars do not agree on how figurines functioned within Formative villages. Indeed, I suspect figurines functioned differently depending on context and audience. I support an interpretation that at least some figurines served in household rituals. Strata 7 and 8 may incorporate debris resulting from household or other rituals conducted in this portion of the site. These discarded ritual items may have been intentionally included in deposits utilized to elevate Floor 2. The high frequency of obsidian blades found in Strata 7 and 8 provide limited support for this interpretation. Although serving more mundane functions, obsidian blades also served in autosacrificial rituals, in which supplicants offered their own blood. No other Etlatongo context exhibits such a high frequency of figurine fragments and blades, and I interpret their presence here as part of a process of sanctifying Mound 1-1 and as a representation of one component in the formalization of ritual activities.

These data remain far from conclusive, but both the high elevation of Floor 2, combined with the heavy concentration of figurine fragments and obsidian blades in the underlying fill, suggest that Mound 1-1 served as public space. While I do not discount the possibility that Unit 1 may represent a higher-status residence, I believe the more parsimonious explanation focuses on public space. By examining the stratigraphic sequence from Stratum 12 through Stratum 6 in Unit 1, the emergence of public space appears as a gradual process, with increasing, more substantial elevation of subsequent surfaces. As documented in the Valley of Oaxaca, Unit 1 exhibits a process of elevating public space and setting it apart from residential areas of the village.

In addition to how they inform us of utilization of the Mound 1-1 vicinity, these figurines provide an extraordinary window into the lives of ancient Etlatongo villagers, providing insights into how these people viewed the human body. Details, such as a female body with patterns of red paint (see Figure 4.5), suggest the kinds of ornamentation with which villagers adorned themselves during certain dances, rituals, or as markers of social identity. Figurines and the contexts in which they are found may also provide visual clues as to the way ancient villagers conceptualized the relationship between biological sex and gender and social roles. While the vast majority of figurines appear consistent with local or regional style and production techniques, I interpret six solid heads as typifying the Olmec style. Unlike the remainder of figurine heads, these six heads feature a white slip, with the surface well burnished to produce a smooth, lustrous finish (Figure 4.6). A face fragment of a hollow figurine also exhibits the Olmec style, a type of artifact often referred to as a "hollow baby" (see text that follows).

Mound 1-1 continued to serve as public space at Etlatongo after the Floor 2 occupation, with two large strata of cultural fill placed atop this surface. Much of Stratum 5 consists of Middle Cruz artifacts, and probably represents a combination of structural collapse of an edifice associated with Floor 2 and fill/debris disposal. Stratum 4, however, documents a major chronological shift in the utilization of this mound. Post–Middle Cruz material comprises the fill utilized in Stratum 4. The surface, Floor 1, placed atop this fill represents a Yucuita/Ramos phase construction that rose 2.5 meters above the base of Mound 1-1 and surrounding structures. Fragments of additional floors visible atop Mound 1-1 indicate the continuing pre-Hispanic utilization of this spot. Mesoamericans constantly rebuilt and reutilized sacred spaces;

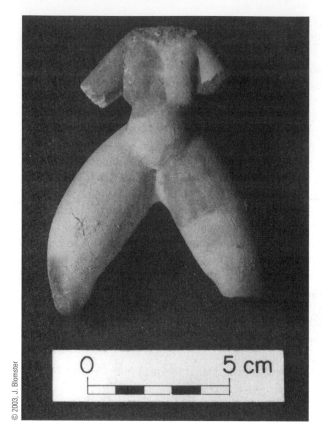

© 2003, J. Blomster

0   5 cm

Figure 4.5 This solid figurine provides a window into the rituals and bodies of Middle Cruz villagers at Etlatongo. The patterned red pigment on this female figurine may represent body paint on a Formative dancer or ritual celebrant. Note the emphasis placed on the disproportionately large thighs.

the Templo Mayor of the Aztecs, in the center of modern Mexico City, represents perhaps the most famous example. This pattern extends back to the sequence of Early Formative structures from Mound 6 at Paso de la Amada, Chiapas, discussed earlier. Each subsequent and larger construction covers earlier episodes. The reutilization of a space enhances its sacredness.

I interpret Mound 1-1 as public or sacred space at Etlatongo as early as the Middle Cruz phase. The utilization of this space may have changed over time. Excavators in the Valley of Oaxaca have documented the appropriation of earlier public space by elites, who utilized these sacred spots as loci for their own houses (Marcus and Flannery 1996). By constructing houses over sacred space, elites enhanced their own legitimacy and ties with the supernatural. The Aztecs exemplify this process, with rulers' palaces constructed adjacent to the sacred precinct at the center of their capital city, Tenochtitlán. Such analogies, however, must be approached with caution. As noted previously, social roles such as "elite" (or more appropriately, higher status) emerged in the Early Formative period. The kinds of vast disparity in material wealth that we associate with such concepts were not yet in place. As I argue later, such roles may have been tied more with control over ritual knowledge and paraphernalia than with economic advantages.

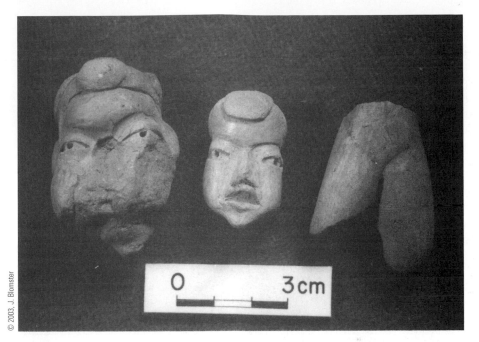

Figure 4.6 A small fraction of figurine fragments from Unit 1 appear quite different in both facial style and finish from the majority of Middle Cruz figurines. Some appear visually associated with the Olmec style, although mixed in with the other figurines found in the midden deposits. A white slip envelops these two heads and body fragment, with extensive burnishing and traces of red paint present as well.

HIGHER STATUS, STORAGE SPACE, AND RITUAL PARAPHERNALIA: UNIT 23

The final sondage unit excavated at Etlatongo lay outside the testing program, a random sample did not dictate its placement. Rather, the accidental discovery of a Postclassic carved stone by a farmer expanding his fields necessitated a salvage unit. Essentially, Unit 23 served to recover data associated with the carved stone. Stylistically, the stone appeared associated with the Postclassic period, depicting a probable warrior with a large headdress similar to those in Mixtec codices. Associated concentrations of large Yanhuitlán Red-on-Cream bowls, diagnostic of the Natividad phase, support this temporal placement. The stone originated just a few meters east of an exposed wall, comprised of shaped rectangular limestone slabs (Figure 4.7). Thick stucco floors, often found with Postclassic palace structures, also lay exposed in the vicinity. One such floor came into direct contact with the wall stones, and was probably directly associated with the wall as an exterior patio or plaza. In order to investigate this context, I placed a unit at the spot indicated by the farmer as the location of the carved stone. Because the approximate location of the carved stone fell within two 1 × 1 meter units on the site grid, I elected to open a 1 × 2 meter unit on the eastern edge of Area 2 (see Chapter 5, Figure 5.1). While

Figure 4.7 This stone wall, located just west of Unit 23, probably dates to the Postclassic period, and is associated with a carved stone that first brought this portion of the site to the attention of the 1992 project.

this unit documented significant Postclassic occupation, it also served to expose an important Middle Cruz higher-status context associated with ritual paraphernalia.

Middle Cruz Deposits

Approximately 2 meters below modern ground surface, excavations exposed a Middle Cruz floor (Floor 5) and associated debris (Stratum 5) lying over this floor. Stratum 5, a homogenous silt-loam, exhibited numerous Middle Cruz ceramic sherds, as well as a ceramic animal head effigy (probably part of a figurine) 3 centimeters above Floor 5. The head depicts a long-snouted carnivore with distinctive Middle Cruz–style eyes, although more gogglelike than the norm (Figure 4.8). An Olmec-style solid figurine head, bald with puffy cheeks, was found in materials redeposited above Floor 5 (Figure 4.9). Stratum 5 represents a combination of materials that accumulated from the use of Floor 5 as a living surface and from structural collapse associated with the abandonment of Floor 5 during the Middle Cruz phase. Additional evidence of structural material in the form of burned daub and plaster fragments was found within Feature 3, the entrance to which was on Floor 5.

Villagers created Floor 5 by transforming a bedrock outcrop into a flat surface, leveling outcrops, and filling in irregularities. From the small sample exposed of Floor 5, this surface represents either a house floor or a prepared outdoor activity area or apron. A discontinuity on the eastern edge of Floor 5 may represent either disturbance from a later cultural feature or a natural drop-off in the elevation of bedrock.

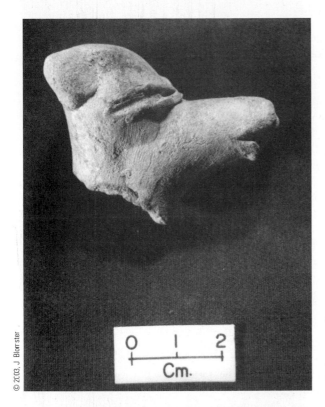

Figure 4.8 This long-snouted ceramic head—possibly representing a dog—was found 3 cm above the Middle Cruz surface in Unit 23. The damp clay preserved a fingerprint placed on it before firing by its creator nearly 3,000 years ago.

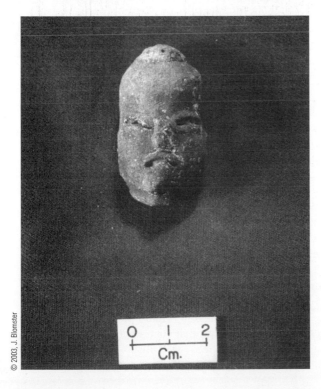

Figure 4.9 This burned Olmec-style solid figurine head lay in materials redeposited above Stratum 5 in Unit 23. Traces of red pigment rubbed onto portions of the head remain visible.

In the latter option, the builders of Floor 5 elevated this surface and associated structure by locating it on a significantly higher bedrock outcrop.

Unit 23 documented one feature (labeled Feature 3) associated with Floor 5; a bell-shaped storage pit. Feature 3's entrance, visible on Floor 5's surface, formed a circle with a maximum diameter of 75 centimeters. Evidence in the form of irregularly placed, roughly shaped masonry blocks at Feature 3's entrance indicates this pit had been purposely sealed. The entrance to the bell-shaped chamber consists of a cylindrical shaft that descends for 70 centimeters until reaching the upper limit of the main chamber of the pit (Figure 4.10). While very few artifacts came from the sediments in this cylindrical shaft, the soil contained heavy charcoal deposits. Artifacts became more abundant as we exposed the main chamber of the storage pit. Except for the initial 5 to 10 centimeters, ancient villagers carved Feature 3 entirely into bedrock. They created a generally symmetrical feature, except for a portion near the top. The plan view of the base, which forms a relatively consistent circle, underscores the symmetrical nature of this bell-shaped pit (Figure 4.10). Further evidence of the exceptional nature of Feature 3 comes from its size. Feature 3 extends for a total of 210 centimeters below Floor 5, with a maximum basal diameter of 182 centimeters, for an approximate volume of 2.79 cubic meters. These dimensions mark Feature 3 as the largest storage feature excavated at Etlatongo; it has a greater volume than the majority of comparable bell-shaped storage pits reported for Early Formative Oaxaca. In the following text I consider the implications of these dimensions.

Two different deposits lay within Feature 3. The upper deposit filled the cylindrical entrance shaft, as well as over half of the bell-shaped portion, for nearly 1.40 meters from Floor 5. This upper deposit, an extremely loose loam, contained heavy charcoal deposits and remains from the structure associated with Floor 5, including numerous cane-impressed burned daub fragments and 13 plaster chunks. The majority of Feature 3 artifacts came from the lower portion of this first deposit, as did the carbon sample with the greatest depth (Figure 4.10). This sample yielded a date of 2740 B.P. plus or minus 70 years (or 790 B.C.); using two sigma statistics, the calibrated range is 1110 B.C. to 793 B.C. cal, with intercepts at 894, 878, and 850 B.C. cal, at a 95% probability level (Stuiver and Reimer 1993). I interpret this upper deposit as secondary refuse, deposited here after Feature 3 had ceased to be utilized for storage.

The lower, and earlier, deposit contained a more compact, silty clay-loam, with less abundant but more partially intact artifacts. At a depth of 1.45 meters into Feature 3, the excavations exposed a hollow figurine, lying on its right side with a small obsidian blade wedged under its right shoulder (Figures 4.10 and 4.11). The hollow figurine lay embedded in this compact silty clay-loam, contrasting dramatically with the looser sediments encountered above it. Approximately 10 to 15 centimeters above the base of the bell-shaped pit lay the partially articulated skeleton of a dog (Figure 4.10). The skeleton, probably deposited fully articulated, had been crushed by the weight of the above sediments. The dog lay in primary context; it appears to have been intentionally deposited here rather than part of the larger secondary refuse disposal above. In fact, the figurine head from 3 centimeters above the floor associated with Feature 3 may allude to this dog (Figure 4.8). Ancient inhabitants of the New World often utilized dogs in ways that contradict our view of these animals as family pets. At the site of Keatley Creek, in British Columbia, Canada, complex hunter/gatherers sometimes sacrificed dogs during particularly elaborate

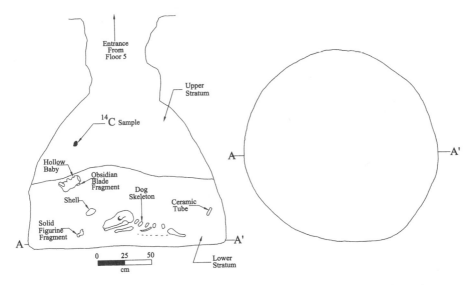

Figure 4.10 Profile and basal plan view of Feature 3, Unit 23, showing the relative location of artifacts within this large bell-shaped pit. © 2003, J. Blomster.

Figure 4.11 The discovery of the nearly complete hollow baby figurine, shown in situ *within Feature 3, Unit 23.*

feasts. They linked dogs with both spiritual importance and displays of prestige (Hayden 1997:98–100). Additional objects in the immediate vicinity of the Feature 3 dog, including a complete shell and two solid ceramic cylindrical tubes (parts of spatulalike objects), may have been deposited as offerings during the closing of this pit or general area. The lower portion of this pit also yielded obsidian, numerous other lithics, one fragment of a large groundstone trough or metate, worked and polished shell, and mica fragments—not common anywhere at Etlatongo.

The Etlatongo Hollow Baby

Hollow figurines represent a rare artifact category compared to solid figurines. Several different types of hollow figurines existed in Early Formative Mesoamerica, reflecting both local and pan-Mesoamerican styles (Blomster 1998b, 2002). The nearly intact hollow figurine found in Feature 3 represents a particularly rare type, often referred to as a "hollow baby" (see Figure 4.12). I address the issue of style in Chapter 6; here it is sufficent to note that hollow babies manifest the Olmec style in the way the physiognomy and representation resemble Olmec figures executed in a variety of media—ceramic, stone, and wood—from Gulf Coast sites such as San Lorenzo and El Manatí (see Chapter 1). Using a robust definition of Olmec style, only approximately 20 ceramic figurines attributed to sites throughout Mesoamerica can actually be identified as hollow babies (Blomster 2002). With the exception of the Etlatongo example, none of these come from meaningful contexts. In fact, all but one have been looted from sites throughout Mexico. Not only are contextual data absent, even the general region from which many of these ceramic sculptures originate remains questionable. As I examined other examples for comparative data, the lack of contextual data surprised me and highlights the appalling loss of data through looting. Apparently due to their generally intact nature, hollow babies have been interpreted as burial offerings (Reilly 1995:27–29). Based on the context of the Etlatongo hollow baby, I reject this interpretation, preferring one that emphasizes a possible multiplicity of uses depending on time, place, and social context.

The Etlatongo hollow baby remains nearly complete, lacking only the top of the head and the lower parts of both legs. The figurine as preserved is 15 centimeters tall and weighs 532.30 grams. By following the general contours of the head, I estimate that it originally stood between 18 and 20 centimeters in height, placing it in the smaller range of the spectrum for hollow babies. As is typical of hollow babies, a white slip envelops the figurine, and the surface has been highly burnished. The artisan cut three holes through the figurine, probably to prevent breakage during firing: one on the bottom side, not visible when the figurine is in an upright position; one that forms a navel; and a third inside the mouth. The mouth hole may have been placed there for other reasons, perhaps related to ritual utilization of this object.

The figure sits with splayed legs, which is the typical pose for hollow babies. Despite its small size, the figure presents an impression of monumentality. Its grave expression gives it a particularly striking and imposing presence. The body combines infant and adult traits; the soft, pudgy infantlike belly contrasts with the strongly sculpted, adultlike pectoral muscles. Also typical for this artifact type is the lack of primary sexual characteristics, although the spread legs reveal the genital area of this naked figure. Gender was not expressed through depiction of genitalia and biological sex on these hollow babies, although it may have been expressed by other, more subtle clues apparent to those who understood the representational system. Secondary sexual characteristics, specifically the realistic and subtle depiction of pectoral musculature, suggest that if the artist intended to illustrate the figure's sex, it probably represents a biological male.

Figure 4.12 At a projected height of 18 to 20 cm, the hollow baby from Feature 3 remains largely intact, except for the upper portion of the head and limbs. A finely burnished white slip envelops the figurine.

The artist emphasized the figure's great corpulence, especially the protruding pudgy stomach, and crafted this object to be seen in the round; the naturalistic modeling on the front continues onto the figurine's back. While the artist invested care and energy in creation of the torso and head of this figure, he or she extended minimal effort in the creation of the limbs. Raised to the sides at shoulder height, the stumpy, fleshy arms appear almost vestigial, and the large, rotund legs appear greatly exaggerated. Such lack of attention to the limbs typifies hollow babies.

The head is at least as large as the entire torso. The carefully modeled face shows the interplay of adult and infant (or nonhuman) traits. While filtered through a stylized template, Olmec-style facial features appear realistic, suggestive of a particular face or type of face. Typical Olmec-style puffed eyelids probably contained L-shaped slit or trough eyes, based on what little remains of the lower portions of the eyes. Fleshy cheeks frame the large, downturned, trapezoidal mouth. Distended ears show careful attention to anatomy. The back of the head features the lower portion of a helmet, with several incisions visible. Red pigment was rubbed onto the helmet and "hairlike" incisions below.

The creator of this figurine crafted an object that emphasized its sense of "otherness" not only by selecting a different medium—hollow and covered with a white, well-burnished slip—but also by choosing to model facial features in a divergent way from contemporaneous solid figurines at Etlatongo. Consistent with the Olmec style, the eyes and the open, downturned mouth distinguish this face from other human images, and the attention paid to the anatomy of the ears is unprecedented at Etlatongo. Nor does obesity frequently appear in contemporaneous figurines, except for those that depict women. In other parts of Mesoamerica, contemporaneous figurines that depict fat males have been interpreted as images of chiefs, persons with a status different from the majority of villagers (Clark 1994a). Contemporaneous solid and hollow figurines also generally display little modeling of the body. The lack of an Olmec-style face also separates hollow figurines from hollow babies. The head of the hollow figurine, excavated at Tlapacoya (a village in Central Mexico), in Figure 4.13 displays only an approximation of some elements of the Olmec style. Thus, the Etlatongo hollow baby differs from contemporaneous figurines in form, image, and underlying symbolism. The extensive modeling and sculpting suggest that the hollow baby was intended for display, not solely as a burial offering. The fact that the Etlatongo hollow baby is broken (indicative of use) found without a burial further contradicts the previous funerary interpretation. The hollow baby appears alien to the Etlatongo representational system, and was probably introduced into it.

Everything You Wanted to Know about Bell-Shaped Pits but Were Afraid to Ask

In assessing the status of the structure represented by Floor 5, the size of Feature 3 provides critical evidence. Unfortunately, Feature 3 represents the only storage feature documented with Floor 5. Formative households generally exhibit a series of pit features in various stages of utilization at any given time; knowing the total storage capacity of this household would strengthen the interpretations regarding the status of this household. With these caveats in mind, here I examine both implications of the size of Feature 3 and the contents of this bell-shaped pit.

With an approximate volume of 2.79 cubic meters, Feature 3 ranks as the largest Etlatongo pit feature. The size of storage pits, receptacles of stored goods and surplus, may reflect a relationship between surplus in a society and social ranking. The size of a bell-shaped pit (or the total capacity of all contemporaneous household storage features) represents the potential volume of goods that could be stored. If emerging elites were accumulating a surplus beyond what was needed for household consumption, these individuals would have required larger and/or more storage facilities. Additionally, the model for development of social inequality in Soconusco relates status to competitive generosity, often expressed in public gatherings such as feasting, which entail elaborate displays of food and serving vessels (Clark 1994a). Thus, individuals or factions within a group that accumulate more materials goods, including some reserved for special occasions, would have required enhanced storage capacity.

How does the volume of Feature 3 from Etlatongo compare with other contemporaneous bell-shaped pits in the Valley of Oaxaca? Based on a sample of 32 storage pits from the site of Tierras Largas, the average bell-shaped pit volume in Early Formative Valley of Oaxaca has been calculated as 1.40 cubic meters (Winter 1972:140). Combining data from both the 1980 excavations (Zárate Morán 1987) and the 1992 excavations at Etlatongo, 13 bell-shaped pits have been excavated from throughout the Formative period (Early through Late). This sample includes only *bell-shaped* pits; I exclude other pit feature types. The average volume of all bell-shaped pits at Etlatongo is 0.86 cubic meter. The nearly 3-cubic-meter capacity of

M.D. Coe.

Figure 4.13 A hollow figurine, found in many pieces, from Tlapacoya, Central Mexico. The highly stylized face, the nonrealistic ears, lack of a white slip, and the small head and tubular body (not shown in the photograph) differentiate this figurine from those in the Olmec style.

Feature 3 is double that of the average contemporaneous Valley of Oaxaca pit capacity and is more than triple that from Etlatongo. In terms of effort involved in the construction of Feature 3, ancient villagers excavated all but the first few centimeters into solid bedrock, making the construction of this feature relatively labor-intensive compared to pits built into soils completely above bedrock.

The great size of Feature 3 supports an interpretation that those who controlled access to it may have been capable of accumulating a great surplus and may have been in the process of negotiating a social identity different from that of the majority of Middle Cruz villagers at Etlatongo. Increased storage capacity has been one of several factors considered in identifying high-status households in the Valley of Oaxaca, along with greater diversity of materials and greater access to nonlocal products (Flannery and Marcus 1983:63–64). The increase in storage pit size may also reflect the responsibilities that emerging individuals or households assumed for guaranteeing resource provisioning (Hirth 1992:25). Throughout the New World, storage capacity often correlates with relative status. Returning to Keatley Creek, a village comprised of pit houses, smaller residences generally contained only a small, or no, storage pit (Hayden 1997). As part of their differential roles in Early Formative society, aggrandizers may have stored surplus food that would have been available to members of the community in times of shortfall.

What about the contents of Feature 3? Clearly, the hollow baby represents one highly unique and scarce item. Although the ceramics will be further considered in

Chapter 6, I note here the high frequency of serving vessels relative to food preparation vessels. Animal bones represent numerous meat-eating episodes involving deer, rabbits, and dogs (in addition to the largely intact dog skeleton at the pit's base). A fragment of a turtle shell, which represents a nonlocal resource, may be from a turtle that was utilized as food; this carapace also may have been employed as a drum. Feature 3 yielded an unusually high quantity of marine shell fragments, representing an additional nonlocal resource. The majority of small shell pieces probably derive from pendants or ornaments. One complete shell, however, emerged from this feature, near the base. Ornamental shell appears to have been an exotic item designating differential status; it has been associated in contemporaneous Valley of Oaxaca sites with high-status areas (see Flannery 1968). The presence of a complete shell, polished but otherwise unworked, in this bell-shaped pit further supports an interpretation of this household's role in ritual paraphernalia and interregional interaction.

One additional line of evidence links the household exposed by Unit 23 with the consumption of exotic goods. Fragments of obsidian, a volcanic glass, abound at sites throughout Mesoamerica. Although obsidian itself is not rare (it served a multiplicity of uses for ancient villagers), it originates from different sources. Obsidian represents an important resource for the archaeologist because sources of obsidian are limited to two major zones of volcanism in Mexico and Guatemala. Because the chemical variability is greater between obsidian sources than within a single source, obsidian fragments retrieved from archaeological excavations can be matched to specific sources. Through compositional analysis, archaeologists can actually identify the source from which ancient Mesoamericans quarried each piece of obsidian; how the obsidian actually arrived in ancient villages, however, requires extensive interpretation about the nature of the exchange mechanism.

Excavations in Feature 3 recovered 16 obsidian fragments, including flakes and blades (see Figure 4.14). I submitted 45 obsidian samples from Early Formative contexts, including the 16 Feature 3 samples, to be compositionally sourced through instrumental neutron activation analysis (INAA), a process further explored in Chapter 6. From the sample of 45 obsidian fragments, Feature 3 contained the only two fragments from Pico de Orizaba, Veracruz. The remaining samples were all from the ParedÛn, Puebla, source—the most frequent source of the analyzed obsidian from Etlatongo. This one Early Formative household exploited the Pico de Orizaba source. Other sources exclusive to two other contexts, with greater ties to Central and Western Mexico, were not present in Feature 3 (Blomster and Glascock 2002). Thus, the group associated with Feature 3 had access to one exchange network from which at least some Etlatongo residents remained excluded; in turn, the Feature 3 villagers lacked access to at least two other obsidian sources. This is consistent with a model of various family or corporate groups vying for prestige but with no one social unit achieving consistent differentiation on a village-wide level.

In addition to artifacts that evince differential access to raw materials, objects that distinguish the Feature 3 artifact assemblage from other contexts can be associated with probable ritual or ceremonial utilization. In addition to the nearly intact hollow baby figurine, two ceramic tubes represent handles of unusual spatulalike objects. I also note that both of the Pico de Orizaba obsidian fragments are prismatic blade fragments, one of which lay in direct contact with the hollow figurine. Prismatic obsidian blades first appear in the archaeological record, along with Olmec-style artifacts, toward the second half of the Early Formative period throughout Mesoamerica

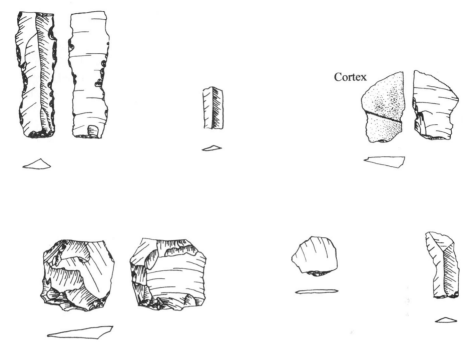

Figure 4.14 Sample of obsidian fragments found in Feature 3 and sourced through INAA. The fragments show a range of forms and production stages, from the finished blade in the top left corner to the piece of debitage in the right corner that exhibits cortex, the outer edge of the obsidian block, indicative of an early stage in the production process. Two views are provided of select pieces; a profile view of each is shown underneath the plan view. Illustrations are at the same scale, with the blade in the top left corner measuring 4.5 cm. © 2003, J. Blomster

(Clark and Lee 1984:253) and may have been part of an emerging suite of new ritual paraphernalia. As noted, obsidian blades have been associated with bloodletting in many Mesoamerican cultures. Their appearance in the archaeological record at this time in Mesoamerica could indicate the initiation of autosacrificial rites, although stingray spines have been cited as more definitive examples of this practice (Marcus and Flannery 1996:62). In addition to storing surplus goods at a scale beyond that of the average household, Feature 3 may represent a place where objects involved in rituals or public ceremonies were stored during their active use-life, or were cached once these objects ceased to function in that capacity.

A reconstruction of the events leading up to the deposits and abandonment of Feature 3 begins with the shift in utilization of this pit from active storage to a place where some items of ritual paraphernalia (such as the hollow baby) may have been cached or simply abandoned in the bell-shaped pit where they had been stored. The closing of the pit may have commenced with the offering of the dog close to the base of the storage pit. As noted, the dog may have been sacrificed as part of a prestige display or a ceremony specifically tied with the closing of Feature 3. Some additional material, such as the intact shell, was either deposited or likewise abandoned here from a previous activity. At some time after this first period, villagers engaged in a second episode of deposition. This time they filled the pit with secondary refuse; the fact that this refuse includes some structural materials (plaster and burned daub) suggests to me that they also abandoned the associated structure at this time. They then partially sealed Feature 3. The ceramic carnivore head found on Floor 5 (Figure 4.8), perhaps related to the dog offered during the first period of deposition, along with the Olmec-style head liberally rubbed with hematite after having been burned (Figure 4.9), may have been offered as part of a closing ritual at different stages of the filling of the pit and abandonment of the associated structure.

This serendipitously placed unit allows for several conclusions on a pan-Mesoamerican level. Hollow baby figurines do not serve solely a funerary function. The discovery of a partially intact but broken example in Feature 3 documents utilization among living people, probably as items displayed in public ceremonies. A much larger hollow figurine, more accurately referred to as a statuette, has been found from an earlier context at a Paso de la Amada platform; this object could have been seen by individuals not directly in contact with it (Lesure and Blake 2002). As I examined other possible hollow babies reported throughout Mesoamerica, I realized that the majority of them do not evince the Olmec style and should be reclassified (such as the one from Tlapacoya illustrated in Figure 4.13). As noted in Chapter 1, archaeologists have used—and abused—the term *Olmec style,* applying it to a wide range of objects that fail to meet a robust definition of the Olmec style. The discovery of the Etlatongo hollow baby and the associated research on hollow babies inspired me to begin to purge the literature of such promiscuous terminology (Blomster 2002). Finally, hollow babies clearly are not primarily Central Mexican phenomena (*contra* Flannery and Marcus 2000). Intact hollow babies, with two exceptions, have no contextual information. We cannot determine their precise context within a site, and there are few clues as to the site or region from which the object was looted. I examined fragments of hollow babies from excavations throughout Mesoamerica and discovered that specimens most consistent with the Olmec style come from San Lorenzo (on the Gulf Coast) and, to a lesser extent, from sites such as Etlatongo and Paso de la Amada. Compositional testing of one such fragment from Paso de la Amada reveals, in fact, a Gulf Coast origin for at least one hollow figurine (Blomster 2002; Neff and Glascock 2002).

Further conclusions about the nature of the contexts exposed in Units 1 and 23 will be provided in the next chapter, which explores occupations encountered in a larger excavation unit.

5/Two Middle Cruz Occupations
Higher-Status or Public Space?

I sat at the base of a black hole, more prosaically known as a test unit, in Area 3 (see Chapter 2, Figure. 2.7). Occasional voices filtered down from field assistants observing me from the surface, close to 5 meters above the base of the unit. After surviving the rigors of documenting the stratigraphy of what became the deepest test unit excavated at Etlatongo, I marveled at the amount of construction and disturbance—i.e., *living*—represented in the stratigraphic profile. From the base of the unit on bedrock to modern ground surface, this profile exhibited 5 meters of surfaces, wall fragments, features, middens and fill—with no strata resulting primarily from natural processes! This humble test unit generated a staggering amount of data from a variety of occupational periods. As I examined the composition of the earliest living surfaces in this unit, I considered the limitations of test units (see "Digging Deeper" section in this chapter). I longed for both additional light and greater horizontal exposure in order to better understand the larger cultural contexts these strata represent. Such pleasant circumstances lay within my grasp, as the project turned to the exposure of larger horizontal areas—robotage.

The interpretations presented in Chapter 4, derived from Units 1 and 23, remain problematic because they are based on test units, which provide a very limited window into the past. Here I present the results of data derived through robotage excavations of a series of Middle Cruz occupations (Excavation Area 2, or EA-2). This type of excavation reveals associations of features and artifacts. I selected EA-2 as a candidate for robotage through an examination of the profile along the road explored by the previous excavations at Etlatongo (Zárate Morán 1987). I reexamined two of the test units excavated in 1980 along the northern boundary of Area 2 with Area 3 (Figure 5.1). It appeared that Middle Cruz deposits lay closer to the surface in this part of Etlatongo, covered by less overburden from later occupations. EA-2 began as a 4 × 3 meter unit, with the longest side running north to south. As I wanted to maintain careful horizontal control, we employed additional subdivisions and continued to record the three-dimensional provenience of all relatively intact artifacts and possible features. Three consecutive expansions enlarged EA-2 for a final size of 7 × 5 meters, or an area of 35 square meters.

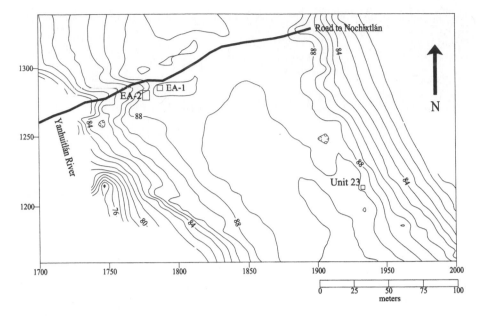

Figure 5.1 Topographic map of the northern portion of Research Area 2, showing the locations of Unit 23 and the two Excavation Areas (EA-1 and EA-2). Contour interval is 1.0 meter; arrow points to magnetic north. © 2003, J. Blomster.

As the EA-2 investigations concluded the 1992 project, I conducted some experiments in methodology. While all cultural materials from these excavations were examined, not everything from the final EA-2 operation was collected. I opted not to save some material close to modern ground surface due to both the overwhelming quantity and poor quality of material, as well as time constraints. After saving all materials throughout the initial EA-2 excavations, during the final horizontal expansion of EA-2 we saved only select materials from the first stratum (see Figure 5.2). Stratum 1 represents a mix of materials recently redeposited during construction of the road that slices through Mound X; the majority of artifacts have been dramatically affected by this disturbance, with ceramic fragments reduced in size to the point of yielding little or no information. For example, we saved all ceramics from Stratum 1 in the initial 4 × 3 meter version of EA-2; here, Stratum 1 disgorged over 6,500 ceramic fragments, less than 300 of which were later deemed worthy of additional analysis. Due to their small size and heavily eroded nature, the other 6,000-plus sherds provide not even basic data on vessel form. Stratum 1 cannot even be construed as reverse stratigraphy, because it contains a mix of at least four ceramic phases rather than a simple inversion of materials. While all soil from this stratum continued to be screened during the final horizontal expansion of EA-2, I allotted only a limited amount of time for the screen to be examined, with only rim sherds and larger, diagnostic materials collected.

EA-2 exposed six separate occupations, yielding a complex stratigraphy of 65 documented strata. While I numbered strata in ascending order, beginning with the top and ending the sequence at the bottom of EA-2, I discuss the occupations in reverse order—the earliest occupation has the lowest number. Here I describe in

DIGGING DEEPER: SONDAGE VERSUS ROBOTAGE: ADVANTAGES AND DISADVANTAGES

With the results from the test units in Chapter 4 and now the EA-2 excavations in mind, I turn to a brief consideration of the advantages and disadvantages of test units (sondage) versus larger excavation areas (robotage). Much of the disadvantage with test units—especially those measuring 1 × 1 meters—lies in the limited amount of area excavated. Due to test unit size, it is impossible to determine if the surfaces exposed in Units 1 and 23 represent internal or external floors. When dealing with deposits that extend as deeply as those in Unit 1, problems with depth emerge. Due to the lack of consistent light in such deep units, often referred to derisively as "telephone booths," photographing and recording strata toward the unit's base becomes increasingly problematic with depth. Preparing and drawing stratigraphic profiles becomes a challenge, with much time spent (resulting in sore leg muscles) on ladders or toeholds excavated into nonrecorded walls. Safety must remain a priority; we constantly tested soil compactness of deep units at Etlatongo to ensure their stability. Ironically, the one cultural feature that safety concerns prevented us from fully excavating occurred not in a test unit but in EA-2 (see discussion of Feature 29).

Why bother with test units, especially at deep sites such as Etlatongo? Without a relatively fast way of subsurface testing, it would not be possible to interpret the changing utilization of the site through time, with the size of the Middle Cruz occupation especially underestimated based only on surface survey (see Chapter 3). I say "relatively fast" because excavations in some deep test units, conducted solely by trowels, lasted over a month!

As evident in this chapter, robotage provides better associations between features and allows for better occupational contexts with which to associate artifacts. As should be clear, deep deposits still present numerous problems—the EA-2 excavations failed to expose an entire Middle Cruz house or floor. So although there are clear interpretative advantages to horizontal excavations, disadvantages relate primarily to time and labor. In addition to the enormous amount of time and labor necessary to excavate EA-2 to bedrock, removal of 3 meters or more of soil within this 35-square-meter block resulted in staggeringly high amounts of cultural materials, many of which do not relate to the Middle Cruz but continue to consume time, space, and effort in the laboratory.

depth only the first two occupations and present relevant stratigraphic data from the north stratigraphic profile (Figure 5.2) and west profile (Figure 5.3). Documentation of EA-2 represented a major challenge. Photographing and drawing the EA-2 stratigraphy lasted over a week, as color, texture, and other relevant data were recorded for each stratum. Despite the fact that recording took place during the rainy season, the Cloud People smiled upon me. A rainfall during the recording of these stratigraphic profiles would have proved disastrous. I had invested a great deal of time defining each strata; if a rainfall "erased" these distinctions, many of which were extremely subtle, I would have to begin the process again. While the rains did not fall for that entire week, a torrential rain began within an hour of finishing the EA-2 documentation. It seemed a fitting conclusion to the field season.

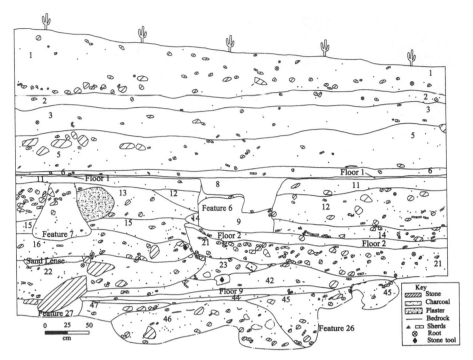

Figure 5.2 North stratigraphic profile of EA-2 showing a complex sequence of occupations, fill, and features. The numbers refer to strata; to simplify the illustration, the stratum number of a particular floor is not included. Note the large artifacts in Stratum 23. The cacti (not to scale!) show the location of modern ground surface. © 2003, J. Blomster.

OCCUPATION 1: STRUCTURE 2-5, FLOORS 10 THROUGH 15, AND FEATURES 28 THROUGH 30

A series of interior surfaces (Floors 10 through 14), a prepared exterior surface (Floor 15), and three associated features represent the earliest occupation within EA-2. Indeed, these deposits remain the earliest excavated at Etlatongo. I interpret the floors as associated with the outline of a largely absent edifice, Structure 2-5 (see Figure 5.4). These deposits represent an occupation that occurred early in the Middle Cruz phase. Most of the relevant strata (Strata 48 to 65) appear on EA-2's west profile (Figure 5.3).

Platform Fill and Structure 2-5 Construction

The oldest deposits in EA-2, Strata 64 and 65, appear to have been placed over bedrock in order to elevate Structure 2-5. These two strata of platform fill underlay Structure 2-5, raising it approximately 50 centimeters above bedrock. This platform-enhanced elevation is actually more substantial than those recorded for many of the raised public structures in contemporaneous Valley of Oaxaca villages (see Chapter 4).

Stratum 65 represents a varied and abundant deposit of platform fill; it underlay Stratum 64 and Structure 2-5, as well as an associated exterior surface or apron (Floor 15) to the east. Numerous fist-sized and smaller bedrock chunks lay in this

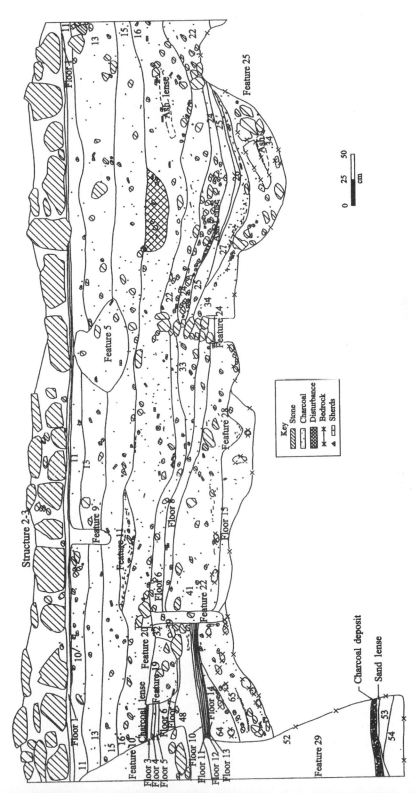

Figure 5.3 West stratigraphic profile of EA-2. The numbers refer to strata; to simplify the illustration, the stratum number of a particular floor is not included. The profile actually follows the alignment of Structure 2-3 (a post–Middle Cruz structure); the strata above Structure 2-3, including modern ground surface, are not included. © 2003, J. Blomster.

light gray loam and may represent debris generated by leveling bedrock outcrops as part of preparing for the construction of Structure 2-5. To the east, the deposition of Stratum 65 provided a level surface for Floor 15, while ancient builders placed a much thicker concentration of this same platform fill under the location where Structure 2-5 would be built. It appears that Stratum 65 was placed directly over exposed bedrock, which exhibits some preparation. Stratum 64 occurred primarily under the earliest surface (Floor 14) inside of Structure 2-5. Stratum 64 has the consistency of a loose plasterlike material. The fact that these two strata lay directly under the structure and the full expanse of the exterior floor (or at least what was exposed of it by the 1992 excavations) further supports the interpretation of these strata as platform fill.

An area of loose soil surrounds the floors that represent the interior of Structure EA-2-5 (see Figure 5.4). I interpret this area as the original location of the foundation stones for the structure associated with these floors; occupants probably salvaged these stones for reuse after the abandonment of this structure. I found only one foundation stone *in situ*. As in contemporaneous Valley of Oaxaca villages, the stone probably represents a foundation of stone that served to anchor wattle and daub walls. Several eroded adobe blocks and burned daub fragments found in this loose area around the interior floors support this reconstruction. Structure 2-5, located atop a platform, contained numerous interior floors as well as an exterior surface (Floor 15) lying 20 centimeters below the interior floors.

Structure 2-5: Exterior

Sloping below the Structure 2-5 platform by 25 to 30 centimeters, Floor 15 extends to the north and east of Floors 10 through 14 (Figure 5.4). Two different strata comprise this exterior surface, although they did not exhibit a distinct boundary (unlike the surfaces in Chapter 7). The strata differed primarily in color, with one being gray and the other almost a pinkish white. This apron appears to have been placed so as to cover the platform fill under Structure 2-5. As seems to be a pattern in terms of different construction of interior and exterior surfaces, Floor 15 is thicker than any interior floors associated with Structure 2-5, ranging from 10 to 30 centimeters in depth. This exterior surface is also less compact than interior floors. Floor 15 forms a level surface, but not as smooth a surface as the interior floors. I interpret Floor 15, present up to 2 to 3 meters away from Structure 2-5, as an apron or a prepared outdoor activity area.

I documented two features associated with Floor 15. Feature 28 extends into the west stratigraphic profile; we excavated only about half of it (Figure 5.4). This feature represents a small pit (diameter is approximately 20 centimeters) excavated by the ancient villagers to a maximum of 20 centimeters in depth from Floor 15. This small, shallow pit, filled with charcoal and ash, may have served as a posthole for an exterior shelter, such as a ramada. Such structures have been documented in the Valley of Oaxaca, often associated with exterior work stations (Flannery and Marcus 1994). The charcoal, which may represent the remains of a burned post, yielded a radiocarbon age of 2930 B.P., plus or minus 80 years. Calibrated using two sigma statistics, at a 95% probability level, this sample produced a range of 1399 to 899 B.C. cal, with an intercept on the calibration curve at 1122 B.C. cal (Stuiver and Reimer 1993)—the early portion of the Middle Cruz phase.

To the east of Structure EA-2-5, Feature 30 represents a large pit feature excavated into the bedrock from Floor 15 (Figure 5.4). The construction of Feature 30

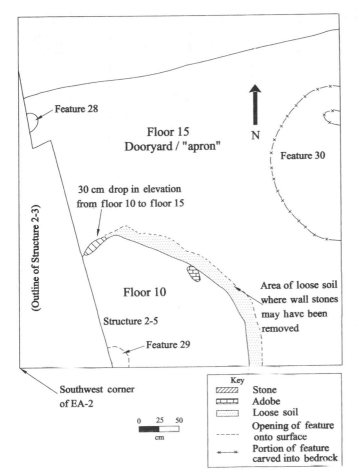

Feature 28

Floor 15
Dooryard / "apron"

N

Feature 30

30 cm drop in elevation
from floor 10 to floor 15

(Outline of Structure 2-3)

Floor 10

Structure 2-5

Feature 29

Area of loose soil
where wall stones
may have been
removed

Southwest corner
of EA-2

Key

	Stone
	Adobe
	Loose soil
-----	Opening of feature onto surface
----	Portion of feature carved into bedrock

0   25   50
cm

Figure 5.4 Plan view of Occupation 1, EA-2, showing the outline of Structure 2-5 and associated interior and exterior surfaces and features. The presence of the post–Middle Cruz Structure 2-3 precluded fully excavating the southwest corner of this excavation area. Arrow points to magnetic north. © 2003, J. Blomster.

also removed part of Stratum 65, the platform fill underlying these surfaces. The entrance to this feature from Floor 15 failed to materialize; it probably lies further to the east of the EA-2 excavations. I estimate we uncovered less than half of this circular feature, which expands in diameter with vertical depth. With a maximum depth of nearly 1 meter below the surface of Floor 15, Feature 30 contained two distinct strata, both of which yielded numerous artifacts, large stones, and bedrock chunks— the latter probably related to the construction of this feature into bedrock. Artifacts include more pre–Middle Cruz ceramics than normal for Middle Cruz contexts, reflecting the dating of this household to the early portion of that phase. Feature 30 probably served in a storage capacity; if Floor 15 continued to be used after Feature 30 fell out of use, residents may have filled it with stones in order to prevent it from collapsing or falling into the former storage pit.

Structure 2-5: Interior Space

Five floors (Floors 10 through 14) define the interior space of Structure 2-5. The four upper floors cover roughly the same area of approximately 2.40 square meters as exposed by the 1992 excavations, while Floor 14 terminates to the east 0.5 meters prior to the other floors. The plan (Figure 5.4) illustrates the latest in this series of surfaces, Floor 10. All five of these floors form very smooth surfaces; however, they all slope approximately 5 centimeters to the south, toward the center of Structure 2–5. As noted in Chapter 4, house floors generally became basin-shaped through use in Early Formative villages.

The five floors vary in construction based on the amount of sand comprising each surface, ranging from a sandy-loam to a loamy-sand. The floors also differ in thickness, from 1 to 3 centimeters in depth. The top surface, Floor 10, remains the thinnest in this series of surfaces; this sandy surface resembles thin (half a centimeter) sand deposits in Valley of Oaxaca houses interpreted as providing a drier surface than floors with less sand content (Flannery and Marcus 1994:26). These floors lay directly on top of each other, without fill or occupational debris separating them. Only Floor 12 exhibited an extremely thin deposit of cultural residue on its surface. Floors 10 through 14 yielded a total of 11 small, nondiagnostic sherds. The lack of surface materials could indicate sweeping of floor surfaces before termination of use, a pattern associated with public or nondomestic space in the Valley of Oaxaca, or may simply be due to a temporally limited utilization of these surfaces. Floors 10 through 13 appear to be resurfacing episodes, based on and expanding the Floor 14 plan. A yellow adobe block, too eroded to determine its original shape, lay on the surface of Floor 10, while several others lay scattered in the soil immediately above this surface. The limited adobe fragments utilized as building materials in Structure 2-5 (which dates to the early portion of the Middle Cruz phase) appear to slightly predate the usage of adobes in construction in Valley of Oaxaca villages, where the first plano-convex (bun-shaped) adobes have been associated with public buildings from the second half of the San José phase (Flannery 1976a:24). The adobes in Structure 2-5 probably formed part of the wall foundation.

FEATURE 29   The excavations exposed only one interior feature in the limited portion documented of Structure 2-5. Feature 29, encountered in the southwest corner of Floors 10 through 14, extends outside the EA-2 boundaries. Inhabitants of Structure 2-5 probably constructed this large bell-shaped pit along with the earliest of these surfaces, Floor 14, and incorporated it in the subsequent resurfacings above Floor 14—none of these later surfaces covered or sealed Feature 29. Due to the presence of a much later pit feature directly above Feature 29, the interior of this pit feature remained unstable, and we only excavated approximately one third of it. Ancient villagers excavated the bell-shaped base of Feature 29 through bedrock and the cylindrical entrance shaft in softer platform fill (Strata 64 and 65). The portions exposed of Feature 29 appear very symmetrical, and I calculate a total volume of 1.70 cubic meters, making this the second largest bell-shaped pit excavated at Etlatongo (Figure 5.3). Considering some of the materials found in this storage pit (see the text that follows), I interpret its large size as a manifestation of the relationship between storage capacity and access to goods.

Feature 29 contained several distinct deposits, the largest of which (Stratum 52) consisted of 50 to 75% charcoal, with charcoal increasing in frequency with depth. We collected numerous large charcoal samples for carbon dating from this material. The amount of burning evinced by this stratum may indicate that Structure 2-5 was partially burned upon its abandonment; some of the burned material may have collapsed or been redeposited in Feature 29 prior to the construction of the later Floor 7. Because the floors themselves did not show burning, the charred material in Feature 29 may originate from burned roof and/or walls. Alternatively, organic material within this pit may have been burned. I found no evidence of this feature being utilized as an oven, kiln, or other production locus. The blackened walls of Feature 29 appear to be an artifact of 3,000 years of contact with the burned organic material contained within it. Feature 29's base did not exhibit significant blackening, nor did the artifacts from the various deposits appear burned. Large stones found in some of the upper strata of Feature 29 may have been wall stones from Structure 2-5. This bell-shaped pit probably originally served as a typical storage pit.

One carbon sample analyzed from Feature 29 yields a date early in the Middle Cruz phase. Calibrated using two sigma statistics, the radiocarbon age of 2900 B.P., plus or minus 60 years, produces a range from 1303 to 899 B.C. cal, with an intercept at 1045 B.C. cal (Stuiver and Reimer 1993). This sample probably postdates the actual occupation of Structure 2-5. The ceramic data support a date in the early half of the Middle Cruz (see Chapter 6).

Two ceramic objects found in Feature 29 appear unique compared to other Middle Cruz assemblages at Etlatongo. We collected a fragment of a cylindrical seal; while not enough remained to reconstruct the complete design, it features two circles between four long bands (Figure 5.5). Objects such as the Feature 29 cylindrical seal may have been dipped in pigment and rubbed over parts of the human body, applying designs through body painting, such as those on the figurine in Chapter 4, Figure 4.5. Feature 29 also contained a ceramic paw (Figure 5.6). Although badly eroded, the upper edge of this ceramic paw appeared to be tapering off into a rim, suggesting that rather than being part of a larger sculpture, this represents a paw-shaped vessel—a form known from later sites in the Valley of Oaxaca such as Monte Albán (see Caso, Bernal, and Acosta 1967).

Feature 29 yielded fragments of at least two hollow figurines. I classify the most complete of these hollow figurines as Group 2 (Figure 5.7). Different from what I describe in Chapter 4 as a hollow baby, it imitates the kind of realistic hollow ceramic baby found in Feature 3, Unit 23, and scattered across Mesoamerica. Too often archaeologists have lumped figurines from these different styles together as "Olmec." I interpret Group 2 figurines as crafted to approximate the posture and Olmec-style face of Group 1 figurines (Blomster 2002). This lack of a fully realized Group 1 face and body may be intentional and represent juxtaposed styles; Mesoamerican art often features such stylistic combinations and juxtapositions to create distinctive styles or messages (Pasztory 1989). Other potential explanations encompass political relations and interactions expressed through different figurine styles. Between villages, different styles often served as boundary mechanisms (Dennis, 1987; see Chapter 3); within villages, they may reflect factional and socio-economic differences. Creators of Group 2 figurines placed less emphasis on the suprahuman imagery that appears on Group 1 figurines; some Group 2 figurines evince both primary and secondary sexual characteristics. Group 2 figurines appear to represent local manifestations of the Olmec style; while they remain rare in the literature, Group 2 figurines are especially scarce in the Gulf Coast, the nexus of Olmec style "baby" imagery. I return to this contrast in Chapter 8.

© 2003, J. Blomster

Figure 5.5 Ceramic cylinder seal from Feature 29, EA-2, associated with Occupation 1 of EA-2—the earliest occupation documented at Etlatongo.

OCCUPATION 2: FLOOR 9 AND FEATURES 26 AND 27

One floor and two features—one of which remains among the largest subterranean features encountered at Etlatongo—represent the second occupation within EA-2. Unfortunately, much of this occupation lay to the north of the confines of EA-2. Due to the road construction just north of EA-2, little additional data from this occupation remain in context at Etlatongo.

Unlike the multiple surfaces associated with Occupation 1, only one (Floor 9), or possibly two (Stratum 44), surfaces were documented for Occupation 2. Floor 9, a compact silt-loam surface, lay only along EA-2's north profile (Figure 5.2); the excavations exposed approximately 0.98 square meter of this surface (Figure 5.8). While Floor 9 formed a relatively smooth surface, it was not a level one, sloping 10 centimeters. The lack of multiple floors and resurfacing episodes could point to a shorter occupation than in Occupation 1. I did not identify a structure associated with this occupation due to the lack of intact walls or spaces where stones may have been removed (as with Occupation 1). Only one potential wall stone was found in the general vicinity of Floor 9. At this time, it is not possible to label Floor 9 as an interior or exterior surface. The position and orientation of Floor 9 does resemble a later occupation in the northeast portion of EA-2; excavations exposed much more of that occupation.

Figure 5.6 Fragment of a ceramic paw from Feature 29, EA-2; probably part of a larger ceramic sculpture.

A possible earlier surface, Stratum 44, lies under Floor 9. A thin, compact deposit, Stratum 44 may have been laid either as a base for Floor 9 or as an earlier surface. Not enough of this irregular stratum was exposed to select the most appropriate interpretation. A thick deposit (Stratum 42) lying atop Floor 9 contained large artifacts and scattered burned daub and stone fragments. I interpret Stratum 42 as structural collapse and postabandonment fill related to Floor 9. Items such as a metate fragment (for grinding corn; see Figure 5.9) may have been abandoned along with the structure. Later midden deposits on the west, and platform fill on the east, covered Stratum 42 as part of the preparation for constructing a new residence in this portion of EA-2.

FEATURE 27   A shallow basin-shaped depression in the bedrock, Feature 27 lay along the southwest portion of Floor 9 (Figure 5.8). Due to being covered by a large stone of more than 50 centimeters, this feature contained very little accumulated soil. This large, roughly shaped stone remains the only potential wall stone found associated with Floor 9. Because of the slumping of the strata above this hollow area, it is difficult to determine if the artifacts found in Feature 27 represent secondary or tertiary deposits; these materials may have filtered down from above. Due to the shallowness of Feature 27, I interpret it as utilized for nonstorage-related activities, but cannot be more precise.

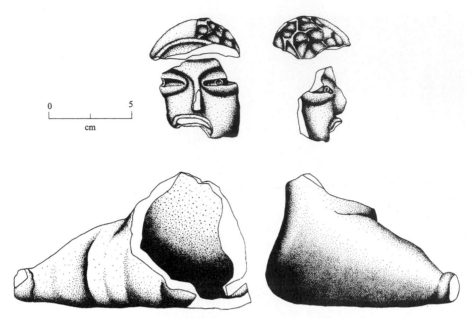

Figure 5.7 Frontal and profile views of three fragments from the same hollow figurine found in Feature 29, EA-2; note the contrast with the hollow baby figurine in Figure 4.12. Red pigment remains in the highly irregular area atop the head. © 2003, J. Blomster.

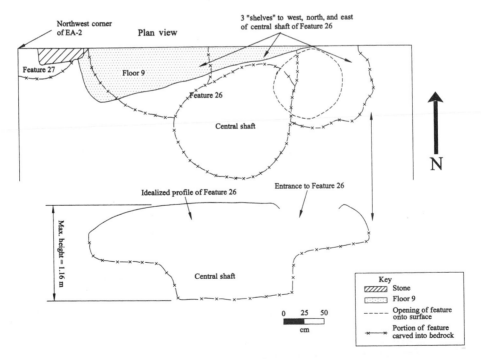

Figure 5.8 Plan view of Occupation 2, EA-2, represented only by the southern tip of Floor 9 and two associated features. In addition to the plan view of Feature 26, a profile view is included of this mushroom-shaped pit feature. Arrow points to magnetic north. © 2003, J. Blomster.

Figure 5.9 Close-up of the north stratigraphic profile of Occupation 2, showing a large metate fragment lying atop Stratum 42 and a ceramic brazier fragment within Stratum 23, a midden deposit used as fill (along with Stratum 21) to elevate Floor 2.

FEATURE 26   A circular area of loose soil directly south of Floor 9, Feature 26 expands dramatically underneath this surface, going under Floor 9 and beyond the limits of EA 2 to the north (see Figures 5.2 and 5.8). Carved mostly into bedrock, Feature 26 exhibits an unusual form: multichambered, with a deep central shaft from which radiate higher "shelves" to the west, east, and north. These shelves project from 46 to 58 centimeters above the base of the deep central shaft, with the east shelf sloping upward to the entrance into this feature south of Floor 9. In profile (Figure 5.8), Feature 26 resembles a giant, squat mushroom. I estimate that the excavations exposed two-thirds of this feature, although due to its nonsymmetrical nature, the exact shape of the northern section of Feature 26 cannot be determined. I estimate a volume for Feature 26 of 2.51 cubic meters.

Feature 26 contained two major strata, representing different depositional episodes. The earliest, Stratum 46, filled primarily the central shaft of Feature 26 and all of the west shelf and lower portion of the north shelf. Packed with artifacts, Stratum 46 alone yielded over 1,000 ceramic fragments. This bounty includes several distinct Olmec-style sherds and fragments of vessels made of a very fine paste; as will be seen in Chapter 6, several of these ceramics represent imports. Part of a large ceramic face in the Olmec style represents possibly a mask or a reworked hollow baby—the piece probably does not extend much below the chin (Figure 5.10). If this does represent a mask, the choice of an Olmec-style face as the "disguise" is particularly intriguing. Six obsidian fragments from this context document three different sources accessed by the Occupation 2 villagers. The villagers associated with Feature 26 utilized one obsidian source, Otumba (in Central Mexico), not present in

Figure 5.10 Olmec-style mask fragment from Feature 26; the mushroom-shaped feature from EA-2 is illustrated in profile in Figure 5.8. Because part of a rim is preserved below the chin, this would not join with a ceramic body.

the sample analyzed from Feature 3 in Unit 23 (Blomster and Glascock 2002). Stratum 45, the later of the two deposits, filled primarily the north and east "shelves."

Feature 26 probably served as a storage container. The so-called shelves lining the deep central shaft would have made ideal storage locations, and would have been easily accessible from the surface. It is not clear if the shape of this feature was predetermined or if the builders simply took advantage of natural irregularities in the bedrock. No evidence of burning or specialized activities was documented, although the enormous quantity of lithic material found in the upper portion of Feature 26 may indicate that the manufacture of stone implements occurred in the Floor 9 vicinity, with the debris piled into Feature 26 once it had ceased serving as a storage pit. The occupants of Floor 9 clearly controlled access to items not common at Etlatongo, although unlike Occupation 1, no platform raises Floor 9 above the surrounding area. One particularly unusual item is a roughly life-size hand or paw sculpture made of baked clay, found on Feature 26's western shelf. This piece has a projection to attach it to a larger sculpture, possibly of a large feline, and is the earliest nonceramic sculpture documented in the Mixteca Alta.

EA-2 after Occupation 2

The EA-2 excavations exposed two additional Middle Cruz occupations (Occupations 3 and 4). Each of these later occupations approximates the locations of Occupations 1 and 2. Occupations alternated between the southwest of EA-2 and the northeast. Occupations 1 and 3 lay in the southwest portion of EA-2, with a series of floors and successive resurfacings that covered nearly identical areas. Neither Occupation 2 nor Occupation 4 in the north of EA-2 showed evidence of resurfacing. Compared with the limited portion exposed of Occupation 2 in EA-2, Occupation 4, with a possible apron, extended much farther to the south than Floor 9. The general outlines of all floors from these four occupations suggest that they were oriented roughly the same way, slightly west of north, but the difficulty in documenting definitive floor boundaries, without extensive walls associated with the surfaces preserved, precludes more specific observations on orientation. Few wall stones were found *in situ*; the fact that wall stones were not generally present suggests that these stones may have been salvaged or reused during each successive shift in household location. Both Occupations 3 and 4 lay atop substantial platforms, as did Occupation 1. Only Occupation 2 appears to have occurred directly over bedrock. Details of these occupations reveal subtle differences in the arrangement of space and features compared to contemporaneous Valley of Oaxaca villages, which provide the best database to compare with Etlatongo occupations for possible public or higher-status contexts.

EVIDENCE FOR SOCIAL COMPLEXITY AND INEQUALITY

Compared to contemporaneous Valley of Oaxaca houses (see Chapter 4), and applying some of the same conditions, I recovered limited evidence that EA-2 occupations may represent public structures or higher-status residences. Occupation 1 features a prepared exterior surface, Floor 15, and an interior surface representing a structure (Structure 2-5) elevated approximately 30 to 50 centimeters above the surrounding area by a platform. Unlike contemporaneous structures built on platforms in the Valley of Oaxaca, interpreted to have served as public structures, the interior floor of Structure 2-5 did not appear to be recessed; the excavators of San José Mogote note that public buildings were not set on platforms but surrounded by them (Flannery and Marcus 1994:33). This may be an architectural difference between the Early Formative Mixteca Alta and Valley of Oaxaca, but a larger sample from the Nochíxtlán Valley is needed in order to assess this comparison. I interpret depressions evident on many of the EA-2 surfaces as resulting from the use and wear of the floors. Comparable, however, to San José Mogote public structures, an apron surrounded all of Structure 2-5 exposed in 1992. None of the floors associated with Structure 2-5 feature plaster, but all were well made and compact.

Feature 29, the storage pit associated with this structure, is the second largest bell-shaped pit yet documented at Etlatongo. Storage capacity appears to roughly correlate with relative social rank; examples from throughout the New World support this association, such as the example discussed in Chapter 4 from Keatley Creek, in British Columbia, where smaller residences had small—or no—storage pits (Hayden 1997). Like the larger bell-shaped pit from Unit 23, Feature 29 contained a variety of objects not common in Middle Cruz deposits at Etlatongo, such as hollow figurine fragments, a cylinder seal, and part of a ceramic feline paw vessel or sculpture. The material in Feature 29, however, represents largely secondary refuse; these objects were not necessarily associated with each other during their use-life, although they probably originated from the same household. It appears that the objects that differentiate Occupation 1 from other contemporaneous artifact assemblages primarily have a ritual association. In terms of economic differentiation, the most provocative evidence is still storage capacity. The ceramics from this context are further assessed in Chapter 6.

Without a larger sample, it is impossible to determine at this time if the adobe fragments, apparently used as building materials in Structure 2-5, reflect a different use of this structure or relate to the status of its occupants. The earliest adobes documented in Valley of Oaxaca villages have been associated with public structures slightly later than the date in which the Structure 2-5 adobes occur (Flannery 1976a).

For Occupation 2, the household shifted to the north, represented by Floor 9 and Features 26 and 27. No evidence of resurfacing was found on Floor 9. It remains unclear if Floor 9 represents an interior or exterior surface due to lack of associated wall stones and postholes. If Floor 9 represents an interior surface, there may have been an apron associated with it to the north; excavations of the post–Occupation 2 households suggest that Etlatongo aprons may not surround the entire structure. Apparently not built on a platform, Floor 9 appears to represent a relatively brief occupation. Feature 26, a multichambered pit feature associated with Floor 9, yielded the earliest evidence of nonceramic sculpture in the Mixteca Alta. While not enough of Floor 9 was excavated to evaluate the nature or status of the associated occupation, clearly large sculptures would not have been present in the majority of Early Formative houses at Etlatongo. Two somewhat later carved stones from San José Mogote were found associated with a public structure in the Valley of Oaxaca (Flannery and Marcus 1983:54).

I contend that these four Middle Cruz phase occupations represent the shifts in location over time of different generations of the same household. Excavations in the Valley of Oaxaca have established that Early Formative houses were usually separated by a space of 20 to 40 meters (Flannery and Marcus 1994:25). The four Middle Cruz occupations at Etlatongo exposed in EA-2 can be divided into north and south occupations. Including the aprons associated with the southern occupations, only 1 to 2 meters of space separates the north and south occupations. These occupations appear to be successive rather than contemporaneous, but all fall within or slightly more than one hundred years. From an early date at Etlatongo, the pattern of household growth and utilization of space centers on successive occupations shifting slightly away from a recently abandoned house. Covered with middens and other debris, the location of the abandoned house was ultimately reutilized, presumably by descendants of the same household group. Residents abandoned Structure 2-5 and occupation shifted to Floor 9, interpreted as having been occupied for a shorter duration than Structure 2-5. After the residents abandoned Floor 9, the household returned to the southern portion of EA-2 for Occupation 3 with a new structure constructed almost directly over the remnants of Structure 2-5. Occupation 4 documents a final shift to the north. Residents probably reutilized foundation wall stones in each successive construction. Burned daub and adobe fragments, which would not have been reutilized, were found associated with some of these surfaces.

While the limited area exposed by EA-2 gives the impression of a simple back-and-forth movement between northern and southern occupations, the reality was probably much more complex. Applying a model of tell (or mound) growth developed in the Near East, it has been suggested that Formative period villages in the Valley of Oaxaca grew in a spiral or corkscrew fashion rather than straight up (Flannery and Marcus 1994:34). Residents built successive houses close to abandoned structures, until the site of an abandoned house served as a platform for a new house. The fragments of houses exposed in EA-2 provide a window into this process at Etlatongo, with additional houses related to the growth and movement of this household probably scattered on all sides of EA-2. This pattern endures through much of the pre-Hispanic occupation at Etlatongo; I examine a similar sequence approximately 400 to 500 years later in Chapter 7.

Higher-Status or Public Space?

Final conclusions regarding status of these EA-2 Middle Cruz households are difficult to make, due to the limited portion of these occupations exposed and the lack of a data set of contemporaneous Mixtec households—thus the comparisons with excavated houses in the Valley of Oaxaca. The fact that Structure 2-5 sits upon a platform, elevating it above the surrounding ground, suggests that this earliest exposed Etlatongo structure may not have been a typical house. It demonstrates early evidence of social complexity, where those individuals associated with this structure visibly set themselves apart from other residents as part of a process of negotiating a different social identity. The platform does not appear to serve for flood protection; bedrock in this portion of Etlatongo is substantially elevated above the level of the nearby Yanhuitlán River. Floods would be a threat to structures built on the alluvium adjacent to this river. The platform may in fact signal that this is an area for more formalized activity, as documented for small-scale societies without significant economic differentiations (Adler and Wilshusen 1990; see Chapter 8). An apron, or prepared exterior surface, surrounds the portion of Structure 2-5 exposed in EA-2. A posthole associated with this apron provides evidence for a possible outdoor shelter or structure. Sheltered outside activity areas have been associated with higher-status households in the Valley of Oaxaca, while prepared aprons generally occur with public space (Flannery and Marcus 1994). Enhanced storage capacity is also evident at Occupation 1. Finally, the large bell-shaped storage pit associated with Structure 2-5 (Feature 29) yielded several objects not common in contemporaneous households. These objects, however, are not indicative of differential economic status.

Similarly, the limited portion exposed of Occupation 2 showed that this household had access to a massive storage feature, the mushroom-shaped Feature 26. The importance of storage capacity for early aggrandizers was considered in Chapter 4. Here I reiterate that the objects found inside Feature 26 included items not common in contemporaneous households in either the Mixteca Alta or the Valley of Oaxaca, including a nearly life-size adobe paw sculpture, which would have fit into a much larger object. Feature 26 also contained a fragment of a large Olmec-style mask. While the residents of Occupation 2 had access to an obsidian source that the occupants associated with Feature 3, Unit 23, did not, the overwhelming impression is that ritual objects encode social inequality—it is access to these objects that differentiated the households of Occupations 1 and 2 in EA-2 from contemporaneous villagers.

So do these two early occupations in EA-2 represent higher-status residences or public space? The problem lies partially in the question. As noted in Chapter 4, archaeologists often seek to segregate higher-status residences and public space— perhaps an unproductive endeavor in societies in which social complexity is first emerging. Archaeological and ethnographic examples document that purported public structures may host both domestic and ritual activities, while the private residence of a "chief" may also serve as a place of ceremonies (Adler 1989). Both Occupations 1 and 2 in EA-2 appear to represent higher-status households rather than public spaces; ample evidence of domestic activities occurs in both occupations. Early social inequality may be manifested in residential architecture, such as platforms, but rather than being linked primarily with heritable economic privileges, the claims to limited authority at Etlatongo may have been based on control of ceremonies and ritual paraphernalia beyond the normal household level. Such control and performance of rituals may have been closely tied with negotiations of social status. This argument also applies to the context exposed in Unit 23. The household associated with Floor 5 and Feature 3 could represent either aggrandizers competing with those of Occupations 1 and 2 in EA-2, or perhaps a slightly later temporal context (see Chapter 6). The occupations in EA-2 and in Unit 23 share a greatly increased storage capacity, which may indicate some economic differentiation, but this does not suggest that these households had established priority over basic subsistence goods. The Middle Cruz context exposed in Unit 23, in fact, is more readily comparable to higher-status households in the Valley of Oaxaca, due to the lack of an obvious platform in Unit 23. Only Unit 1, with a more substantial platform (especially the one underlying Floor 2) and high frequency of ritual paraphernalia, may truly represent a public space. The reality is that additional exposure, especially in the Unit 1 vicinity, is necessary in order to test any of these hypotheses. Ceramic analysis, to which we now turn, can also inform these interpretations.

6/Interregional Interaction at Etlatongo
Ceramic Style, Compositional Analysis, and Radioactive Fire-Serpents

Excavations of ancient Mesoamerican villages yield enormous quantities of ceramic fragments. The humble pot sherd, representing part of a ceramic vessel, is the most common artifact category. From a modern perspective, a world filled with metal and plastic vessels, it is difficult to imagine a time when nearly every container was made of clay. The tens of thousands of sherds found at sites such as Etlatongo remain as mute witnesses to such a time. Their durability enables sherds to survive in nearly any environment. They represent important markers of time; regional chronologies are based on diachronic changes in ceramic styles (see Chapter 1).

Ceramic cross-ties based on stylistic similarities inform the relative chronologies constructed for adjacent contemporaneous regions (see Table 1.2). Even small-scale, nonhierarchical societies were rarely autonomous but, rather, engaged in wide-ranging interactions (Hegmon et al. 1997). Sherds document activities that otherwise would be invisible, and are crucial informants in examining interregional interaction. While archaeologists have generally assumed that the degree to which shared designs appear between or within communities is directly proportional to the amount of interaction, other factors account for stylistic intensity besides level of communication. For example, based on ceramic designs, competing Formative period ceremonial centers in the Valley of Oaxaca engaged in less interaction than would be predicted based on distance and village size (Plog 1976b). As will be seen in the following text, ceramics can be used to examine interregional interaction as well as intrasite connections and relations. Such intrasite analyses have been used, for example, to determine residential groups (Hill 1970). In terms of a world systems perspective, ceramics can be employed to explore relationships between and within regions, assessing the degree to which regions imported or exported finished products.

Ceramics selected for analysis from Etlatongo derive from well-defined contexts, in order to permit intrasite comparisons. In fact, most of the sherds discussed in the following text originated in the contexts featured in Chapters 4 and 5. In order to examine interregional interaction, I compare Middle Cruz ceramics with contemporaneous materials from other regions—primarily the Valley of Oaxaca and the Gulf Coast. As part of the Etlatongo research strategy dealing with interregional interaction, ceramic

DIGGING DEEPER: CERAMIC ANALYSIS WITHOUT TEARS

In order to acquaint readers with some of the ceramic terminology used in both this chapter and subsequent ones, here I present the basic ceramic vessel shapes used during the Middle Cruz phase. A basic distinction centers on whether the vessel is restricted or unrestricted (Figure 6.1). An unrestricted vessel has an orifice (opening at the top) equal to or greater than the maximum diameter of the vessel's body, while a restricted vessel has an orifice less than the maximum diameter (Rice 1987:212). Not including the necks, the wall (body) of a restricted vessel extends away from the orifice (Figure 6.1a); the opposite is true for unrestricted vessels (Figure 6.1b). Because of this, unrestricted vessels often have proportionately larger rims than restricted vessels. One result is that restricted vessels may be overrepresented in ceramic counts consisting primarily of body sherds. In the Etlatongo analysis, we examined body sherds to determine if they represent a restricted or unrestricted vessel. Analyzing the surface finish of the sherd's interior and exterior allows this distinction; the interior of restricted vessels generally receives only limited, if any, finishing. This basic technique empowers the lowly body sherd, making this pariah of the archaeological set (in fact, undecorated body sherds are often disposed of

with no analysis) into a useful informant (see Blomster 1998a). The distinction between unrestricted and restricted sherds allows for limited functional interpretations for areas having disproportionately high percentages of one or the other, given the earlier caveat regarding overrepresentation of restricted vessels based on body sherds. Of course, rim sherds remain the most useful vessel fragments for determining shape.

Villagers employed restricted vessels in food preparation, cooking, and storage. Middle Cruz restricted vessels at Etlatongo include: ollas (globular bodies with necks), tecomates (similar to ollas but without necks), and—rarely— bottles. Utilized primarily in serving food and drink, unrestricted vessels include: hemispherical bowls (with a rounded base), conical bowls (with out-leaning walls and a flat base), and cylindrical bowls (with walls that form a rough right angle with the base) (Figure 6.4). Additional shapes will be described in Chapter 7. Specialized vessels that would not fit into either category were treated separately during the analysis, and will be discussed only as needed.

The analysis includes other aspects of ceramic vessels. While some vessels show the original color of the clay on their exterior, others have an additional

analysis included two components. Traditionally such comparisons center on stylistic similarities of ceramics from different regions. I combine this conventional approach with a more robust criterion for examining interregional interaction: chemical composition analysis. Given the periphery status generally assumed for the Mixteca Alta (see Chapter 2), Etlatongo should have few, if any, Olmec-style designs or imported vessels, and should show an overall lesser frequency of both Olmec-style designs and foreign ceramics compared to the Valley of Oaxaca. The data discussed in the text that follows directly contribute to these issues.

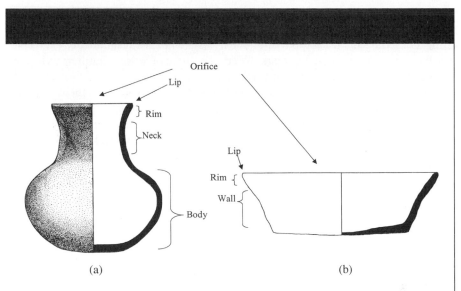

*Figure 6.1 Restricted and unrestricted vessels from Etlatongo demonstrate basic
ceramic anatomy, with major features labeled. The thick dark band on the right side of
each vessel shows the pot's profile, documenting its shape and thickness. The vertical
line shows the midpoint of each vessel. In addition, stippling has been used to indicate
the contours of the left pot's body. (a) A restricted vessel, with an orifice smaller in
diameter than its body. The neck is just short enough for this to be an olla. This
contrasts with (b) an unrestricted vessel with an orifice wider than any other part of
the body. Due to the angle of its walls, this is a conical bowl. Vessels are not to scale;
olla height = 10 cm, bowl height = 7 cm. © 2003, J. Blomster.*

coating of a fluid suspension of fine clay and water referred to as a slip. The "finish" of a vessel refers to modification of the surface, such as burnishing of the unfired vessel while leather-hard to achieve a lustrous appearance. Decoration involves additional alterations of the vessel, and includes application of local and Olmec-style designs. For further information, Prudence Rice's (1987) textbook on pottery analysis includes a useful glossary.

STYLE AND THE SAN LORENZO HORIZON

The formal qualities of the Olmec style were briefly outlined in Chapter 1. There are numerous difficulties in comparing styles across space, one of which involves the various ways anthropologists and art historians employ the concept of style. The formal qualities (shapes, composition, subject matter) in the art of a group often constitute style (Layton 1981; Schapiro 1953). Style is a way of doing something, and reflects a choice among varying alternatives (Hegmon 1992). Some of these choices reflect intentionality, a notoriously difficult concept for archaeologists when dealing with works produced by a long-dead artist. While recognizing variability, a given style expresses an internal order and consistency in various media and objects. Much to the archaeologist's frustration, different styles are not always mutually exclusive, nor does one style conveniently mark the art of a group or artisan. Further, style does not account for all material culture variation.

Anthropologists have defined different types of style and assigned them differing sociocultural significance (Hegmon 1992; Sackett 1977). Styles can be viewed as expressions of elements significant to the artist and/or the audience, as styles vary widely among groups using nearly identical techniques (Layton 1981:163). Style serves many roles, both inactive and active, from symbolic representations to marking social distinctions, interactions, and individual or group identities (Pasztory 1989). In the Valley of Oaxaca, styles may have served as boundary maintenance mechanisms between hostile villages (Dennis, 1987). Given the discussion of practice theory in Chapter 1, it should come as no surprise that I favor a view of style where, in some circumstances, active human agents manipulate it as part of their larger agenda. Style may communicate one's social identity to others, and actors may embrace—or reject—styles as part of their social negotiations. In fact, archaeologists working on the Pacific Coast of Chiapas hypothesize that the oldest, and fanciest, pottery was created as an exotic item and used in feasts to enhance the status of competitive aggrandizers (Clark and Blake 1994).

Style can, however, display ambiguous information that may not be interpreted according to the sender's intentions. Furthermore, issues of production and perpetuation of style are often excluded from an overemphasis on information exchange in style (Hegmon 1992). Ultimately style, and information transmitted by it, is context-dependent, and varies accordingly. Recognizing that many perspectives on style may be applicable based on research agendas, I see style as both formal elements of material culture and potentially as a means of communication and information exchange (Blomster 2002; Wobst 1977). Messages communicated through style ultimately are multivalent, dependent on both the sender and the audience. Here I focus on Olmec-style motifs expressed on San Lorenzo horizon ceramics.

The Olmec created the first monumental sculpture in Mesoamerica, executing art in a consistent style. This style is also expressed on portable objects, primarily ceramic figurines and vessels, found throughout Mesoamerica. Although not all elements encompassed by the Olmec style originated on the Gulf Coast, these elements were first synthesized and most fully expressed in this region. The distinctive style in which Olmec artists depicted human physiognomy at San Lorenzo finds expression in ceramic figurines (referred to as hollow babies) scattered across Mesoamerica (see Chapter 4).

The elements of the Olmec style that appear on ceramic vessels during the San Lorenzo horizon are largely symbolic, but also have a basis in monumental Gulf Coast sculpture. Many of these symbols abstract Olmec ideological themes, with stylized representations of supernaturals. There are examples, however, of possible explicit depictions of deities or animistic forces worshipped by the Olmec and contemporaneous groups on Gulf Coast and Central Mexico ceramics (see Figure 6.2). Such explicit depictions rarely appear in Oaxaca. These more explicit representations allow possible reconstruction of the more frequent abstract images, although obvious problems abound in attempting analysis of Olmec religion. It is probably a mistake to look for distinct, separate deities. The Aztec, for example, worshipped a host of deities, many

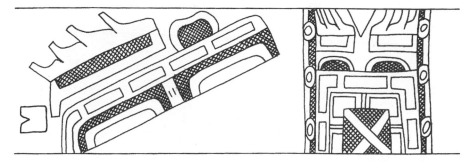

Figure 6.2 A more detailed, naturalistic Olmec-style head on a vessel from an unspecified site in Central Mexico. This "roll-out" drawing of the vessel shows a front view and profile view of the same creature, what some have interpreted as two different images—fire-serpent ("lightning") and were-jaguar ("earth"). Adapted from Joralemon 1971:Figure 120. Drawing courtesy of Dumbarton Oaks.

of which had interchangeable attributes, leading to a very useful analytical concept of "deity complexes" rather than a focus on unique deities (Nicholson 1971).

The ceramics analyzed in the text that follows generally have been associated with two separate mythological beings or forces (Covarrubias 1957; Pyne 1976). Archaeologists' conceptions of these creatures, based on scattered static images, may be wildly different from how the creators of this imagery envisioned them. Stylized depictions of the "fire-serpent" feature large, broad horizontal excised bars, with upside-down "U" elements that represent the serpent's gums. Symbolic flames generally rise from the eyebrow area, and at the base is the so-called "paw-wing" motif (see Figure 6.3a). Similarly, an abstract version of the "were-jaguar," a cleft-headed creature that figures prominently on Gulf Coast monumental art, includes the cleft motif, often framed by "music brackets." While these motifs appear to be mutually exclusive, some design elements appear on both—such as the St. Andrew's cross, a large "X." In addition, as the more literal depiction of these concepts in Figure 6.2 demonstrates, these may be different aspects of a similar or related entity.

San Lorenzo Horizon Ceramics from the Gulf Coast

From 1966 to 1968, the Yale University Río Chiquito Project documented occupations at San Lorenzo, Veracruz—the earliest of the large Olmec centers (Chapter 1). One important contribution of this project was the definition of the San Lorenzo A and B ceramic phases (referred to here collectively as the San Lorenzo horizon; see Chapter 1, Table 1.2). Two pottery types were defined as exclusive to the San Lorenzo horizon, Calzadas Carved and Limón Incised (Coe and Diehl 1980:159). The appearance of this pottery at other sites remains central to the debates on Olmec influence and interregional interaction. Two additional ceramic types critical in understanding Formative interaction come from the San Lorenzo excavations: Xochiltepec White and Conejo Orange-on-White.

Calzadas Carved pottery, decorated by carving the surface while still leather-hard, exhibits distinctive Olmec-style symbols, including the jaguar-dragon paw-wing motif (and variations of it), as well as more explicit supernatural images (Figure 6.3a). The carving of this pottery imbues it with a very sculptural appearance.

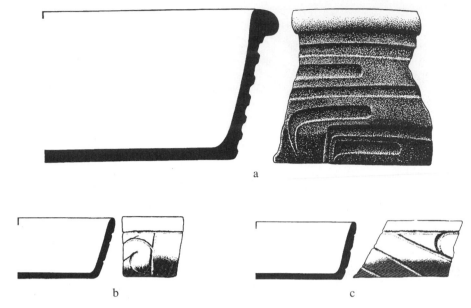

a

b   c

Figure 6.3 Examples of (a) Calzadas Carved and (b) and (c) Limón Incised cylindrical bowls excavated from San Lorenzo. Note the difference between the thick, excised lines of "a" and the thin, curving lines, alternating with vertical or diagonal lines, incised on "b" and "c." The two examples of Limón Incised are part of the sample analyzed through INAA. Decoration is shown to the right of each profile, indicating it occurs on the vessel's exterior. Not to scale; height of a = 9 cm, height of b and c = 5 cm. Adapted from Coe and Diehl 1980:Figures 138g and 144c, d. Drawings courtesy of M. D. Coe.

This ceramic type displays stylized elements of the creatures defined earlier as the fire-serpent and were-jaguar, such as flame eyebrows, crossed bands, opposed lines, and music brackets. Some incising is present as well. The design usually occurs on the exterior of bowls with vertical or slightly inclined sides (cylindrical bowls). Determining vessel color at San Lorenzo remains difficult due to erosion; the potters either slipped or self-slipped the vessels gray, brown, or black (Coe and Diehl 1980:162–166).

Limón Incised designs appear on vessels that are similar in paste and temper to Calzadas Carved pottery, but are often differentially fired to obtain combinations of black and white. Poor preservation also precludes assigning specific colors to this type. The designs, generally on the exterior of the vessel, appear on cylindrical bowls as well as vessels with slightly out-leaning sides. Incised, rather than carved, lines form curvilinear designs, emphasizing the *ilhuitl* or opposed volutes motif (see Figure 6.3b, c). Thin vertical lines often separate the sloping, curving lines. Coe and Diehl (1980:171) note that this pottery occurs less frequently than does Calzadas Carved outside of the Gulf Coast. Even at San Lorenzo, both Calzadas Carved and Limón Incised are rare.

The San Lorenzo excavations also encountered numerous white paste ceramics, including Xochiltepec White, made of clay so low in iron that it fires pure white. Possibly related examples have been documented throughout Mesoamerica. In terms of vessel shape, this type is most frequently expressed in tecomates, often in the shape of a squash; bowls appear infrequently. Documented by a few fragments at San Lorenzo, Conejo Orange-on-White represents a related, and even scarcer, type (Coe and Diehl 1980:179). It exhibits the same paste as Xochiltepec White, but has been slipped an orange-red. Potters sometimes carved designs through the slip. Vessel shapes correspond with those of Xochiltepec White. Prior to the Etlatongo research, this type of pottery had not been documented archaeologically outside of the Gulf Coast.

The San Lorenzo Horizon in Oaxaca: Fire-Serpents and Were-Jaguars

In the Valley of Oaxaca, the local manifestation of some San Lorenzo horizon elements—the San José phase (see Chapter 1, Tables 1.1 and 1.2)—represents a dramatic change in material culture. In terms of physical properties, graywares, characterized by a fine gray clay body, appear for the first time, as do a variety of slip colors, including white, orange, red, and pink (Blomster 1998a; Flannery and Marcus 1994; Winter 1994:135). New vessel forms are introduced as well, including *braseros* (used for fires), spouted trays, phytomorphic vessels (generally squash-shaped), and cylindrical bowls (often executed as graywares). Conical bowls become frequent during the San José phase. Whitewares resembling Xochiltepec White appear at this time; they may be imports. The problem is, from where did these possible imports come? Excavators in the Valley of Oaxaca have complained that no objective measurement for accessing goods transported by any Formative society exists (Flannery and Marcus 2000:8). The Etlatongo research contributes to resolving this issue.

Stylistically, San José phase pottery is marked by the adoption of some San Lorenzo horizon elements, which appear in addition to already existing local designs. Although examples of Limón Incised ceramics largely have not been documented for the Valley of Oaxaca, some vessels exhibit designs similar to Calzadas Carved pottery. On cylindrical bowls, the designs, generally singular, are carved onto the exterior; on conical bowls, designs—often in several groups—appear on the interior vessel wall. These designs show variations of the fire-serpent and were-jaguar symbols, with some expressed in a manner nearly identical to Gulf Coast pottery and others more similar to Olmec-style expressions in other regions of Mesoamerica (Flannery and Marcus 1994:377). Oaxaca manifestations of the Olmec style generally do not include naturalistic representations of supernatural forces. The similarities lie in abstract designs, often variations of San Lorenzo horizon motifs expressed on the Gulf Coast. Whole Olmec-style vessels mark prestige and/or authority, and have been found with either adult male burials or infant burials in Oaxaca, indicative of associations with ascribed (inherited) status (Drennan and Flannery 1983:67; Winter 1972).

In Oaxaca, some scholars dismiss any impact or significance between these symbols and Olmec interaction or contact. Initially interpreted as evidence of local Oaxaca elites imitating Gulf Coast elites (Flannery 1968), any link between these symbols and the Olmec has been broken with the reinterpretation of San José Mogote, the major Valley of Oaxaca village, at roughly the same level of sociopolitical complexity as San Lorenzo (see Chapters 1 and 8). Through this reinterpretation of political organization, the Olmec have been "stripped" of any priority in the manifestation of these symbols. Projecting early Spanish missionaries' accounts of Zapotec religion back 2,500 years, these designs have been interpreted as ancient

Zapotec symbols for "earth" (were-jaguar) and "sky" or "lightning" (fire-serpent) (Marcus 1989).

No precedent, however, exists for these symbols in Oaxaca, nor is there continuity with later Zapotec art and iconography. Joyce Marcus (1989) links the expression of earth or earthquake on ceramic vessels with the Zapotec glyph for earthquake (Glyph E), which appears on a stone slab at San José Mogote dating between 600 and 300 B.C. (depending on which authority is consulted). In addition to problems with assuming that elements on different media (ceramic versus stone) relate to roughly similar designs a millennium later, an alternative identification of the supposed earthquake glyph from San José Mogote further undermines this argument (Urcid 1992:157).

In an analysis of 595 decorated sherds, Nanette Pyne identifies 18 freestanding motifs. With 4 symbols considered distinctive to Oaxaca and not Olmec-related, she labels 7 as fire-serpent motifs and 7 as were-jaguar motifs (Pyne 1976:273). Based on their purported mutual exclusivity within and between villages, some archaeologists interpret these two motifs (actually many motifs lumped into two categories) as representations of descent lines within San José Mogote and other early Valley of Oaxaca villages. The mutual exclusivity of these motifs is not absolute (Marcus 1989:169), casting doubts on an interpretation linking them to descent lines. The conflation of many disparate designs into 14 motifs representing two "forces" remains especially problematic. Several motifs consist of highly abstract elements that should not be identified as either "earth" or "sky." In fact, these motifs may not represent contrasting forces. A cylindrical vessel from Central Mexico, often enlisted to support these motifs as separate "forces" (Flannery and Marcus 2000), actually shows the same creature but from a front and profile view (see Figure 6.2). Finally, the supposed mutually exclusive nature of these motifs has been hypothesized to be reflective simply of chronological variation (Winter 1994:135).

Stylistic arguments have not convincingly demonstrated a primary Oaxaca affiliation for these symbols. What about raw material analysis? One previous study did focus on compositional analysis of San Lorenzo and Oaxaca Valley sherds. After working with Valley of Oaxaca ceramics, Nanette Pyne examined San Lorenzo material, identifying a small number of Olmec-style motifs indistinguishable from those on graywares from the Valley of Oaxaca (Flannery and Marcus 1994:262). Pyne selected eight San Lorenzo sherds for further stylistic and compositional analysis. Unfortunately, the majority of these sherds' motifs have never been published, so it is impossible to assess the veracity of Pyne's stylistic interpretations.

Using microscopic analysis, William Payne (1994) compared the eight San Lorenzo sherds with those from the Valley of Oaxaca. Seven sherds were seen as indicative of a connection, with four of the San Lorenzo sherds apparently manufactured from the same materials as Oaxaca graywares. Kent Flannery and Joyce Marcus (1994:263) interpreted these data to demonstrate that some San Lorenzo ceramics with Olmec-style motifs were actually manufactured in Oaxaca and exported to the Gulf Coast. They deployed these data to support the "sister" model, where each Formative group manufactured its own variation of Olmec-style symbols, with the San Lorenzo Olmec producing and receiving Olmec-style symbols from other Formative groups (see Chapter 1). While problems abound with interpretations based on eight sherds, a more thorough program of compositional studies can test the resulting conclusions. I report the results of just such a program in the following text.

MIDDLE CRUZ CERAMICS AT ETLATONGO

Preliminary analyses have been conducted on all Early Formative ceramics recovered from the 1992 excavations. As the ceramic analysis is still in progress, type names have largely not been established for Middle Cruz pottery. Instead, as the focus here is on interaction, I present Etlatongo ceramics that resemble, or are identical to, those from contemporaneous sites, with an emphasis on sites in the Valley of Oaxaca and the Gulf Coast. To facilitate these comparisons, I apply binomial names (such as Xochiltepec White) established for Mesoamerican Formative ceramics to those from Etlatongo; these names refer to similar clay body and surface treatment, but with different vessel forms and decorations possible within each "type." I also perform synchronic analysis—examining roughly contemporaneous ceramic assemblages—in order to explore intrasite differences and implications for emerging social complexity. These comparisons are informed by chemical characterization of 53 ceramic samples from Etlatongo, San Lorenzo, Central Mexico, and Valley of Oaxaca sites.

Diachronic Change in Middle Cruz Vessel Form and Slip at Etlatongo

In order to understand relative frequencies of vessel shapes and slips through time, I perform a seriation analysis on ceramics from 10 Middle Cruz proveniences at Etlatongo (Table 6.1). These contexts are summarized by numbers such as "B. 715," with "B" referring to *bag,* and 715 to the specific bag number. Each bag generally represents a discrete context, most of which are discussed in Chapters 4 and 5. To assess diachronic change, contexts were placed relative to each other based on both ceramic styles/cross-ties and radiocarbon dates. Sherds linked by style with the previous phase, the Early Cruz, proved especially useful in identifying earlier contexts, as these materials were transitional (left over from that earlier time). Ideally, the seriation analysis should begin with a pure Early Cruz sample, but as noted previously, I encountered no primary Early Cruz occupation; earlier ceramics lay scattered in later deposits. Several of the contexts in adjacent rows in Table 6.1 are roughly contemporaneous and allow for synchronic analysis. For example, contexts represented by Bags 714, 715, 594, and 681 probably originate from within one generation, while those represented by Bags 18 through 14 are separated from the first group by a relatively substantial amount of time (perhaps as much as 100 years).

Analysis focused on calculating the minimum number of vessels (MNV) for each context; several sherds from the same vessel were counted as one vessel. In determining MNV, only rim sherds—and in rare cases, basal sherds that show the angle of the vessel wall—were counted. A total of 575 vessel fragments comprise the Middle Cruz sample in Table 6.1. In order to illustrate frequencies in the form of vessels from more "common" status houses (see following text), and to examine larger patterns of diachronic change, I augmented this sample with 186 vessel fragments from the Yucuita phase—approximately 350 years after the Middle Cruz phase (see Chapter 7).

This analysis highlights several general trends in vessel form through time (Figure 6.4). Tecomates, especially decorated ones, generally decrease in frequency through time, while ollas are usually one of the most frequent and consistent forms present. In this sample, hemispherical bowls, the most common unrestricted form during the

TABLE 6.1   VESSEL SHAPE IN TEN MIDDLE CRUZ AND TWO YUCUITA PHASE PROVENIENCES*
(ARRANGED FROM EARLIEST TO LATEST)

Provenience	Ollas & Bottles #	%	Tecomates #	%	Hemispherical Bowls #	%	Cylindrical Bowls #	%	Conical Bowls #	%	Apaxtles (Basins) #	%	Olmec Style #	%	MNV[†]
Middle Cruz Phase															
B. 714: EA-2, Stratum 65	9	32	3	11	2	7	5	18	7	25	2	7	1	4	28
B. 715: EA-2, Feature 29	9	36	1	4	3	12	6	24	4	16	2	8	1	4	25
B. 594: Unit 23, Feature 3	35	25	12[‡]	8	16	11	27	19	51	36	1	1	5	4	142
B. 681: EA-2, Feature 26—Stratum 46	9	13	5[‡]	8	4	6	16	24	32	48	1	2	5	8	67
B. 693: EA-2, Feature 25—Stratum 34	26	31	5[‡]	6	5	6	13	16	34	40	1	1	13	16	84
B. 678: EA-2, Feature 25—Stratum 25	6	14	1	2	1	2	19	43	16	36	1	2	1	2	44
B. 18, 17: Unit 1, Strata 12 (Floor 3) & 11	7	19	1	3	1	3	5	14	22	61	0	0	0	0	36
B. 16: Unit 1, Strata 10 (Floor 3) & 9 (bottom)	12	29	4	10	1	2	4	10	20	49	0	0	0	0	41
B. 15: Unit 1, Strata 9 & 8	15	25	4	7	1	2	7	12	34	56	0	0	3	5	61
B. 14: Unit 1, Stratum 7	14	30	0	0	1	2	5	11	27	57	0	0	1	2	47
Total for Middle Cruz	142	25	36	6	35	6	107	19	247	43	8	1	30	5	575
Yucuita Phase															
B. 94: Unit 6, Feature 4	50	45	5	4	4	4	1	1	51[§]	46	0	0	NA		111
B. 569: EA-1, Feature 10 (Burial 4 fill)	31	41	2[‡]	3	3	4	1	1	38[§]	51	0	0	NA		75
Total for Yucuita phase	81	44	7	4	7	4	2	1	89	48	0	0	NA		186
Total—All	223	29	43	6	42	6	109	14	336	44	8	1	NA		761

*Percentages are rounded off to nearest whole number.
[†]MNV (minimum number of vessels) does not include braziers, miniature vessels, and other forms excluded from this analysis.
[‡]Includes phytomorphic (vegetable-shaped) vessels.
[§]Includes a composite silhouette bowl and/or a plate.

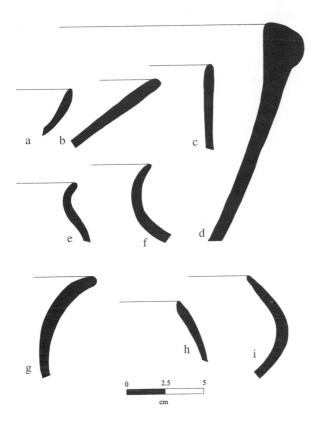

Figure 6.4 The range of Middle Cruz shapes at Etlatongo, featuring rim sherds excavated from the two earliest EA-2 contexts (Feature 29 and Stratum 65). The first four shapes are unrestricted: (a) a hemi-spherical bowl, (b) a conical bowl, (c) a cylindrical bowl, and (d) part of a large basin (or apaxtle). *The remaining five represent restricted shapes: (e), (f), and (g) show the variety of olla forms, while (h) and (i) illustrate tecomates. ©2003, J. Blomster.*

Early Cruz, are most frequent early in the Middle Cruz, swiftly declining in frequency to 2 or 3% of the ceramic assemblage afterward. None of the hemispherical bowls are decorated. Cylindrical bowls become more frequent in the early and especially middle portion of this sequence. Throughout the Middle Cruz, conical bowls are generally more common than cylinders. In one of the earliest contexts explored at the site (Feature 29 in EA-2), more cylinders are represented than conical bowls. This pattern repeats for one of the final strata deposited in Feature 25, EA-2. Cylinders begin to decline approximately midway through the sequence, and conical bowls become even more frequent, generally comprising nearly half of the total ceramic assemblage.

These observations regarding change in vessel form at Etlatongo parallel those for the Valley of Oaxaca. The shift away from hemispherical bowls and the heavier frequency of cylindrical bowls early in the Middle Cruz phase appears to match the pattern for the San José phase (Winter 1994), with conical bowls more frequent in the later half of both phases. Large basins are also present in the earlier contexts examined (see Figure 6.4d); these appear most frequently during the middle part of the San José phase in the Valley of Oaxaca, where examples with diameters between 56 and 60 centimeters have been found and interpreted as washtubs or dyeing vats (Flannery and Marcus 1994:192). These may be similar in function to ethnographic *apaxtles,* large ceramic vessels that can be over 70 centimeters in diameter. Rather than serving solely as large washing vessels, I suggest they may also have had a function in commensal rituals, such as feasting.

Diachronic analysis also reveals changes in slip color through time. The earliest contexts in Table 6.1 feature a small proportion of Early Cruz ceramics, where potters employed slip colors primarily of buff or tan and red—generally a brick red. In many examples, the underlying color of the clay body is allowed to show. The available slip palette greatly expands early in the Middle Cruz, not just in total colors but also in variety of each color category. White slips dominate the Middle Cruz ceramic assemblage, occurring in a range of yellow whites to gray whites. While some of the variation relates to color changes during firing, many of the varieties of a given color appear consistently across the site. Potters also introduced gray slips during this time, as well as orange and black slips. Red slips diversify into a broad spectrum of colors, which occasionally includes the brick red so diagnostic of the Early Cruz phase.

People often assume crafts improve through time. We cloud the question, of course, by our own perceptions of what defines "better." In terms of decoration, this assumption has been proven incorrect in Mesoamerica. As noted previously, in the Soconusco region of coastal Chiapas, some of the most exquisite ceramics (such as elaborate tecomates, for serving drinks) ever produced appear as the *first* pottery in the archaeological record. In the highlands, the pattern is somewhat different. Earlier pottery undergoes an initial period where villagers created basic forms with little elaboration. In the Nochixtlán Valley, the Middle Cruz represents an explosion in new forms, slips, and decorative techniques—a transformation in the potters' craft from the Early Cruz. Approximately 350 years later, the Yucuita phase evinces more consistent manufacturing techniques but a reduction in the color palette and decoration.

Synchronic Analysis

Exploring synchronic change in ceramics can reveal intrasite variability. For example, at contemporaneous Valley of Oaxaca sites, greater frequencies of decorated vessels and possible import wares mark relatively higher-status residences, while lower-status houses have higher frequencies of coarse utilitarian wares and relatively undecorated pottery (Flannery and Marcus 1994). Houses 13 and 17 at San José Mogote exemplify this pattern; the pottery of House 13 is relatively undecorated, featuring utilitarian wares (undecorated ollas, etc.). Only one sherd illustrates a possible Olmec-style fire-serpent design, which suggests lack of equal access to these materials. House 17, in contrast, yielded numerous decorated and luxury wares. Coarse, utilitarian wares appear more frequently in House 16, a sheltered work area associated with House 17 (Flannery and Marcus 1994:329–330). Unfortunately, the Valley of Oaxaca ceramic data are presented as sherd counts rather than MNV, preventing direct comparisons with Etlatongo data.

Etlatongo ceramic assemblages appear to conform to this pattern. Higher-status residences exhibit higher frequencies of decorated vessels, especially those with Olmec-style designs. Table 6.2 summarizes these data, conflating the vessels seriated in Table 6.1 as either restricted (ollas and tecomates) or unrestricted (bowls and *apaxtles*), reflective of their function. Restricted vessels primarily have storage and cooking functions, while unrestricted vessels have serving and presentation associations. In fact, Table 6.2 underestimates serving vessels, as many of the small, fancy tecomates included as restricted vessels undoubtedly functioned as proposed in Soconusco—as drinking vessels. By analyzing data related to vessel function,

TABLE 6.2 SUMMARY OF RESTRICTED
VERSUS UNRESTRICTED VESSELS*

Provenience	Restricted		Unrestricted		Total
	#	%	#	%	
Middle Cruz Phase					
B. 714	12	43	16	57	28
B. 715	10	40	15	60	25
B. 594	47	33	95	67	142
B. 681	14	21	53	79	67
B. 693	31	37	53	63	84
B. 678	7	16	37	84	44
B. 18, 17	8	22	28	78	36
B. 16	16	39	25	61	41
B. 15	19	31	42	69	61
B. 14	14	30	33	70	47
Total for Middle Cruz	178	31	397	69	575
Yucuita Phase					
B. 94	55	50	56	50	111
B. 569	33	44	42	56	75
Total for Yucuita phase	88	47	98	53	186
Total—All	266	35	495	65	761

*See Table 6.1 for full provenience data.

unusual spikes in the data, such as a higher percentage of unrestricted vessels, may relate to contexts that represent more of an emphasis on serving and less on cooking.

The earliest context in Table 6.2, Stratum 65 in EA-2—a deposit of platform fill placed under the first in a succession of possibly higher-status houses (see Chapter 5)—is instructive, as this deposit, drawn from materials probably not related to the earliest higher-status structure, exhibits the highest frequency of restricted vessels. I interpret the remaining contexts, which have higher frequencies of unrestricted vessels (ranging from 60 to 84%), as higher-status or public areas. Because the contexts presented in Tables 6.1 and 6.2 are not contemporaneous (see earlier text for relative groupings), some of these patterns could be related to diachronic changes. Nevertheless, striking patterns emerge. The four proveniences from Unit 1 (represented by Bags 14 to 18) originate from a probable public context. These have a consistently high percentage of unrestricted vessels, yet one vessel type—the large basin (*apaxtle*)—is absent. This could support an interpretation of basins associated with individuals engaged in competitive displays, rather than in public settings. Of course, this could also just be a sampling error or reflective of a bias in trying to separate higher-status contexts from public contexts (see Chapters 4 and 5).

One higher-status context illustrates this pattern. Feature 3 in Unit 23, reported in Chapter 4, yielded a total of 2,548 ceramic fragments, including vessels and figurines. Based only on sherds, nearly 80% of the ceramics originated from restricted vessels. As noted earlier, restricted vessels yield more body than rim sherds. The ceramic totals for Feature 3 exemplify why sherd counts are inadequate to accurately assess vessel frequency. Based on the 142 vessel fragments presented in Table 6.1, Feature 3 follows the higher-status pattern of a high percentage (67%) of unrestricted vessels. Additionally, restricted vessels from this context show an unusually high frequency (50%) of decoration, including some designs that appear unique to Etlatongo. Fragments of fancy decorated tecomates, including two phytomorphic (in this case, pumpkin-shaped) vessels, indicate that Table 6.2 underrepresents the frequency of serving vessels. An *apaxtle* fragment is present, as is a spouted tray fragment and at least two solid tubes or handles to spatulalike objects. The frequency of Olmec-style decorations (4%) is average. This pattern is further amplified in the roughly contemporaneous context represented by Bag 681, with 79% unrestricted vessels and many additional exotic items not included in Table 6.2.

A sampling problem, however, plagues these data. With the exception of Stratum 65, all of the Middle Cruz contexts in Tables 6.1 and 6.2 can be linked with higher-status or public areas. This sampling bias has been detailed in Chapters 4 and 5. Thus, although test units exposed several possible average Middle Cruz contexts at Etlatongo, additional robotage excavations are necessary to more fully document such contexts. To augment the sample with "average" status houses, two later Yucuita phase contexts have been included in Tables 6.1 and 6.2. The frequencies of restricted versus unrestricted vessels appear to reflect the limited data available from Middle Cruz contexts of comparable status, with an average frequency of restricted ceramics of 47% in the two Yucuita phase contexts. Since the Yucuita phase represents diachronic change, these limited observations about unrestricted/restricted frequency merely represent expectations to be tested about ceramic assemblages of average Middle Cruz houses.

OLMEC-STYLE DESIGNS AT ETLATONGO

Table 6.1 also designates the presence of freestanding Olmec-style motifs. To be designated as Olmec style, the design must be characteristic of those defined for Calzadas Carved or Limón Incised pottery. Only sherds that exhibited a substantial portion of the design were counted; the estimates of Olmec-style motifs are conservative and represent an effort to employ a more robust definition and selection of these symbols. Olmec-style designs are relatively rare throughout the sequence. Contrary to expectations based on projected comparisons with the Valley of Oaxaca and the supposed peripheral status of the Mixteca Alta, Etlatongo shows neither a reduced range of designs nor a lesser frequency. These designs occur most frequently toward the middle of the sequence presented in Table 6.1; they are present on about 5% of the total vessels, usually cylindrical bowls.

Olmec-style motifs appear extremely early in the Etlatongo ceramic sequence. In Stratum 65 in EA-2, the earliest context analyzed from Etlatongo, we encountered an Olmec-style fire-serpent carved on a grayware cylindrical bowl (Figure 6.5a). In Feature 29, the storage pit constructed through this fill and into bedrock, a fragment of an extremely well-made black cylinder with a fine and deeply incised exterior Olmec-style fire-serpent was recovered (Figure 6.5b). Red pigment still remained in the incisions! Here I discuss the kinds of Olmec-style designs at Etlatongo, reiterating that

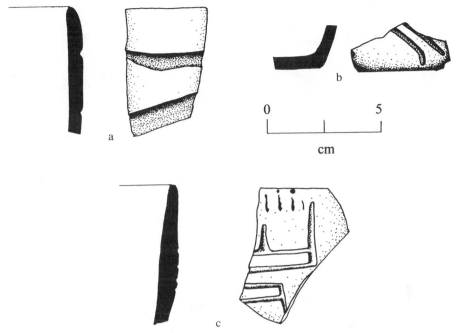

Figure 6.5 Three cylindrical bowl fragments with Olmec-style designs: (a) and (b) originate from EA-2 (Stratum 65 and Feature 29, respectively) and show variations of the so-called fire-serpent design. INAA classifies sherd "a" (Sample #22) with San Lorenzo ceramics. In (c), sherd comes from Zárate Morán's excavations, and shows a possible were-jaguar related motif. © 2003, J. Blomster.

Middle Cruz ceramics exist with designs unrelated to the Olmec style. At Etlatongo, these local designs generally do not occur on graywares; the nonlocal symbols are the only designs at Etlatongo that appear on new forms (cylindrical bowls and spouted trays) and also on a new clay body, grayware. In Feature 3 from Unit 23, restricted vessels have a variety of impressed designs. The manufacturing technique remains unclear for some of these impressions; I suspect potters made at least one local design by impressing a small bone into the damp clay (see Figure 6.6a).

Calzadas Carved: Fire-Serpents and Were-Jaguars at Etlatongo

Olmec-style motifs in pottery have often been characterized as fire-serpent and were-jaguar designs. Although, as noted earlier, the symbolism behind these motifs may not represent a clear dichotomy, I employ this basic division here in order to compare Etlatongo data with those from the Valley of Oaxaca. The Etlatongo data fail to support the interpretation that these symbols represent local descent groups, as both fire-serpents and were-jaguar designs are present in some of the same deposits, although fire-serpent designs are much more common at Etlatongo.

Based on a strict definition of what constitutes a were-jaguar design, examples of this design form a very small portion of the overall assemblage of Olmec-style designs at Etlatongo. The frequency would increase if numerous partial "cleft" elements, cross-hatching, and scrolls (or even fragments of carved lines) such as those

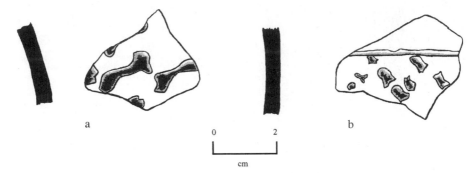

a

b

0   2

cm

Figure 6.6 Two restricted vessel sherds (probably from ollas) from Feature 3, Unit 23, with apparently local designs. The designs on "a" may have been impressed with a small bone while the clay was still moist. © 2003, J. Blomster.

utilized in the Valley of Oaxaca were included (Marcus 1989:172). Unlike fire-serpent designs, which occur early at Etlatongo, no definitive were-jaguar design appears in the earliest Middle Cruz deposits. Zárate Morán actually recovered the most diagnostic example of a were-jaguar motif from Etlatongo, although out of context (Figure 6.5c). Unlike fire-serpent designs, it occurs on the exterior of an Etlatongo Orange cylindrical bowl fragment.

The excavations recovered several complete or partially complete examples of freestanding fire-serpent designs (Figures 6.7 and 6.8). As in the Valley of Oaxaca, fire-serpent motifs occur primarily on gray cylindrical bowls (Figure 6.7), but some elements occur on spouted tray fragments, as well as black-slipped tecomates, where the fire-serpent is expressed through a combination of the upside down "U" motif and the deeply excised bars (Figure 6.8). Some examples have fine incising, usually interpreted as flame motifs, while others have one "X" or several (Figure 6.7). Other designs from Etlatongo bear a striking resemblance to San Lorenzo motifs not easily classified as fire-serpent or were-jaguar.

Limón Incised at Etlatongo

Not only does Etlatongo show as full (if not more) a range of carved Olmec-style designs as the Valley of Oaxaca, but the appearance of Limón Incised ceramics at Etlatongo further distinguishes the Nochixtlán Valley. Not a single sherd of this ceramic has been published among the hundreds of thousands of ceramic fragments from the more extensive San José Mogote excavations. Limón Incised at San Lorenzo appears most commonly on bowls with out-leaning walls and bolstered rims. Similarly at Etlatongo, Limón Incised designs occur primarily on the exterior of cylindrical to slightly out-leaned bowls with bolstered rims; these vessels usually are not graywares (Figure 6.9). At Etlatongo, Limón Incised designs appear slightly later but roughly contemporaneously with Calzadas Carved–style designs, although never as frequently as the latter.

Examples of Limón Incised nearly identical to those illustrated from San Lorenzo occur at Etlatongo. Limón Incised rarely occurs in contemporaneous sites in Mesoamerica. Virtually absent from all Valley of Oaxaca sites, only one published sherd from Valley of Mexico excavations resembles those from San Lorenzo

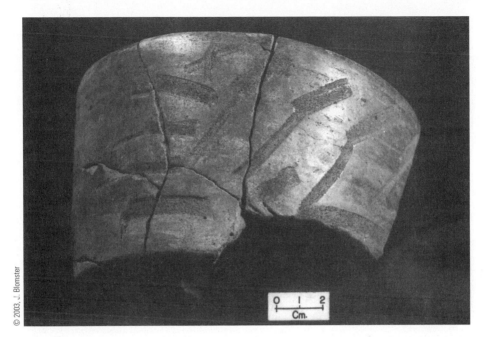

Figure 6.7 Grayware bowl from Feature 12, EA-2, with fire-serpent motif. INAA classifies this vessel (Sample #03) with San Lorenzo ceramics in terms of its composition.

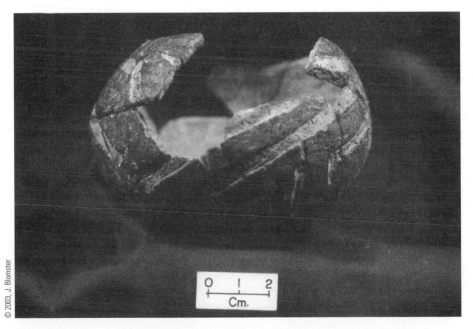

Figure 6.8 Pieced together from several adjacent strata in EA-2, this black-slipped tecomate exhibits a carved fire-serpent motif. The exterior is highly burnished, and red pigment remains inside the excised areas. INAA classifies this vessel (Sample #06) with local Etlatongo ceramics.

© 2003, J. Blomster

Figure 6.9 Large fragment of a Limón Incised bowl from midden deposits north of Occupation 1, EA-2. Thin incised vertical lines alternate with curving lines on this cylindrical bowl fragment.

(Niederberger 1987:Figure 393). Materials illustrated from the Soconusco region of Coastal Chiapas (Clark 1994b:Figure 12.9) manifest the range in colors and design from both Etlatongo and San Lorenzo, and represent the most comparable Limón Incised assemblage (outside of the Gulf Coast) to that of Etlatongo. Locally manufactured examples have been documented at San Carlos in the Soconusco region (Neff and Glascock 2002:Table 1).

INSTRUMENTAL NEUTRON ACTIVATION ANALYSIS OF MIDDLE CRUZ CERAMICS

Style-based analysis of ceramics provides little data in determining where a vessel was actually manufactured. One of the key arguments in Oaxaca archaeology has been that Olmec-style designs at Formative villages simply represent locally manufactured versions of such symbols. Compositional analyses complement the examination of vessel shape, surface treatment, and decoration. Here I present a selection of Middle Cruz ceramics encountered at Etlatongo, with the organization into groups informed by chemical compositional analysis, specifically instrumental neutron activation analysis (INAA).

The INAA process determines the basic chemical composition of a sample through the measurement of various forms of radiation emitted as the radioactive isotopes in an irradiated sample decay. Essentially, samples are made radioactive—a strange fate for a 3,000-year-old sherd. Fortunately, the procedure utilizes only a tiny fraction of each sherd. Gamma rays are of primary importance for INAA, as these rays can be measured for the wavelengths characteristic of each element (Rice 1987:397). The process can detect 75 of the 92 naturally occurring elements; it also measures the abundance of trace elements, which is useful for distinguishing between clays (Hegmon et al. 1997).

I submitted 53 samples to the University of Missouri Research Reactor Center (MURR) under the direction of Dr. Hector Neff (these analyses were partially funded by a National Science Foundation grant to the reactor, SBR-9503035). At MURR, the INAA consists of two irradiations, including a short and a long irradiation, and three gamma counts. The three different counts essentially measure the concentrations of 32 elements. The MURR procedures are fully explained elsewhere (Neff and Glascock 2002). After counts have been performed, the chemical data are then analyzed in order to recognize compositionally homogeneous groups within the sample; these groups represent geographically similar zones. Samples that fall within these groups originate from the same geologic zone and are more similar to each other than samples from other zones.

Although archaeologists have only recently begun to see the possibilities of INAA for ceramic compositional studies, the technique has been utilized with great success in analyzing obsidian. The unique chemical fingerprint allows each sample of this volcanic glass to be linked with its source (Blomster and Glascock 2002). Approximately 40 obsidian sources have been identified in Mesoamerica, providing crucial data in examinations of interregional exchange and interaction (Glascock et al. 1994). Ceramics, however, represent a much more varied material; INAA will not provide the same level of specificity in determining a sherd's origin.

Sample Selection

The 53 samples submitted to MURR consist of 29 from Etlatongo, with the remainder from other contemporaneous sites: 14 from San Lorenzo (including a kaolinite clay sample), 3 each from San José Mogote and Tierras Largas in the Valley of Oaxaca, and 2 from Hacienda Blanca, also in the Valley of Oaxaca. Additionally, 2 samples come from a surface collection made at Tlapacoya, Central Mexico, and donated to the Yale University Peabody Museum as a study collection in the 1960s. All samples, Etlatongo provenience information, and ultimate group assignation are listed in Table 6.3. All rim sherds from Etlatongo and San Lorenzo have been documented either photographically or through a line drawing. Those published from San Lorenzo (Coe and Diehl 1980) are noted in Table 6.3, while I present a representative selection of the Etlatongo samples in this chapter.

As the focus is on Etlatongo, I selected samples from undisturbed contexts from the 1992 excavations; 22 of the samples originate from four of the contexts in Table 6.1, while the other 9 are from additional EA-2 Middle Cruz contexts. In order to contrast locally made ceramics with potential imports at Etlatongo, I included sherds that appeared to be local products rather than actual Nochixtlán Valley clay samples. As has been well documented in the Valley of Oaxaca, the idea many archaeologists have of a well-defined, unique clay source utilized by potters, to which they add temper, founders upon close observation. Research in the Valley of Oaxaca documents that clays readily accessible to ancient potters lay within close proximity to their villages; these clays already had "inclusions" within the clay body (Payne 1994). Thus, in order to include samples of ceramics that appeared truly local, I submitted samples from coarse, utilitarian cooking vessels. This entails an admittedly simplistic assumption: Vessels important for daily activities and subject to frequent breakage and replacement, such as some of the thin-walled ollas or large fire-blackened tecomates, would probably be manufactured locally. The vessels selected for the general coarseness of their paste with large nonplastic inclusions did group together, and I interpret them as results of local ceramic production. Hindsight, of course, is twenty-twenty. In retrospect, I wish I had submitted samples from several ceramic wasters—vessels damaged during formation and firing processes—found in Unit 1. In lieu of finding kilns (which is unlikely, as formal kilns probably were not utilized at this time), these represent the ultimate artifactual evidence for on-site ceramic production.

An important part of the analysis involves comparison with Gulf Coast ceramics. Chemical characterization of Olmec ceramics had not been systematically undertaken prior to this. In selecting samples from the Olmec site of San Lorenzo curated at the Yale Peabody Museum, I combed the collection for any of the eight sherds Pyne and Payne analyzed. While not marked (an unfortunate oversight), I probably found at least one of these samples. I was especially interested in ceramics classified as Xochiltepec White, often cited as a possible Gulf Coast export even without the benefit of compositional analysis. I also included samples of a related ceramic type, Conejo Orange-on-White. A sample of raw kaolinite that Coe collected in 1967 from La Chogostera, near San Lorenzo, seemed especially important, as it may be the parent material for at least some Xochiltepec White vessels, a possibility first suggested by Coe and Diehl (1980:171). Rather than serving only for pottery manufacture, the Yale project documented that clay from this source was made into balls, smoked for flavor, and eaten.

I selected samples from the Valley of Oaxaca villages of Tierras Largas and Hacienda Blanca in cooperation with the excavator of these sites, Marcus Winter, who provided provenience information. The sample from the Valley of Oaxaca is small, and intrasite comparisons will not be attempted. In sample selection, I emphasized possible imports as well as locally made graywares. I also deployed sherds from a study collection presented to the Peabody Museum from San José Mogote. These samples, probably all from the surface, had been identified as to "type," using the binomial nomenclature scheme discussed earlier.

The sample I submitted to MURR was admittedly small, serving as the basis for interpreting movement of Formative ceramics, especially between the Nochixtlán Valley and the Gulf Coast. Fortunately, the results of an additional and much more expansive sourcing project have both verified and modified the results of my own humble sample, allowing for more secure group discrimination (compare Blomster 1998a:Table 10.2 with Neff and Glascock 2002:Table 1). This larger sample includes over 1,000 samples, although not all from contemporaneous sites. Unfortunately, these samples have not been illustrated. Many of the supposed Olmec designs would fail to meet my criteria for such a designation; nor are the identifications of ceramic "type" always secure. While I focus here only on material that enhances the samples from sites that formed the basis of my own project, this study has broad implications for the movement of Olmec pottery throughout Mesoamerica, some of which I consider in the final chapter.

Results of the INAA Sample

Table 6.3 summarizes the results of the analysis; full presentation of the chemical composition of each sample is beyond the scope of this chapter. These groups have been renumbered for the purposes of this presentation, and represent only a portion of the groups recognized in the larger analysis of Formative pottery. Here I discuss six groups into which the majority of samples segregate. Four samples do not fall into these groups. Two sherds (#36 and #37) represent the entire sample from Hacienda Blanca, a Valley of Oaxaca village that appears to be especially important immediately before the San Lorenzo horizon. Due to the possible earlier date of these sherds, they may not be comparable to the rest of the sample. Although in the same Etla subsector of the Valley of Oaxaca as San José Mogote, different clay sources may have been employed at Hacienda Blanca, which has been interpreted as a center for Early Formative figurine manufacture (Ramírez Urrea 1993). Sample #30, from San José Mogote, remains unassigned, but I suspect it would most likely fall within Group 4. One unassigned Etlatongo sample, #09, probably pertains to Group 5.

These data graphically illustrate the movement of Early Formative ceramics, and provide robust support for the conclusion that the San Lorenzo Olmec exported ceramic vessels to contemporaneous groups throughout Mesoamerica. Utilizing the 32 elements retained in the analysis, the segregation into groups is unambiguous, with one exception—Group 3, which (as will be seen later) forms essentially a composite of Groups 1 and 2. Several elements, such as chromium, thorium, tantalum, cesium, and calcium, are particularly useful in discriminant analysis. Groups 1, 2, and 3 all feature low concentrations of calcium, distinctive of a lowland (Gulf Coast) origin. This contrasts with clay sources from highland Oaxaca, which generally have a high calcium concentration, such as those derived from geologic formations surrounding Etlatongo, the Yanhuitlán beds. A problem was identified in calcium concentrations of some later Oaxacan graywares—both archaeological and ethnographic—and clay sources near San Lorenzo, but a multivariate perspective has made it clear that these samples have been segregated into appropriate groups (Neff and Glascock 2002:10).

Groups 5 and 6: Made in Etlatongo

Groups 5 and 6 appear restricted to Etlatongo; 10 samples segregate into Groups 5 and 6. I interpret these sherds as representing ceramics made at Etlatongo. All of the fragments of coarse utilitarian wares submitted cluster into Group 6. In fact, an interesting compositional difference manifests itself in these two groups. While the material in Group 5 is comprised largely of "fine brownwares," Group 6 consists of most of the examples of "coarse brownware." The composition of Groups 5 and 6 differs in the inclusion of larger, and more frequent, nonplastics in the Group 6 clay body, a distinction utilized prior to this chemical segregation by categorizing some brownwares as "fine" and others as "coarse" or "sandy" (Blomster 1998a; Zárate Morán 1987). Further, fine brownwares generally are fired more completely. The inclusion in this group of a tecomate with a complete fire-serpent design (Sample #06, Figure 6.8) indicates at least some local manufacture of these symbols, although the identities of the potters remain unknown. This nearly complete (although found in many pieces!) black-slipped tecomate features a fully realized, albeit typically abstract, depiction of

TABLE 6.3 GROUP ASSIGNMENTS FOR 53 CERAMIC SAMPLES FROM ETLATONGO, THE VALLEY OF OAXACA, CENTRAL MEXICO, AND THE GULF COAST*

Group	Sample	Site/Provenience	Ceramic Type	Comments
		Group 1, or "San Lorenzo White"		
1	01	Etlatongo, EA-2, B. 693	Xochiltepec White tecomate	Gourd-shaped; see Figure 6.10
1	02	Etlatongo, EA-2, B. 672	Conejo Orange-on-White conical bowl	Not decorated
1	10	Etlatongo, Unit 1, Strata 9 (top) and 8	Conejo Orange-on-White cylindrical bowl	Not decorated, but exterior similar to Conejo
1	11	Etlatongo, EA-2, Feature 26, Stratum 46	Conejo Orange-on-White tecomate	Elaborate incised design; see Figure 6.11
1	20	Etlatongo, EA-2, Feature 26, Stratum 46	Xochiltepec White tecomate	
1	21	Etlatongo, EA-2, Feature 26, Stratum 46	Xochiltepec White tecomate	Exterior similar; interior different
1	29	Etlatongo, EA-2, Feature 29	Xochiltepec White tecomate	
1	38	Tlapacoya; surface	Xochiltepec White hemispherical bowl	
1	40	San Lorenzo, La Chogostera	Kaolinite sample	Collected June 11, 1967
1	41	San Lorenzo	Conejo Orange-on-White tecomate	Illustrated in Coe and Diehl 1980: Figure 150e
1	42	San Lorenzo	Xochiltepec White tecomate/phytomorphic	Illustrated in Coe and Diehl 1980: Figure 146e
1	43	San Lorenzo	Xochiltepec White tecomate	Illustrated in Coe and Diehl 1980: Figure 146f
1	51	San Lorenzo	Conejo Orange-on-White tecomate	Illustrated in Coe and Diehl 1980: Figure 150a
		Group 2, or "San Lorenzo Local"		
2	07	Etlatongo, EA-2, Feature 26, Stratum 45	Grayware Coatepec White-rimmed Black	
2	12	Etlatongo, Unit 1, Floor 3 surface	Streaky Grayware conical bowl	Similar to Delfina Gray from Valley of Oaxaca
2	13	Etlatongo, Unit 1, Strata 9 (top) and 8	Grayware cylindrical bowl	
2	19	Etlatongo, EA-2, Feature 26, Stratum 46	Black-slipped Brownware cylindrical bowl	Not decorated
2	26	Etlatongo, Unit 23, Feature 3	Fine Brownware cylindrical bowl	Not decorated

Group	Sample	Site/Provenience	Ceramic Type	Comments

Group 2, or "San Lorenzo Local" (continued)

Group	Sample	Site/Provenience	Ceramic Type	Comments
2	27	Etlatongo, EA-2, Feature 29	Coatepec White-rimmed Black cylindrical bowl	Some angle to walls
2	32	San José Mogote, surface	La Mina White restricted vessel	Body sherd from a bottle?
2	35	Tierras Largas	Delfina Fine Gray cylindrical bowl	Not decorated
2	39	Tlapacoya, surface	Grayware cylindrical bowl	Carved Olmec-style design
2	44	San Lorenzo	Calzadas Carved cylindrical bow	Illustrated in Coe and Diehl 1980: Figure 140f
2	45	San Lorenzo	Calzadas Carved jar with outflaring neck	Illustrated in Coe and Diehl 1980: Figure 139e
2	46	San Lorenzo	Limón Incised bowl	See Figure 6.3b
2	47	San Lorenzo	La Mina White tecomate	Illustrated in Coe and Diehl 1980: Figure 149x
2	48	San Lorenzo	La Mina White tecomate	Illustrated in Coe and Diehl 1980: Figure 149r
2	49	San Lorenzo	Limón Incised cylindrical bowl	See Figure 6.3c
2	50	San Lorenzo	Calzadas Carved cylindrical bowl with bolstered rim	San Lorenzo B; not illustrated; Pyne sherd?
2	52	San Lorenzo	Tular Black-and-White conical bowl	Illustrated in Coe and Diehl 1980: Figure 154q
2	53	San Lorenzo	Calzadas Carved cylindrical bowl	Illustrated in Coe and Diehl 1980: Figure 140m

Group 3, "San Lorenzo White" or "San Lorenzo Local"

Group	Sample	Site/Provenience	Ceramic Type	Comments
3	03	Etlatongo, EA-2, Feature 12	Grayware carved conical (almost cylindrical) bowl	Complete Olmec-style fire-serpent; Figure 6.7
3	04	Etlatongo, EA-2, B. 661	Grayware carved cylindrical bowl	Olmec-style fire-serpent
3	22	Etlatongo, EA-2, Feature 29	Grayware cylindrical bowl	Fire-serpent design; see Figure 6.5a
3	25	Etlatongo, EA-2, Feature 26, Stratum 46	Brownware or La Mina White tecomate	Possible phyto-morphic vessel; with flange
3	28	Etlatongo, EA-2, Feature 26, Stratum 46	Black-slipped Fine Brownware	Olmec-style design
3	31	San José Mogote, surface	Coatepec White-rimmed Black bowl	Identical in style to Sample 27

TABLE 6.3 *(continued)*

Group	Sample	Site/Provenience	Ceramic Type	Comments
		Group 4, "White-2"		
4	33	Tierras Largas	Xochiltepec White conical bowl	
4	34	Tierras Largas	Xochiltepec White	Similar to Xochiltepec White on exterior only
		Group 5, "Etlatongo-1"		
5	08	Etlatongo, EA-2, Feature 26, Stratum 46	White-slipped Fine Brownware	Distinctive white slip
5	16	Etlatongo, EA-2, Feature 26, Stratum 46	Black-slipped Brownware conical bowl	White strip around interior rim
5	18	Etlatongo, EA-2, Stratum 65	Etlatongo Orange-slipped Brownware conical bowl	Distinctive orange slip
5	23	Etlatongo, EA-2, Stratum 65	Etlatongo Orange-slipped Brownware cylindrical bowl	Body sherd
		Group 6, "Etlatongo-2"		
6	05	Etlatongo, EA-2, B. 676 (posthole)	Etlatongo Red-on-White restricted vessel	Similar to San José Red-on-White
6	06	Etlatongo, EA-2, B. 672	Black-slipped tecomate	Olmec-style fire-serpent design; see Figure 6.8
6	14	Etlatongo, EA-2, Unit 23, Feature 3	Coarse Brownware hemispherical bowl	Thin white slip
6	15	Etlatongo, EA-2, Feature 26, Stratum 46	Coarse Brownware conical bowl	Distinctive off-white slip
6	17	Etlatongo, EA-2, Stratum 65	Coarse Brownware conical bowl	Distinctive off-white/greenish slip
6	24	Etlatongo, EA-2, Feature 29	Black-slipped Brownware shallow bowl	Red pigment rubbed onto roughened surface of exterior
		Unassigned		
None	30	San José Mogote, surface	Xochiltepec White tecomate	
None	09	Etlatongo, Unit 1, Strata 10 (Floor 3) and 9	Fine Brownware tecomate	Possibly equivalent to La Mina White
None	36	Hacienda Blanca	Possible conical bowl	Late Tierras Largas phase
None	37	Hacienda Blanca	White-slipped Brownware conical bowl	Late Tierras Largas phase/early San José phase

* As explained in the text, the groups have been retitled from Neff and Glascock 2002 for the purposes of this chapter.

the fire-serpent, without the absence of some motifs and "coarser" design noted in other regions exhibiting possible local manufacture (Agrinier 1989:20).

Many of the Group 5 ceramics represent fine brownware vessels with a distinctive orange slip, which I refer to as "Etlatongo Orange." Perhaps a more descriptive title would include modifiers such as "hot" or "bright" orange (we informally referred to it as "vomitus" orange). Etlatongo Orange ceramics, executed in fine brownware, often feature a distinctive surface finish; the slipped surface has been burnished so that it appears matte or even waxy rather than lustrous. Potters applied this slip primarily to conical and, less frequently, cylindrical bowls. Decoration rarely appears—the were-jaguar illustrated in Figure 6.5c is unusual.

Both Groups 5 and 6 feature brownwares with a variety of white slips. Several types of white slips, generally burnished to achieve a lustrous finish, have been identified; these variations in slip colors represent exploitation of different kaolinite sources, at least one of which is known in the Mixteca Alta (Marcus 1994, personal communication). The white slip is often worn down by burnishing so that streaks of the underlying color of the clay body show through—a phenomenon also observed on white-slipped brownwares in the Valley of Oaxaca (Flannery and Marcus 1994:204). White-slipped ceramics represent a large category of the total Middle Cruz assemblage at Etlatongo, generally expressed in unrestricted vessels (especially conical bowls). White-slipped brownware vessels are sometimes decorated, but generally not with "Olmec-style" designs—a situation that contrasts with that documented in the Valley of Oaxaca (although I would be more selective in what to label as "Olmec designs").

Groups 1, 2, and 3: Made in San Lorenzo

A total of 18 samples from the 1992 Etlatongo excavations segregate into Groups 1, 2, and 3, along with 19 other samples from the Valley of Oaxaca, the Valley of Mexico, and especially the Gulf Coast Olmec site of San Lorenzo (Table 6.3). The ceramics comprising Group 1 feature a white kaolin clay body with either no or extremely tiny nonplastic inclusions. With two exceptions (see Group 4 discussion that follows), all ceramics selected for the analysis that appeared similar to Xochiltepec White (or its variant, Conejo Orange-on-White) segregated into Group 1.

XOCHILTEPEC WHITE   One of the most distinctive ceramics in Formative Mesoamerica, Xochiltepec White exhibits no slip (or is self-slipped) and is extremely well burnished. Xochiltepec White vessels at Etlatongo are usually restricted in form, in the shape of tecomates or squashlike vessels, and occur early in the Middle Cruz sequence at Etlatongo, but are never common. While such vessels often occur in elaborate shapes, such as a squash or pumpkin, additional decoration is not common. Two examples from early contexts, Features 26 and 29 in EA-2, are included in Table 6.3 (see Figure 6.10).

The origin and production of Xochiltepec White ceramics have long eluded archaeologists, although generally they are suspected to have a Gulf Coast origin. Due to the inclusion of an actual kaolinite sample (#40 in Table 6.3) collected near San Lorenzo, this issue has been resolved. The kaolinite sample and 7 samples of

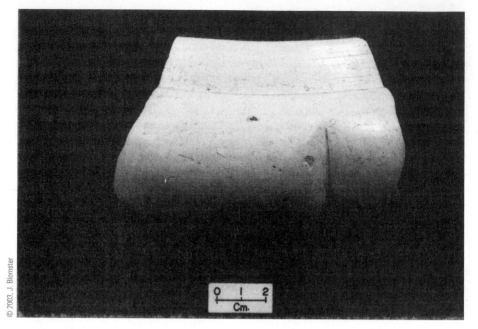

Figure 6.10 Large fragment of a Xochiltepec White vessel from Feature 25, EA-2. INAA classifies this squash-shaped vessel (Sample #01) with San Lorenzo ceramics.

ancient ceramic vessels from Etlatongo, 1 from Tlapacoya (Central Mexico), and 4 from San Lorenzo all clearly segregate into the same compositional group. This conclusion has been strengthened by additional clay samples collected from the San Lorenzo area (Neff and Glascock 2002). Additional INAA of excavated sherds add four more contemporaneous sites to the list of villages receiving Xochiltepec White ceramics from the Olmec or intermediaries: San José Mogote, Laguna Zope (on the Pacific Coast of Oaxaca), and San Carlos and Paso de la Amada, in the Soconusco region of coastal Chiapas.

CONEJO ORANGE-ON-WHITE   A second, and especially rare, type of pottery made from the same kind of iron-free kaolin utilized in Xochiltepec White is Conejo Orange-on-White, which is also an Olmec export. First illustrated at San Lorenzo (Coe and Diehl 1980:179), this ware might be more accurately called Conejo Orange-on-Yellow, as the fired clay body consistently appears as an off-white to light yellow rather than the pure white of Xochiltepec White. The potters applied an orange slip, sometimes in zones; they often incised designs, reminiscent of Calzadas Carved, through the orange slip, exposing the underlying clay body. A sample included from San Lorenzo (#41) had an elaborate incised design, similar to a large tecomate fragment from Etlatongo (#11; Figure 6.11). The fact that Sample #02 from Etlatongo came from a bowl, rather than the more typical restricted vessel for this type, initially led me to call this a local imitation of Conejo Orange-on-White. The INAA analysis shows this sherd clearly segregates into Group 1.

Rare both within and beyond the Gulf Coast, Conejo Orange-on-White appears at Etlatongo, currently represented by an MNV of four. Hundreds of thousands more

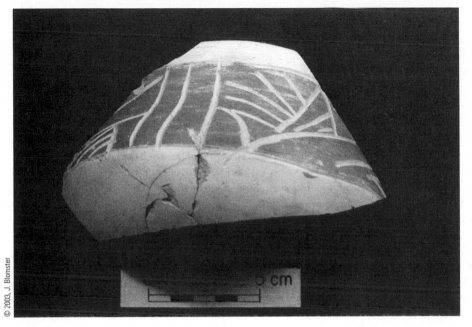

Figure 6.11 Large fragment of a Conejo Orange-on-White tecomate fragment from Feature 26, EA-2. Orange slip has been applied in a band; incisions made in this orange area dramatically expose the underlying white to yellow color beneath. INAA classifies this vessel (Sample #11) with San Lorenzo ceramics.

sherds have been excavated in the Valley of Oaxaca than in the Nochixtlán Valley, but no examples of Conejo Orange-on-White have been identified. I believe, however, there is one example of this type in the Valley of Oaxaca, illustrated as an "unusual vessel" of Xochiltepec White (Flannery and Marcus 1994:Figure12.140). The description of the slip leads me to interpret this as a fragment of a Conejo Orange-on-White vessel. The fact that it was the only fragment of this type found from the much more extensive excavations at San José Mogote and other Valley of Oaxaca sites emphasizes its rarity. Its more frequent appearance at Etlatongo further dispels the notion of the Nochixtlán Valley as peripheral in terms of access to nonlocal goods compared to the Valley of Oaxaca. An additional example, with incisions, comes from San Carlos, Chiapas—the Soconusco site where the most Olmec features have been documented (Clark and Pye 2000).

Group 2: San Lorenzo Local

The INAA revealed an additional surprise—the San Lorenzo Olmec also exported many non–Xochiltepec White ceramics, including examples featuring distinct Olmec-style symbolism. All San Lorenzo sherds with distinctive Calzadas Carved or Limón Incised analyzed from this sample are clustered in Group 2 and include a wide range of vessel shapes: conical and cylindrical bowls, tecomates, and an olla fragment. Additional examples from San Lorenzo include many coarse utilitarian wares. One San Lorenzo sample, #50, appears to have been one of the sherds identified by

Pyne as an Oaxacan import present at San Lorenzo. The INAA data contradict this interpretation. The low calcium concentrations, and comparison with clays analyzed from San Lorenzo, definitively demonstrate that Group 2 ceramics were manufactured at San Lorenzo. This is especially interesting, as Group 2 includes three graywares from Etlatongo, and one each from Tierras Largas (Valley of Oaxaca) and Tlapacoya (Central Mexico); the Tlapacoya example features a prominent fire-serpent design. Based primarily on the Pyne and Payne study cited earlier, it has generally been assumed that the Valley of Oaxaca had a monopoly on the production of graywares, particularly Delfina Gray, a fine "rock-hard" highly burnished pottery. Scholars suggest that ancient Oaxacans actively exported Delfina Gray pots, especially those with purported Oaxaca variants of Olmec designs, to other parts of Mesoamerica, including the Gulf Coast and Central Mexico (Flannery and Marcus 1994). While such movement may have happened, no robust data exist at this time to support such an argument.

Prior to the INAA, it would have been assumed that fine grayware pottery at Etlatongo, similar to Delfina Gray, originated in the Valley of Oaxaca. The INAA data demolish this assumption. Additional Etlatongo graywares have been analyzed that also segregate into Group 2; many of these samples purportedly feature Olmec-style designs (Neff and Glascock 2002). Thus, the Olmec actively exported their complex iconographic symbols outside of the Gulf Coast and into regions such as the Mixteca Alta and the Valley of Oaxaca. All of the graywares included in the sample I submitted originate in the Gulf Coast, including a fragment (#35) of a Delfina Fine Gray excavated in the Valley of Oaxaca. Some graywares may have been manufactured at Etlatongo. Additional, albeit problematic, Etlatongo samples referred to as graywares in the larger INAA project segregate into Groups 5 and 6. Additional samples that cluster into Group 2, San Lorenzo local, originate from San José Mogote (#32), Laguna Zope, San Carlos, Aquiles Serdan, and San Isidro (the last three from Chiapas).

Two Etlatongo examples (#07 and #27) and one San José Mogote sample (#31) of a type called Coatepec White-rimmed Black segregate into either Group 2 or the related Group 3. This extremely well-made ceramic features a white, ivory band along the rim of a black vessel, an effect achieved by differential treatment of the rim while firing the vessel in an oxygen-reducing atmosphere. Etlatongo examples are confined to cylindrical and conical bowls, and occasionally feature incised designs. This rare ceramic type, once interpreted solely as a highland product (Flannery and Marcus 1994:338), also appears to include Gulf Coast exports. Analysis of additional samples may reveal a highland variant.

Group 3: San Lorenzo White and Local

Additional ceramics that definitely originate at San Lorenzo cluster in Group 3, a problematic group. The six samples in Group 3 (five from Etlatongo and one from San José Mogote) could cluster either in Group 1 or 2; thus I have placed them in their own group, reflecting their common San Lorenzo origin. For samples #22 and #28, the probability is highest for Group 1 affiliation; the remaining four would statistically segregate into Group 2. Because neither Sample #22 nor #28 appears to have a white clay body, my interpretation is that all six sherds should be included with Group 2. These have been excluded from placement in Group 2 so that they play no role in defining the centroid and variance-covariance structure of that group (see Neff and Glascock 2002:8). As with Group 2, however, these samples include numerous graywares from Etlatongo, including the most intact fire-serpent design found on an Etlatongo grayware (see Figure 6.7). The walls of this vessel out-lean just a bit more than the norm for a cylindrical bowl, but the design wraps around the vessel's exterior—the usual location for cylindrical bowl designs.

Group 4: Whitewares

Several varieties of whitewares were manufactured in Formative Mesoamerica, with some possibly imitating true Xochiltepec White. Samples #33 and #34, both from Tierras Largas in the Valley of Oaxaca, represent one such variety and form a separate cluster—Group 4. Six additional samples have been segregated into this group, all of which originate from two additional Valley of Oaxaca sites—Hacienda Blanca and San José Mogote (Neff and Glascock 2002:Table 1). In terms of synchronic analysis within Oaxaca, it is noteworthy that no true example of Xochiltepec White came from secondary sites, in terms of regional site hierarchy, such as Hacienda Blanca and Tierras Largas. Several of the specimens in this group exceed 1% probability of membership within the San Lorenzo White group and may originate from the Gulf Coast (Neff and Glascock 2002:11). None of the Etlatongo whitewares segregated into this group, nor do any Etlatongo whitewares appear to have been locally manufactured.

Olmec Designs and INAA: Radioactive Fire-Serpents

Of the five vessel fragments analyzed that exhibit clear Olmec-style designs from Etlatongo, four (80%) originated at San Lorenzo. The four Etlatongo fire-serpent vessel fragments with Olmec origins are executed either on graywares or fine brownwares. The one with a local manufacturing affiliation (#06) appears on a well-slipped and burnished tecomate made from a coarse clay body (Figure 6.8). Compositional analysis provides a link between style and manufacturing locus. While potters did fashion additional examples of Olmec-style designs on clays from the Etlatongo area, these symbols did not originate in Oaxaca, divorced from Olmec iconography (*contra* Flannery and Marcus 1994). In fact, the one locally manufactured fire-serpent at Etlatongo does not come early in the sequence; one imported fire-serpent vessel (#22) comes from Feature 29, EA-2, one of the earliest contexts excavated at the site. This is significant as it shows an association of Olmec imports with one of the earliest occupations at Etlatongo. It appears that one group, the Olmec, played a central role in the expression and dissemination of these motifs. It remains to be determined what—if anything—ancient Oaxacans contributed to this multiregional symbol system.

CERAMICS AND EXCHANGE AT ETLATONGO: SUMMARY

For the first time, it is possible to discuss movements of ceramic objects in Formative Mesoamerica based on scientific data rather than style comparisons and hunches. INAA provides robust data from which I conclude that the San Lorenzo Olmec exported pottery throughout Mesoamerica, often with Olmec-style iconography, as evidenced at Etlatongo by Groups 1, 2, and 3. Rather than Etlatongo being on the periphery, it received decorated and undecorated vessels from the Gulf Coast. Considering the peripheral status usually accorded the Nochixtlán Valley and Mixteca Alta, the INAA results are startling: 18 of the 29 samples submitted from the 1992 Etlatongo excavations segregate into compositional groups (Groups 1, 2, and 3) originating from San Lorenzo. Over half of the Etlatongo ceramics sampled through INAA (62%) represent Olmec manufacture, not local production. Of course, the sample contains bias, as I selected ceeramics specifically to explore this kind of interaction.

The compositional analysis provides new insights into the ceramic changes during the Middle Cruz. New iconography introduced into the Nochixtlán Valley early in the Middle Cruz phase corresponds with a new clay body, grayware, and new vessel shapes—cylindrical bowls and spouted trays. Olmec-style symbols, often manifested on these new forms, demonstrate the participation of the ancient villagers of Etlatongo in interregional interaction. Olmec-style symbols appear both on imported pottery as well as locally manufactured vessels. It remains unclear how local production of Olmec-style pottery was organized: Did all potters have the ability, or perhaps more importantly, the authority to manufacture them?

Rather than being peripheral to the Valley of Oaxaca, Etlatongo evinces a wider range of Olmec-style ceramics than does the more intensively investigated Valley of Oaxaca. Both stylistic analysis and chemical characterization demonstrate a different, and perhaps more intensive, involvement in importation of Olmec pottery and symbols than in contemporaneous Valley of Oaxaca villages. Conejo Orange-on-White is absent or is possibly represented by one sherd in the Valley of Oaxaca; it is more frequent at Etlatongo. Limón Incised pottery, a marker of the San Lorenzo horizon virtually absent in the Valley of Oaxaca, appeared at Etlatongo with less frequency than Calzadas Carved pottery.

Until the sample size from Etlatongo increases, intrasite synchronic distribution analysis remains difficult. Imported pottery and vessels decorated with Olmec-style designs appear in the higher-status or public spaces excavated at Etlatongo, but as noted previously, the sample is biased toward such contexts. The contexts with more frequent imported pottery often contain other exotic objects, ranging from ceramic to adobe sculpture fragments.

A synchronic analysis across Mesoamerica, using the San Lorenzo horizon as one large slice of time, reveals that the sites with the most imported pottery are large regional centers, such as San José Mogote in the Valley of Oaxaca and San Carlos in Soconusco. While comparable data from other Mixteca Alta sites are not yet available, the appearance of this pottery at Etlatongo, as well as the site's size and position in the regional settlement hierarchy, argues that rather than being a mere periphery of the Valley of Oaxaca or on the fringes of Formative Mesoamerica, Middle Cruz Etlatongo was a regional center on the same scale as San José Mogote. Each region engaged in a different level of interaction with the Gulf Coast Olmec, and this interaction centered on the largest site in each region.

From a practice perspective, it is easy to theorize that agents vying for status at regional centers such as Etlatongo may have deployed contact with foreign, exotic symbols—such as Olmec iconography—to their own end. Research on exotic goods in Panama (Helms 1979) documents such manipulation of foreign goods by nascent and established elites. In the 1960s, when the Olmec were more commonly considered a precocious group, a similar argument was presented to explain Valley of Oaxaca participation in this symbol system (see Chapter 1). But this argument fails to explain several aspects of this interaction. Why adopt such similar symbols? By disposing of the argument that this iconography has a Valley of Oaxaca origin, the significance of these linkages must be examined. Also overlooked in these reconstructions is the perspective of Olmec agents. What did they take from this interaction? We shall return to this question in Chapter 8.

While we shall return to how Etlatongo and the Mixteca Alta relate to larger Formative Mesoamerica, the compositional analysis reveals some remarkable evidence regarding the relationship between Etlatongo and the nearest regional center at San José Mogote. Extensive INAA has been performed on graywares from the Valley of Oaxaca. Many graywares manufactured in the Valley of Oaxaca exhibit Olmec symbols. None of these vessels, however, traveled to the Nochixtlán Valley. Based on the sample analyzed, Etlatongo graywares were either Olmec exports, or some may have been locally manufactured. In terms of vessel movement and iconography, it appears that there was more contact between Etlatongo and San Lorenzo than between Etlantongo and the much closer village of San José Mogote.

7/Life and Death at Late Formative Etlatongo
Ancestors and the Yucuita Phase

Archaeologists adapt to situations encountered in the field. Often they make discoveries that contribute to the understanding of a host of issues, many of which may not have been included in the original research design. As noted in Chapter 2, a well-designed research strategy includes flexibility to deal with the unexpected. After all, there would be no point in doing archaeology if we could predict exactly what we would find prior to going to the field. Beginning with the accidental discovery of part of a Late Formative burial, the 1992 excavations contributed a wealth of data relating to both death and life at Etlatongo. These data address issues including treatment of the dead and their relation with the living. Additionally, the documentation of roughly contemporaneous ceramics from a series of discrete and well-defined contexts, ranging from burials to midden deposits, contributes to the definition of a new ceramic phase for the Nochixtlán Valley—the Yucuita phase.

DEATH AND ANCESTORS IN OAXACA

Anthropologists have had a long-standing interest in the study of matters relating to death, especially in term of how it affects social life, the significance of ritual, and the relationship between ritual and emotion (Durkheim 1938; Metcalf and Huntingon 1991). Mortuary rituals in particular highlight the relationship between the individual and society, the constant negotiations of social roles, and fundamental social and cultural issues. Additionally, cross-cultural comparisons reveal the great variety in concepts of death, responses to it, and treatment of the corpse.

Archaeologists especially look for meaning and expression in burials—one of the few types of deposits that express intentional behavior of the ancients. Burials reflect the positioning of objects and bodies actually arranged by ancient humans. The corpse and its placement reveal issues of sex, gender, disease, nutrition, status, and concepts of the body, and can lead to broader understandings of social ranking, demography, and pathology within the community. Although death is often considered the ultimate leveler, many times funeral rites reinforce social status, as seen in huge funerary monuments dedicated to powerful individuals, such as Egyptian pyramids. Of course, numerous problems abound in reconstructing past social organization using the presumed social rank of the dead, generally assessed through the amount of labor invested in the burial and its offerings; material culture can lie (Ucko 1969). Attempts to show an egalitarian community, such as the burials of New England Puritans, or even to inflate the social rank of the deceased may be active negotiations on the part of the living to construct a social order that may never have existed. Armed with a practice perspective, archaeologists interpret the social order reflected in burials with great caution.

Ethical issues also have an impact on the study of burials. In the United States, archaeologists have become increasingly sensitive to the concerns of the living descendants of the deceased; this has resulted in a generally positive dialogue as archaeologists and Native Americans strive to find a common ground between research, respect, and religion (see Swidler et al. 1997).

Death, in Western society, generally involves physical separation of the deceased from the living. In the United States, most of the familiar, and surprisingly uniform, funerary rituals took shape between 1830 and 1920 (Farrell 1980). Quickly removed from the physical space of the living to a morgue or funeral parlor, the corpse is embalmed, displayed, and visited for a brief time. Ultimately, the body is buried in a cemetery, usually some distance from the family home. In some ways, death is the ultimate taboo—it is kept at a great distance, the remains are disposed of far from the living family, and the deceased ceases to be an active member of the family. To many non-Western cultures, the American way of dealing with death and corpse presentation is particularly elaborate, costly, and exotic (Metcalf and Huntingon 1991:23).

Comparisons through time and space reveal that death does not always involve such a separation. Deceased Inka rulers, for example, continued to have active political and social lives long after their death (Conrad and Demarest 1983). The mummies of Inka rulers visited each other, and their descendants consulted them on political and economic matters. Among the Aztecs, family members maintained the estates and palaces of deceased rulers. This Aztec practice has roots deep in Mesoamerica, where the importance of the dead and ancestors goes back to the earliest villages that arose between 2000 and 1500 B.C. These early villagers buried their dead under or close to their house; the family shared their living space with the ancestors (Miller 1995). Throughout Mesoamerican societies, the relationship between death and life remained reciprocal. Through death and blood sacrifice, humans returned a debt to both the earth and the deities that sustained them. Ancestors continued to play a role among the living.

With some exceptions, early Mesoamerican villagers did not conceive of some distant place or structure, such as a cemetery or mausoleum, in which the dead should be housed. Instead, the dead remained close to the family, and probably continued to be considered part of the family's everyday life. The archaeological record documents that later Zapotec elites frequently revisited and reused tombs of their ancestors. Maintaining a very physical connection with the ancestors proved so important that villagers sometimes removed burials and their offerings when the family abandoned and changed their residence, reinterring the materials at the family's new location (Miller 1995). Connections with dead ancestors validated and could redefine the power or rank of the living.

While the meanings and specifics behind these practices obviously differ through time and space in Oaxaca, the interaction between the dead and the living remains strong. Perhaps this is best expressed in contemporary communities in Oaxaca, and throughout Mexico, on November 2nd, the "Day of the Dead," when families welcome deceased relatives back into their homes. They prepare household altars with favorite beverages and foods of the deceased and hold festive vigils at graves (although burials are no longer within close proximity to the house—a Spanish "innovation"). Lists of deceased family members are often read at these occasions; a written list with over 32 names has been documented in the Zapotec village of Yalalag, while even longer lists have been recited from memory (Miller 1995:242).

In order to discuss the relationship of the dead with the living at Etlatongo, it is necessary to go into some detail about the stratigraphic sequence of a series of burials and house floors.

EXCAVATION AREA 1 (EA-1)

Exploring Etlatongo through larger areas of excavation—robotage—rather than a sole reliance on 1 × 1 meter test units—formed an integral part of the 1992 plan of operations (see Chapters 2 and 5). Excavation Area 1 (EA-1) actually began as a 1 × 1 meter test unit located close to the northern boundary of Research Area 2 (see Chapter 5, Figure 5.1). Placed in order to assess the depth of Middle Cruz deposits exposed just over a meter to the north in 1980, that earlier project documented several features, including a burial consisting only of the femora down to the feet; the remainder of the body had been destroyed by construction of the adjacent road (Zárate Morán 1987:20).

This initial test unit revealed a more complex stratigraphy than that recorded in 1980. Also, this unit showed that not even the lowest (and thus oldest) stratum contained solely Middle Cruz phase deposits. Despite the absence of a primary Middle Cruz occupation, I decided to expand this test unit to an excavation area due to the presence of a substantial masonry wall and the hypothesized presence of a burial in the vicinity, signaled by several intact vessels. As seems inevitable in archaeology, we encountered the first whole vessel from the 1992 project at the end of the day. Much to the surprise of most nonarchaeologists who see only complete vessels in museums, archaeological ceramics are rarely found whole; burials are one of the few contexts where this occurs.

In order to better track the horizontal location of artifacts, EA-1 grew through a series of 1 × 1 and 1 × 2 meter units. All expansions of EA-1 after the initial test unit were excavated by natural—or, more accurately, cultural—stratigraphy, with subdivisions of 20-centimeter levels imposed on those strata that exceeded 20 centimeters in depth. The EA-1 excavations exposed an area of 14 square meters, or roughly 4 × 4 meters (with a 1 × 2 meter portion unexcavated in the southeast corner). Excavations continued until bedrock, for a maximum depth of 3.25 meters, not including features constructed into bedrock (Figure 7.1). Twenty-one strata were identified and described, including seven floors, ten features, and four burials containing a total of six individuals (Figures. 7.2 and 7.3).

The strata result from four discrete occupations. While in the field I numbered strata in ascending order (i.e., in the order in which we encountered them), here (as in Chapter 5) I discuss the occupations numbered in the reverse, so Occupation 1 is the earliest in EA-1. As the fourth, most recent occupation is much later and unrelated to the three earlier occupations, I do not discuss it. The thick deposit closest to

Figure 7.1 The eastern half of Excavation Area 1 (EA-1), showing completed excavations and the variety of features associated with Occupation 1. Arrow points to magnetic north; scale in photograph is 30 cm.

modern ground surface—Stratum 1 (Figures 7.2 and 7.3)—was deposited recently as part of the road construction that cut through this part of the site, resulting in mixing of deposits from a variety of phases (see Chapter 5).

We begin our story with the earliest of the occupations—Occupation 1.

OCCUPATION 1: FLOOR 7, BURIALS 1–4, AND FEATURES 7–10

An extremely well-constructed floor, plus four features, represents the earliest occupation in EA-1. Four burials associated with this occupation contained six individuals. I discuss the floor and associated strata prior to a detailed examination of the burials.

Floor 7

Floor 7, built during the earliest occupation preserved in EA-1, extends throughout all 14 square meters of this excavated space. Constructed of clay-loam soil, Floor 7 was either partly placed over bedrock exposed circa 500 B.C., or earlier debris covering bedrock may have been scraped away prior to floor construction. Installation of Floor 7 varied. In the eastern portion of EA-1, much of Floor 7 consists of modified bedrock, with patches of clay and loam used to fill in gaps in the bedrock (Figure 7.2); to the west, because bedrock elevation varies, villagers laid a consistent 2- to 5-centimeter

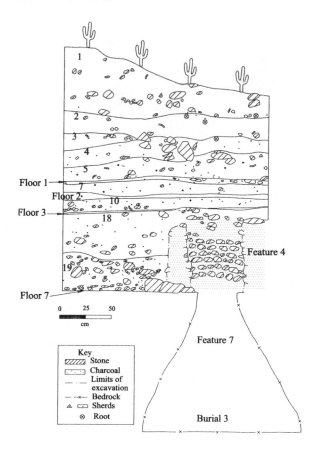

Figure 7.2 East stratigraphic profile of EA-1. The numbers refer to strata; to simplify the illustration, the stratum number of a particular floor is not included. © 2003, J. Blomster.

thick floor over fill placed to level this surface (Figure 7.3). The builders inadvertently included some ceramics from earlier periods in this fill. Much of the same red clayey material that occurs in bedrock in EA-1 was used to construct this floor. Extremely level and smooth, Floor 7's elevation barely varies 1 centimeter across this surface. Possible wall fall lay in the south profile of EA-1, immediately above Floor 7. This floor probably formed an interior surface. Because no intact walls or foundation stones remained in place, I did not assign a structure number to this floor.

Four features are associated with Floor 7 (Features 7 through 10). Interred during and after the use of Floor 7, the six individuals documented from the four burials probably were members of this Yucuita-phase household.

Burial 1/Feature 8

Feature 8, a slab-lined chamber covered with large stone lintels, contained Burial 1 (Figure 7.4). The individual fit snugly within this enclosure, designed specifically to encase Burial 1. Villagers constructed the chamber of slightly larger than fist-sized unshaped stones, packed together to form walls averaging 30 centimeters in height. Family members covered this individual, placed inside this chamber along with offerings, by four large lintels, only one of which evinces substantial shaping. They interspersed smaller stones between the four large lintels.

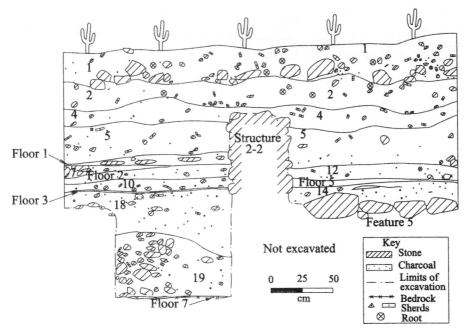

Figure 7.3 West stratigraphic profile of EA-1. The numbers refer to strata; to simplify the illustration, the stratum number of a particular floor is not included. © 2003, J. Blomster.

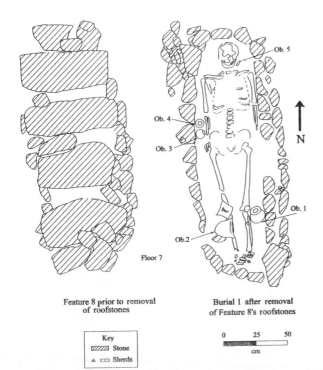

Figure 7.4 Plan view showing Feature 8 (left) and its interior with Burial 1 (right), with the stone lintels removed. Arrow points to magnetic north. © 2003, J. Blomster.

DIGGING DEEPER: BURIALS TYPES FROM LENIN TO MONTE ALBÁN

Just as there is a variety of ways of treating the living body, groups across the world differ greatly in their treatment of the corpse. In some groups, such as with royal Inka mummies (or the body of Lenin in the former Soviet Union), the corpse is never disposed of at all—it is preserved and displayed. In terms of practices that remove the body from constant viewing by the living, archaeologists generally make a distinction between cremation, or burning of the body, and burial/interment, where the body is placed in a variety of positions (flexed, extended, etc.) and buried. Two basic types of burials are commonly recognized: primary, where the deceased is found in his or her original place of deposition; and secondary, where the remains have been moved (generally after decomposition of the flesh) from their primary site and then redeposited. Scattered body parts, such as trophy skulls, included with primary burials fall under this category. In some parts of the world, such as Borneo, secondary burials are actually common, as they are part of a belief in death as a gradual process. A secondary burial occurs after the final rotting of the flesh, which signals the deceased soul's arrival in the land of ancestors (Metcalf and Huntington 1991:34). The distinction between primary and secondary may not always be clear. Different generations of elite families, for example, used many of the tombs at Monte Albán continuously. In this case, previous interments within the tomb may simply have been pushed to the side to make way for the new arrival.

Interred in an extended position from north to south, Burial 1 lay oriented almost directly magnetic north, placed face up, with head pointing north. While the legs were extended, the feet pointed inward and on top of each other—a necessary measure in order to conserve space and fit the individual into this small chamber. With this detail, we catch glimpses of ancient life, such as the realization that the chamber had been built slightly too small! The individual lay directly on Floor 7. Poorly preserved, much of Burial 1's torso was present only in the form of bone powder. All bones were found in proper anatomical position; this is a primary burial (see the "Digging Deeper" section in this chapter). Two independent osteologists examined all bones from the 1992 excavations. While too poorly preserved to permit identification of sex, the bones indicate this individual was definitely an adult.

Relatives included five objects with Burial 1 as offerings—four ceramic vessels and a cylindrical greenstone bead, located immediately adjacent to the left of the mandible (see Table 7.1 and Figure 7.5). Perhaps the bead initially lay in the mouth of the deceased—a common practice in Mesoamerica—but fell out during decomposition. These ceramics will be discussed in the following text, as they form part of the sample utilized to define a new ceramic phase (the Yucuita phase) and inform the chronological placement of Burial 1.

TABLE 7.1   OFFERINGS ASSOCIATED WITH BURIAL 1

Object Number	Description
1	Small brownware olla (globular, necked jar) with everted rim
2	Brownware cylindrical bowl
3	Miniature olla with short neck and direct rim
4	Grayware "bule"—miniature vessel—with incised cross-hatching and lines on the exterior
5	Greenstone cylindrical bead

Burial 2/Feature 9

Burial 2 lay just over half a meter to the east of Burial 1, oriented parallel to it. As with Burial 1, a series of large stone slabs—Feature 9 (Figure 7.6)—covered Burial 2. Unlike the stones covering Burial 1, these limestone slabs are all amorphous in shape. Burial 2 also differs from Burial 1 because no chamber of smaller stones surrounded it; the lintels were placed almost directly over the human remains. A final difference lay in the placement of Burial 2 on a small earthen platform rather than directly on Floor 7.

The arrangement of the burial goods also differed from Burial 1. Thirteen objects—all ceramic vessels—accompanied Burial 2 (see Figure 7.7 and Table 7.2). Unlike the vessels accompanying Burial 1, I found only one vessel (Object 12) in close proximity to the skeletal remains and covered by a lintel. Ten vessels, located to the southwest of the leg bones, lay either uncovered or only partially covered by the roofstones. A plate (Object 1) sat west of and above a lintel.

The eleven vessels clustered to the southwest of Burial 2 lay oriented with rims up, although several had fallen over. Two miniature plates (Objects 10 and 11) were placed so that their orifices touched each other, forming an ellipse. One plate has red pigment smeared in it, with burned vegetal material atop the pigment. A recent microscopic analysis of this burned material by Margaret Houston (2002, personal communication) suggests it may be residue from copal, an incense especially well known among the Maya. Broken into two large pieces, half of Object 3 lay at the western extreme of the ceramic assemblage and the other half to the east. I argue that this vessel was fractured prior to its placement with this burial, because intervening vessels between these two fragments would have prevented such postdeposition positioning.

Perhaps due to the lack of a chamber enclosing it on the sides, the individual in Burial 2 is in an extremely poor state of preservation. Only the femora (upper leg bones) are relatively intact, while parts of both tibiae and one fibula fragment are present. Except for a small portion of the left pelvis, and fragments of the lower arm bones and left clavicle, the skeleton above the femora is absent. Although we encountered numerous bone fragments among the lower portion of the skeleton (representing eroded bones), few fragments lay in the soil where the upper portion of the

Figure 7.5 Ceramic vessels and a greenstone object found as offerings with Burial 1.

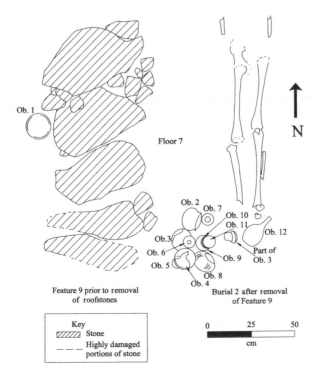

Ob. 1

Floor 7

N

Ob. 2
Ob. 7
Ob. 10
Ob. 11
Ob. 12
Ob. 3
Ob. 6
Ob. 9
Part of Ob. 3
Ob. 5
Ob. 8
Ob. 4

Feature 9 prior to removal
of roofstones

Burial 2 after removal
of Feature 9

Key

Stone

Highly damaged
portions of stone

0   25   50
cm

*Figure 7.6 Plan view
showing Feature 9 (left)
and its interior with Burial
2 (right), with the stone
lintels removed. Arrow
points to magnetic north.
© 2003, J. Blomster.*

Figure 7.7 Ceramic vessels found as offerings with Burial 2.

skeleton should have been—certainly not enough to account for the dearth of preserved bones. The absence of the humeri (upper arm bones) and all craniodental bones remains striking and suggests that either the burial was damaged after interment or that it is not a primary burial.

The possibility remains that the missing skeletal material may be the result of poor preservation. This interpretation, however, fails to convince, due to the scarcity of bone fragments in the area where the torso and cranium should have been, and the lack of teeth—usually the best-preserved body part. Nor did later disturbance destroy these bones, as this would have been clear in the stratigraphy (unless vibrations from the construction of the road, approximately 1 to 2 meters to the north, pulverized these bones). Preservation, erosion, and later disturbance are probably not the primary factors in the disappearance of certain bones.

An additional possibility is that the descendants of the individual in Burial 2 curated certain bones, a practice documented in later periods both in Oaxaca and elsewhere in Mesoamerica. The data from Burial 2 do not support this explanation. In one much later example from the Valley of Oaxaca, only the highest-level Zapotec lords, referred to as *coquis,* utilized this practice. They removed the femora of ancestors and displayed them (Lind and Urcid 1983:88)—a very graphic example of showing one's lineage and social status. In the case of Burial 2, the femora are present, while many other bones—primarily ones generally not curated—are absent. Furthermore, I do not interpret Burial 2 as a high-status burial, although it remains to be proved that this practice was confined to the elite nearly 1,000 years before the example documented in the Valley of Oaxaca.

TABLE 7.2   OFFERINGS ASSOCIATED WITH BURIAL 2

Object Number	Description
1	Brownware plate with direct rim
2	Brownware olla with short neck and everted rim; band of red slip on interior rim and below the exterior rim, and painted exterior design (Figure 7.13)
3	Fine brownware cylindrical bowl with everted rim; distinctive "Yucuita yellow" slip
4	Brownware tecomate
5	Miniature conical bowl with direct rim
6	Miniature brownware cantaro or bottle
7	Miniature brownware olla, with direct rim
8	Brownware squash effigy vessel (Figure 7.12)
9	Small brownware kidney-shaped bowl
10	Small grayware plate, with incised cross design (Figure 7.15)
11	Small grayware plate, with red pigment and vegetal material at base—possibly copal
12	Creamware bottle with highly polished red-slipped exterior; probable Valley of Oaxaca import
13	Miniature hemispherical bowl; found inside Ob. 9

Instead, several lines of evidence point to Burial 2 as a secondary interment. In this scenario, the individual in Burial 2 died prior to the individual in Burial 1 and was interred elsewhere. Upon the death of the Burial 1 individual, this earlier corpse was disinterred in order to be placed parallel to Burial 1. The fact that these two burials are clearly associated, based on the stratigraphy and their parallel position on Floor 7, supports reinterment. While the individuals in Burials 1 and 2 did not expire at the same time, they may have been linked in life and thus placed together in death.

In the Valley of Oaxaca, the paired burial of individuals linked in life has been documented as far back as 1000 B.C. Paired burials of men and women, possibly husband and wife pairs, have been documented at Tomaltepec and San José Mogote (Whalen 1981; Marcus and Flannery 1996:97–98). A burial pair at San José Mogote was arranged similarly to Etlatongo Burials 1 and 2, with the husband on the left, surrounded and covered by limestone slabs (similar to Burial 1), while the wife (or female interment) lay beside him but without slabs (Marcus and Flannery 1996:97–98). The bones from Burials 1 and 2 at Etlatongo remain too poorly preserved to definitively determine biological sex of these individuals.

The lack of roofstones over the area where the torso and cranium of Burial 2 should have been is also suggestive of reinterment. If these bones were not available for reinterment, there would be no reason to cover this area with lintels. Additionally, no offerings were placed with the largely absent upper portion of the body. The pieces of one offering, Object 3, lay in positions that indicate the vessel may have been broken prior to interment; perhaps it was reused from the initial interment of this individual. Finally, the one well-preserved upper body bone of Burial 2, the left clavicle, was placed only in approximate anatomical orientation. Bones of the lower body were also slightly out of position relative to each other. Thus, while the biological sex of Etlatongo Burials 1 and 2 could not be definitively determined, I conclude they may represent the interment of a husband and wife; the individual in Burial 2 died first, and was reinterred upon Burial 1's death so that they could face eternity together.

Burial 3/Feature 7

Burial 3 consists of three individuals at the base of a bell-shaped pit (Feature 7) excavated into bedrock from Floor 7 (see Figure 7.2). With a roughly circular base, Feature 7 has a volume of 1.42 cubic meters. A plasterlike limestone powder covers the surface of Feature 7. Like most bell-shaped pits that eventually were used to house burials, Feature 7 was probably used initially for storage. Unlike all other burials excavated during the 1992 season at Etlatongo, the skeletal remains in Burial 3 are well preserved, with nearly every bone still in anatomical position (Figure 7.8). Two of the individuals had their legs at least partially flexed or bound; the other individual did not appear to have received this type of preparation.

The three individuals covered parts of each other, allowing a possible reconstruction of the order in which these individuals were deposited (Figure 7.8). I argue that the remains were interred in at least two separate events. While ten offerings (nine ceramic vessels and one shell decoration—see Table 7.3) come from Burial 3, only two of these can be associated with one particular individual. In fact, one vessel—Object 10 (not included in Figure 7.8)—lay 10 centimeters above the highest human remains. Due to both placement and size of the majority of vessels, all whole vessels were probably deposited as part of the interment of the final individual in Burial 3, rather than thrown down through a later cylindrical chamber (Feature 4) constructed over Feature 7 (see following text). We found additional partially intact vessels some distance above Burial 3 within Feature 7.

The grave goods provide a consistent relative date or association with the Yucuita phase (500 to 300 B.C.) for Burials 1 to 3. Feature 7 and Burial 3 have also been analyzed using absolute dating techniques. A concentration of burned organic remains, retrieved directly above Burial 3, was submitted for radiocarbon dating and produced a date of 420 B.C., plus or minus 90 years, precisely within the proposed time span for the Yucuita phase.

In addition to frequent ceramic artifacts, Feature 7 also contained nearly 20 broken adobe blocks. Most of these lay above Burial 3, with only 3 blocks in close proximity to any of the bones. The adobe blocks were probably deposited in order to fill Feature 7 and its burial. This could have happened after the construction of Feature 4 atop Feature 7.

BURIAL 3, INDIVIDUAL 2   The earliest interment in Burial 3, Individual 2 lay nearly completely covered by the torso of Individual 1 and partially by the right arm of Individual 3. Located in the northern half of Feature 7 with the head to the south, Individual 2 appears to have been in a kneeling or seated position, but fallen so as to lie completely on the base of Feature 7 (Figure 7.8). Tightly flexed, the lower leg bones doubled back under Individual 2's femora. Prior to interment, the lower body of Individual 2 was probably bound in order to maintain this position. The cranium

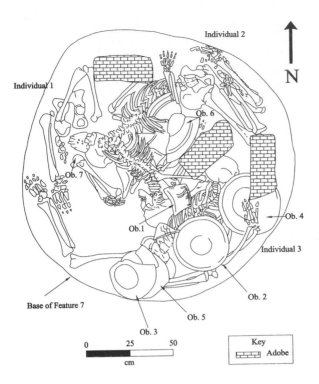

Figure 7.8 Plan view of Burial 3 within a bell-shaped pit (Feature 7), showing the arrangement of three overlapping individuals, associated offerings, and adobe blocks. Arrow points to magnetic north. © 2003, J. Blomster.

lay on the base of Feature 7; a miniature, undecorated bottle (Object 7) lay by the skull. It was the only offering directly on the base of Feature 7, covered by soil and the later remains of Individual 1. If individual 2 originally sat upright, then Object 7, on the base of Feature 7, cannot be directly associated with this individual.

Independent osteologists variously identified Individual 2 as both a biological male and female. I support the interpretation of this individual as a male, as the analyst made the identification based on all bones; the subsequent analysis only looked at the skull. This individual was a subadult (between 15 and 17 years) at the time of death, because the upper left and lower molars remain unerupted. The skeleton evinces no clear sign of trauma, so the cause of death could not be determined.

BURIAL 3, INDIVIDUAL 1   Interred after Individual 2 but prior to Individual 3, the slightly higher elevation of Individual 1 relative to Individual 2 (which lay mostly on the floor of Feature 7) suggests that at least some time passed between these interments. While Individual 1 covered a large portion of Individual 2, only limited contact occurred between Individuals 1 and 3; the lower left arm of Individual 3 covered the left humerus and scapula of Individual 1 (Figure 7.8). A large conical bowl covered this area of overlap between Individuals 1 and 3. While the precise amount of time between these interments cannot be determined, the fact that they occupied separate portions of Feature 7, with only minimal overlap, as well as the arrangement of offerings and lack of soil between the bodies, suggests little time separates the interments. Of course, much of the body position—and the interpretation—may have been affected by postdepositional processes.

TABLE 7.3   OFFERINGS ASSOCIATED WITH BURIAL 3

Object Number	Description
1	Grayware conical bowl, with everted incised eccentric rim and interior design of three wavy incised lines alternating with three straight lines
2	Brownware conical bowl, with everted rim
3	Brownware conical bowl with direct rim, and mat impressions on the exterior base
4	Brownware conical bowl with everted rim
5	Large brownware olla, with red slip on neck
6	Brownware conical bowl with divergent rim; mat impressions on base; interior has two incised lines under rim
7	Miniature brownware short-necked bottle with remains of a thin red micacious slip
8	Small shell ornament probably in the shape of a human face
9	Brownware olla, smaller than Object 5
10	Brownware conical bowl, with direct rim

Individual 1 may have originally had its lower body flexed in a seated position, rather than kneeling (as was Individual 2). It is difficult to determine the exact position of Individual 1's legs, because during the decomposition process—and with the weight of materials pressing down from above—the lower part of the body separated from the torso; it was lying partly in a state of disarray (Figure 7.8). The legs were probably positioned so that Individual 1 sat cross-legged or "tailor-style," defined here as legs flexed and knees extended away from the torso, with the feet close together. The arms could be in variable positions. Represented on a Formative fig-urine from San José Mogote, this position has also been described as "yoga-style" (Flannery and Marcus 1976:382). I see tailor-style burials, with probably unbound arms, as one type of seated burial (e.g., burials can also be seated and tightly flexed). With a small comparative sample from the Nochixtlán Valley, it would be premature to assign any status to these positions.

Identified as an adult female between the ages of 30 and 35, Individual 1 stood 1.58 meters tall based on long bone measurements. Pathology is present in some internal depreciation of the bone, along with caries on the teeth and an abscess.

BURIAL 3, INDIVIDUAL 3   Probably interred shortly after Individual 1, Individual 3 filled the southeastern portion of Feature 7 (Figure 7.8). Individual 3 occupied the space not filled by Individual 1; even after the presumed collapse of Individual 1, they overlap only at one point. Not placed in a flexed or seated position, Individual 3 sprawled on its dorsal side against the southeast boundary of Feature 7, with the left leg flexed and the right almost fully extended.

The deposition of Individual 3 involved less attention to the position of the body than with Individuals 1 and 2; the placement of Individual 3 seems designed prima-rily to minimize overlap with Individual 1. The left forearm and hand of Individual

3 reached into Object 4, a large conical bowl that partially covered the cranium. A small shell ornament lay on the pelvis and may been part of the clothing or jewelry worn by Individual 3.

Identified by both osteologists as an adult female, Individual 3 may have stood 1.57 meters tall. In addition to osteoarthritis on the lumbar vertebrae, extensive dental pathologies are present. Several teeth were lost prior to death (evident because the mandible shows signs of healing in these places), and numerous caries and abscesses are present. Particularly painful caries destroyed the lower right second molar, with the bare root exposed and abscessed.

After villagers interred Individual 3, they deposited the majority of offerings in Feature 7. A series of vessels (Objects 2, 4, 5, 6, and 9) covered Individual 3. While Objects 2 and 4, two bowls, had been placed rim side up, as if ready to use and perhaps holding food offerings, an additional conical bowl—Object 3, positioned rim side down—covered parts of the legs. Placed further above Burial 3, Object 10 may have been deposited later, from Feature 4. Most of the adobe blocks were also deposited at this time. The fact that several of the adobe blocks lay close to the base of Feature 7 suggests at least some were deposited soon after the final burial. These adobe blocks may have been from the house wall associated with Floor 7. Perhaps their placement within Feature 7 represents a dismantling and abandonment of the Floor 7 house at the time of the interment of Burial 1 (see following text).

Sometime after the deposition of the whole vessels, Feature 7 began to be filled with secondary refuse. While several partially intact vessels were found—and could have been later symbolic offerings through Feature 4—generally Feature 7 became a trash receptacle. The entrance of Feature 7 was eventually sealed with several large stones cemented by a loose plaster mix. Later villagers from Occupation 3 placed Feature 4 (Figure 7.9), a cylindrical chamber, directly atop the entrance to Feature 7. The course of basal stones in Feature 4—substantially larger than the other small, tightly packed stones that make up this feature—perfectly match Feature 7's entrance. Feature 7 may have remained at least partially opened after the construction of Feature 4; the plasterlike material that sealed Feature 7 did not extend under all of Feature 4's basal stones. It may have been initially possible for additional materials (such as Object 10) to be deposited in Feature 7 from Feature 4. As I argue later, this cylindrical shaft represented continued access, at least symbolically, to Feature 7. I argue that ancient Etlatongoans deposited all of the interments and probably intact vessels prior to the construction of Feature 4 (with the possible exception of Object 10). The dimensions of both the vessels and burials preclude their deposition from Feature 4, even if access to Feature 7 remained uncovered.

Additional individuals in bell-shaped pit burials excavated in 1980 reposed in the vicinity of Feature 7 (Zárate Morán 1987:23–28). One of these pits, excavated just 4 meters to the west of EA-1, also contained three individuals. Like Feature 7, this pit had also been excavated into bedrock. A carbon sample produced an uncalibrated date similar to the one recovered from Feature 7 (Zárate Morán 1987:108). The three individuals excavated in 1980 may have been descendants of the household represented by Feature 7, with the house in a slightly different location (see following text).

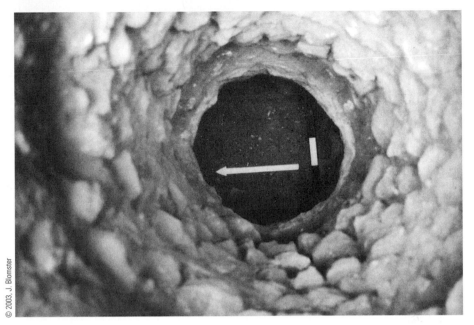

Figure 7.9 Feature 4, the cylindrical chamber constructed atop Feature 7, the bell-shaped pit associated with Occupation 1 in EA-1. Arrow, at the entrance of Feature 7, points to magnetic north; scale measures 30 cm.

Burial 4/Feature 10

Burial 4 consists of one individual (and three teeth from another) interred in an irregular shallow pit—Feature 10—in the northwest section of EA-1 (Figure 7.10). The entrance to Feature 10 from Floor 7 contrasts dramatically with that surface because it was never resurfaced. Roughly circular, Feature 10 becomes more expansive horizontally, with increased vertical depth below Floor 7. A stone wall that runs roughly northwest to southeast at an orientation of N15°W divides Feature 10 into two compartments. The wall, constructed of fist-sized and larger unshaped stones, stands at a maximum of three courses high.

The western, and smaller, section of Feature 10 contained Burial 4. This section received substantial subsurface amplification; the area directly north of the skull was expanded to accommodate Burial 4. This suggests that Feature 10 was already in use prior to the interment of this individual, at which time the western segment with the human remains was closed. The stone wall may have been erected to divide Burial 4 from the eastern portion of Feature 10, which may have continued in use.

The individual in Burial 4 reclined in an extended position on its dorsal side from northwest to southeast, with the skull at the north. The orientation maintained that of the stone dividing wall; the similarity of orientations further supports the association of the wall and Burial 4. While the body lay extended, the arms were flexed so that the hands rested below the skull, with palms facing up. The poorly preserved bones from Burial 4 limit possible osteological observations. It appears, however, that all

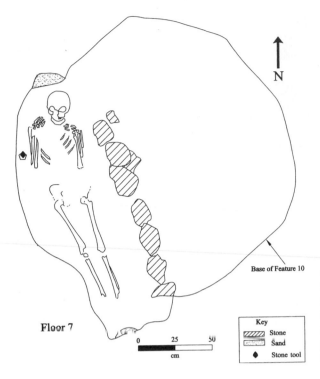

Base of Feature 10

Floor 7

0   25   50

cm

Key

Stone

Sand

Stone tool

Figure 7.10 Plan view of Burial 4 within Feature 10, with wall separating the burial from the eastern half of this pit feature. Arrow points to magnetic north. © 2003, J. Blomster.

bones are present and in proper anatomical orientation. Burial 4 is a primary burial, probably of a female. No vessels were found associated with Burial 4, although a largely intact stone tool, probably a scraper, lay to the west of the right arm.

The original function of Feature 10, before half of it was used to contain a burial, remains unclear. If plastered, this shallow basin may have been similar to what has been referred to as a "casting pit" from Formative Valley of Oaxaca (Marcus 1998), employed in household ritual for divination through casting of materials, such as corn kernels, into shallow water-filled basins. Because the sides of Feature 10 were not plastered, it would probably have been too porous to contain liquid. No evidence of burning, indicative of a hearth, was recovered from Feature 10.

OCCUPATION 2: FLOOR 6 AND FEATURES 5 AND 6

Prior to Occupation 3 and after Occupation 1, most of the area exposed by EA-1 formed a large midden. The southwestern portion of EA-1, however, exposed part of an additional occupation—the second EA-1 occupation.

Of several exposed wall fragments associated with Occupation 2, the most recent is Feature 5, a wall of which one course—comprised of four large stones (and numerous smaller stones)—remains (Figure 7.3). Feature 5 may have served as a retaining wall or foundation of some sort; some of the stones may have been reused in the later Structure 2-2. The wall and associated deposits probably represent structural collapse and debris associated with the abandonment of this occupation. An additional (and earlier) wall fragment, Feature 6, was exposed and associated with Occupation 2.

The EA-1 excavations exposed one surface, Floor 6, from Occupation 2. A homogenous pinkish-gray sandy-loam, Floor 6 extends slightly beyond Feature 6 and probably represents the southeast corner of a Yucuita phase house, with Feature 6 the foundation of the south wall. Due to the close proximity of Occupation 1 to the east, this occupation may represent the same household group shifting location through time. A burial excavated in 1980 probably contained members of this household, and an additional member of this household—represented by part of a human long bone—lay in a disturbed area that bounds Floor 6 to the north. An intact phytomorphic bottle came from this portion of EA-1 in Stratum 18 and may be associated with the human remains lying largely outside of EA-1.

Midden and Fill: Strata 18 and 19

Found throughout EA-1, except for the Floor 6/Occupation 2 vicinity, Stratum 18 forms a thick deposit, averaging 0.40 to 0.50 meter, with abundant inclusions (Figures 7.2 and 7.3). I interpret this stratum as a household midden, probably deposited by the household represented by Floor 6. After the abandonment of the Floor 7 occupation and the deposition of Stratum 19 (see the following text), members of the household may have moved directly to the west of the abandoned house and used the space of the abandoned house to deposit trash. The 1992 excavations documented this pattern of employing abandoned houses as refuse loci throughout Etlatongo. Although this household largely lay outside of EA-1, the 1992 excavations captured a small portion of it (Strata 14 through 17).

Stratum 19, an additional thick deposit, lay under Stratum 18, but had a different composition. Large, generally unmodified stones dominated this stratum and gave the impression that Stratum 19 represents a deposit of intentional fill and wall collapse. The discovery of Burials 1 and 2, associated with Floor 7, supports this interpretation. These burials lay on Floor 7, deposited while Floor 7 was still exposed and then overlaid by Stratum 19, deposited largely as intentional fill over burials and the wall collapse associated with the abandonment of Occupation 1.

OCCUPATION 3: STRUCTURE 2-2, FLOORS 1 THROUGH 5, AND FEATURES 3 AND 4

Part of a structure and a series of exterior and interior floors represent the third occupation in EA-1.

Structure 2-2

A well-preserved wall running roughly north to south in the central southern portion of EA-1 and a less well-preserved east-to-west wall comprise Structure 2-2 (Figure 7.11). These walls unite to form a well-defined corner—the northwest corner of a structure, probably a house. The construction of Structure 2-2 occurred later in the Yucuita phase, based on ceramics recovered from floors associated with these walls. Villagers constructed Structure 2-2 over the thick midden deposit and fill discussed previously.

Construction techniques differ among the exterior and interior walls. The west wall runs north to south; four to five courses of it still stand. Two rows of large,

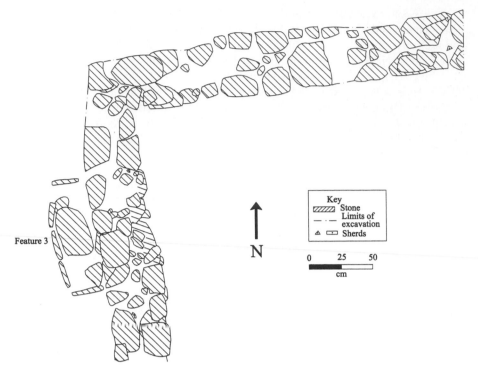

Feature 3

N

Key
Stone
Limits of
excavation
Sherds

0   25   50

cm

*Figure 7.11 Plan view of Structure 2-2 and the adjacent Feature 3. Arrow points to
magnetic north. © 2003, J. Blomster.*

minimally shaped limestone blocks (averaging about 25 centimeters in length) laid
roughly side by side form the west wall, with the interior space between the blocks
filled by smaller stones. We found no evidence of mortar. Villagers expended some
effort on the stones that make up the exterior side of the structure, shaping them to
form a roughly rectangular shape. They placed these stones to form well-defined
vertical courses and created a relatively even, but by no means smooth, facade.
There appears to have been less concern for the interior side of the wall; these
stones appear unshaped and placed in irregular courses. While the exterior side may
have been plastered, as were contemporaneous house walls at Yucuita (see Robles
García 1988), no stucco remains. The exposed portion of the poorly preserved north
wall, running west to east, appears to be constructed similar to the west wall.

An additional feature protrudes from the exterior of the west wall of Structure 2-
2—Feature 3 (Figure 7.11). This feature extends approximately 0.95 meter long,
defined by several slender stones that bound it and form a rectangle surrounding a
large, rounded stone. The feature stands one course of stones high. Initially, I thought
Feature 3 represents a doorway or threshold—these are known from the Valley of
Oaxaca to be about 1 meter long and one course of stones high (Flannery and Marcus
1994:25). Unfortunately, no doorway appears on the wall adjacent to this feature.
Several large figurine fragments were found within this feature, including a woman
with one hand touching her groin, and a large (approximately 10-centimeter) head;

perhaps this represents a locus of figurine activity or disposal. Alternatively, Feature 3 may have been a bench, or associated with an outside activity area.

Interior of Structure 2-2: Floors 1 through 3 and Feature 4

The excavations revealed a series of floors (and strata resulting from their occupation) within Structure 2-2. The strata separating these floors—either deposited during the use of a floor or sometimes added/modified in preparation for resurfacing a floor—exist only within Structure 2-2. Floor 1, a compact slightly undulating silt-clay surface with large nodules of orange clay, formed the third (and final) of three surfaces used as house floors within Structure 2-2. Generally separated from the earlier Floor 2 by 5 to 10 centimeters of soil, Floor 1 represents a resurfacing of Floor 2 and ultimately of Floor 3, following the extent of those earlier surfaces.

Two distinctly colored materials—an orange clay-loam (Stratum 8) and a pinkish-gray clay-loam (Stratum 9)—comprise Floor 2. Juxtaposed against each other, these two materials form a relatively level and smooth surface. The contrast between the two strata is well-defined; the strata form discrete zones within Structure 2-2. While the contrast may merely be the result of different construction materials being randomly selected, I consider the possibility that the ancient builders of Structure 2-2 intentionally created this opposition. There is almost no mixing of the two materials—the builders segregated them. Further exposure of this surface would demonstrate if this pattern continues across all of this interior surface.

Floor 3, the first surface laid down with the occupation of Structure 2-2, contacts the bottommost course of stones of Structure 2-2, indicating that the wall was probably constructed immediately prior to the laying of Floor 3. Nearly identical in color to the pinkish portion of Floor 2, this floor forms the thinnest and most consistent of the surfaces associated with Structure 2-2.

Floor 3 is associated with the previously discussed Feature 4. Floor 3–type clays and several stones block the entrance to Feature 4 from Floor 3. Access to this feature probably ended prior to the abandonment of Floor 3 and its subsequent resurfacing. Feature 4 forms a roughly cylindrical chamber, although wider at its top (42 centimeters) than its base (Figure 7.9). Feature 4 extends 76 centimeters from Floor 3 down to Floor 7, for an approximate volume of 0.10 cubic meters. Seven to eight courses of very similarly sized stones are tightly packed in ever wider concentric bands from bottom to top, with only the bottom course composed of much larger stones. The stones form a very solid wall due to the limited use of a strong mortar, traces of which remain. Probably used prior to and during the occupation of Floor 3 as a symbolic connection to Burial 3, this feature also may have served as a storage pit, although its shape is anomalous within the Etlatongo sample.

Positioned directly over the opening of Feature 7, Feature 4's base matches this opening, with the basal stones extending 2 to 5 centimeters over Feature 7's entrance. The preciseness of the junction between Features 4 and 7 precludes the possibility that villagers constructed Feature 4 without prior knowledge of the location of Feature 7. Furthermore, the stratigraphy demonstrates that Feature 4 was built prior to Floor 3, probably during Occupation 2 after they abandoned Floor 7 but before Floor 7 was covered with fill and midden. Feature 4 was incorporated into the construction of Floor 3 and continued to be used during the first portion of Occupation

3. The location of Feature 4 may have helped guide the location of Structure 2–2. There may have been an interest in maintaining access to Feature 7 and the ancestors it contained even after the abandonment of Floor 7. As was discovered during the excavation of Feature 4, field assistants from the town of Etlatongo could thrust their upper bodies into the top of this feature with ease (more corpulent gringos found this to be a difficult endeavor). If Feature 7's entrance was not completely sealed, access to this bell-shaped pit would have been difficult but feasible. Even with Feature 7's closure, Feature 4 would have still provided symbolic access to those individuals and could have served as a place for rituals and offerings.

Exterior of Structure 2-2: Floors 4 and 5

With Floor 3 representing the earliest occupation within Structure 2-2, two additional floors lay exterior to it. Floor 4, the most recent of these surfaces, is similar in color to Floor 1, but less compact than that interior surface. Villagers probably installed Floor 4 as a formal patio or outside activity area. Outside patio or activity areas have been documented at roughly contemporaneous houses in the Nochixtlán Valley at Yucuita (Robles García 1988). Floor 4 represents a resurfacing of the earlier Floor 5 roughly contemporaneous with Floor 1 (inside of Structure 2-2). Floor 5 appears virtually identical to Floor 3 within Structure 2-2. The floors on the interior of Structure 2-2 have substantial (5 centimeters plus) amounts of deposits separating them, unlike the exterior surfaces. Perhaps both human and natural agents kept the exposed exterior surfaces clear of accumulating debris close to this house. Ultimately, the occupants abandoned this household and shifted occupation beyond the area exposed by EA-1.

LIFE, DEATH, AND THE GROWTH OF VILLAGES

The data gathered from the EA-1 excavations provide a glimpse of Yucuita phase life, and death, at Etlatongo. EA-1 documents at least four occupations, the three earliest of which probably belonged to the same household or lineage, or descendants of the members of the original family, showing the great continuity in the use of this locale.

The construction of Floor 7 initiated the Yucuita phase occupation of EA-1. The occupation associated with this surface may have been a temporally limited one, with no evidence of resurfacing Floor 7. During and immediately after its use as a living surface, four burials were interred on or under Floor 7. Burial 4 may have been interred first. After Burial 4 was interred in the western half of a shallow, circular pit, the burial was covered and separated from the eastern portion of the pit by a stone wall, indicating that the eastern part of the pit—and therefore Floor 7—continued in use after Burial 4.

Placed in a subterranean bell-shaped pit, one of three individuals in Burial 3 was almost certainly placed in this pit some time prior to the other two. The exact timing of this, and how it relates to the other burials, is difficult to determine. After all the individuals had been interred and offerings placed among the bodies, adobe blocks and other fill were deposited, probably in an effort to cover the burials. These adobe blocks, mostly broken, may have come from the walls of the structure associated with Floor 7, and may relate to the abandonment of this occupation.

In understanding the placement of the burials and the abandonment of Occupation 1, the relationship between Burials 1 and 2 is particularly instructive. The individual in Burial 2 probably died first, but was probably the last of the six individuals associated with Occupation 1 interred on Floor 7. I interpret Burial 2 as representing a secondary burial, originally buried elsewhere. The death of Burial 1, interpreted here as the last of these six individuals to die, probably prompted the reinterment of Burial 2. Burials 1 and 2 may have been a married pair, the heads of this household. The death of the remaining member of this pair also may have prompted the abandonment of Floor 7. The abandonment of a structure due to the death of a prominent household member has been ethnographically documented across the world from as far away as the Luo of western Kenya (Dietler 1993, personal communication). The placement of Burial 1 directly on Floor 7, in a slab-lined chamber sealed with large lintels, effectively precluded further use of Floor 7 as a living surface. Although the remains are too poorly preserved to determine biological sex, Burial 1 may have been the head of the household. Burial 2, possibly the spouse of Burial 1, was reinterred and placed next to and parallel with Burial 1, with the majority of the skeleton missing above the legs. As part of the abandonment of this structure, occupants probably threw adobe blocks from the structure's wall (no intact walls associated with Occupation 1 remain) into the bell-shaped pit that housed Burial 3. After depositing a layer of fill (Stratum 19) and probably constructing Feature 4 over the abandoned surface, occupation shifted to the west. Floor 6 may represent this second occupation.

Despite the slight shift to the west of the household, the ancestors continued to be venerated and play an important role in daily life. Descendants maintained access, at least symbolically, to the individuals in Burial 3 through a cylindrical chamber (Feature 4) built with tightly packed stones, constructed directly over the entrance to the bell-shaped pit. Villagers constructed this chamber prior to covering Floor 7 with fill. The precise fit of Feature 4's base with the entrance to Feature 7 supports an interpretation that Feature 7's entrance (probably at least partially sealed) remained visible during this construction. While maintaining access to Feature 4, the Occupation 2 residents utilized the surrounding area (Stratum 18) for a household midden.

Occupation 3 returned to the approximate location of Occupation 1, marked by construction of Structure 2-2 and Floor 3 over the southeastern portion of Floor 7. Over 75 centimeters of fill and midden separate this new occupation, probably by the same household group or family, from Floor 7. In fact, Feature 4 may have played an important role in the exact location of Structure 2-2; occupants incorporated the opening of this cylindrical chamber into Floor 3, thus maintaining access and a symbolic connection to Burial 3. The occupants of Floor 3 may have been only several generations removed from their ancestors in Burial 3. They finally sealed access to this feature prior to the resurfacing of Floor 3. Given the amount of fill that separates Floor 2 from the earlier Floor 3, additional construction would have been necessary in order to raise Feature 4 to the level of Floor 2.

Two major resurfacings (Floors 1 and 2) were undertaken within Structure 2-2; in both cases, fill separates these new surfaces. Upon the abandonment of Floor 1 (the final floor associated with Structure 2-2), this structure and the area surrounding it served as a midden for a nearby household, possibly the descendants of the same family that built Structure 2-2. The possibility exists that this occupation occurred to the north of Structure 2-2. The 1980 excavations found a fragment of a stone wall that may have been a house wall (Zárate Morán 1987:18–19), and the 1992 excavations encountered several centimeters of a thick, compact, red clay surface in the north profile of EA-1, above the level of Floor 1. Due to the construction of the road to Nochixtlán, this possibility cannot be further explored, as all material north of EA-1 has been removed.

I argue that the earliest three occupations in EA-1 represent the same household unit and their descendants. I conclude this partially from the effort that was invested in maintaining access to some of the burials associated with the earliest occupation—the three individuals in Burial 3. Additionally, what the 1992 excavations exposed of these households suggests that these occupations lay situated very close together. It has been suggested that in Formative period Oaxaca, there was a distance of 20 to 40 meters between households (see Chapter 5). As with the EA-2 occupations, the EA-1 occupations literally lie atop each other, which I interpret as representing the shift in location of the same household through time. Staggered over time, the EA-1 occupations illustrate shifts in household location and how parts of the village grew through time. Within the general vicinity occupied by this household, the actual location of the house itself shifted slightly. Abandoned structures, covered by fill or middens by the new household, ultimately provided a base upon which a subsequent house could be constructed.

Comparisons of Etlatongo Burials

While the four burials excavated in EA-1 illustrate a wide spectrum of Yucuita phase interments, showing a range of burial types, the sample remains too small to look for patterns of status differentiation within the burial assemblage. Even augmenting the four burials from the 1992 excavations with five Yucuita phase burials excavated in 1980 forms too limited a sample to assess status and rank. It does appear as if burials in bell-shaped pits housed multiple individuals; those excavated in 1980 were generally flexed or in less formal positions—probably part of the reality of dealing with such a circumscribed space.

In addition to the three extended burials excavated in 1992, all roughly north to south, one of the extended burials recovered in 1980 also lay north to south, but face down, with the skull to the south—in contrast to the other extended burials. In terms of labor invested, Burial 1 evinces the most effort from this sample, placed in a chamber prepared by stone slabs and covered with large lintels, at least one of which was shaped. This supports the interpretation of Burial 1 as the head of the Occupation 1 household.

DEFINING THE YUCUITA PHASE
AND LATE FORMATIVE CERAMIC PRODUCTION

One advantage of excavating a number of roughly contemporaneous burials is the number of intact vessels they provide, documenting vessel form, slip, and decoration (Figures 7.5 and 7.7). This sample, combined with additional primary and secondary deposits from contemporaneous storage pits (Feature 7 and another in Area 2), fill (Stratum 19 in EA-1), and a midden (Stratum 18), evince a series of similar traits, contrasting with ceramics from earlier and later contexts. Many of the designs stylistically correlate with those from the early portion of the Monte Albán I phase for the Valley of Oaxaca (Caso, Bernal, and Acosta 1967) and represent a more chronologically restricted ceramic phase than had previously been recognized for this region. Refining ceramic sequences is crucial; since ceramic phases represent periods of chronological time, more discrete phases allow more precise, and valid, placement of occupations based on ceramic styles.

The distinct nature of these Late Formative materials was initially identified at Yucuita, a Nochixtlán Valley site about 10 kilometers north of Etlatongo (see Chapter 2). Archaeologists recovered abundant samples in both primary and secondary contexts from a residential section, Areas C, D, and E (Winter and Cruz Hernández 2000). The similarity of these well-provenienced samples from Yucuita and Etlatongo allows for collaboration—combining samples from both sites in order to define a phase that will truly serve the region as a whole. Defining ceramic phases based on more than one site in a region has been crucial since the first ceramic chronology was proposed for the Nochixtlán Valley (Spores 1972). Because this new phase was first recognized at the site of Yucuita, it has been named accordingly. Ultimately, the Yucuita phase may parallel ceramic phases outside the Nochixtlán Valley; similar materials have been recovered from Yucunama (Matadamas 2002) and at Tequixtepec in the Mixteca Baja (Rivera Guzmán 2002). Below I present a brief overview of the Yucuita phase. Based on carbon samples from both sites (see previous text for the Etlatongo sample) and stylistic parallels with the Valley of Oaxaca, the phase is estimated to run from 500 to 300 B.C.

Based on the pioneering ceramic analyses of Alfonso Caso, Ignacio Bernal, and Jorge R. Acosta (1967), whose large blue volume on the subject is often referred to as "the Blue Bible," ceramics contemporaneous with those from Monte Albán are generally divided by paste. This distinction refers to color when fired, texture, and inclusions—essentially macroscopic properties. By defining a certain number of paste types, it is not assumed that these pastes all share the same "recipe" or that they are chemically or petrographically similar. Some of the inclusions—nonplastic materials within the paste—may have been in the clay itself, while potters added others intentionally as temper. Research at the modern pottery village of Atzompa, in the Valley of Oaxaca, has shown potters' high degree of discrimination in extracting and combining clays and tempers based on what they will produce (Thieme 2001).

Three pastes are frequent during the Yucuita phase: brown, with a coarse clay body and a variety of inclusions (ranging from quartz/quartzite and mica to limestone, calcite, and other materials); fine brown, with a more consistent, compact, fine clay body, ranging in color from medium to dark brown, and with fewer inclusions (usually tiny quartz, mica, as well as flint and feldspathic fragments); and gray, an extremely consistent clay body with small inclusions, generally quartz, with or without tiny mica fragments, and occasionally other nonplastic inclusions. At least one additional paste has been recognized from Etlatongo: cream. This paste appears identical to Valley of Oaxaca ceramics, and recent analysis (using INAA) of several Etlatongo sherds demonstrates a match with those Valley of Oaxaca clay sources (Thieme 2002, personal communication). A large bottle recovered in Burial 2 (Object 12, Table 7.2) is an example of a creamware vessel with a bright red slip (referred to as a C.4 in the Valley of Oaxaca, with "C" standing for cream paste, and "4" referring to vessel finish). The infrequent cream-paste vessels signals importation from the Valley of Oaxaca.

Brownwares

Both continuity and change characterize the Yucuita phase compared with the final Cruz ceramic phase. This is especially evident in the persistence of forms but with new variations and a somewhat different brownware paste recipe. Brownware bowls often have thicker walls than in the Cruz phase, and while slip and decoration are less elaborate (see text that follows), potters produced these Yucuita phase brownwares more consistently than the coarse brownwares of the preceding phases. The paste is generally not as packed with inclusions; the clay recipe appears more consistent. Vessel firing appears less wildly variable and often more complete than previously, while fireclouding on the surface of Yucuita vessels is uncommon compared to the Cruz phase. These changes are indicative of more standardized, or at least more routinized, practices in some elements of ceramic production. This may signal increased part-time specialization at the household level. While I do not interpret pottery production at Yucuita phase Etlatongo as a full-time specialization, fewer people may have been engaging in it more regularly than in the Cruz phase. Many scholars caution that increasing standardization does not automatically signal specialization or intensification in the organization of production. Specialization itself exists on many levels, including that of household production, and does not always correlate with increased production and sociopolitical complexity (Stark 1995).

The potters also expended less effort in burnishing. Generally, burnishing is employed to apply the final finish to a vessel. In modern pottery communities in the Valley of Oaxaca, a smooth stone may be used to create the surface finish; the amount of burnishing results in how lustrous a vessel appears. Surfaces are less lustrous than in the Cruz phase, and individual burnishing marks are much more frequent. Also, it is more common for exterior walls of serving vessels, such as bowls, to be either unfinished or simply smoothed or wiped. Probably associated with changes in the organization of production is the more uniform shape of Yucuita phase bowls.

The vast majority of brownware bowls are conical in shape, generally with sharper angles (usually greater than 40 degrees) than in the Cruz phase; shapes such as plates (a short-walled, steeply angled conical bowl) become more frequent. Previously frequent bowl shapes, cylindrical and hemispherical bowls, are rarely employed compared to Middle and Late Cruz phases. While ollas remain common, other restricted orifice vessel shapes—such as tecomates, a type of neckless olla—appear less frequently. Although a few forms dominate the majority of the assemblage, there is still a variety of less frequently occurring vessel forms, as shown in the diverse Burial 2 assemblage (Figure 7.7). In addition to many miniature vessels, distinct forms such as phytomorphic vessels (in this case, shaped something like a squash) continued to be used (Figure 7.12). Potters introduced new forms, such as the *comal*—a platelike vessel for grilling tortillas (Winter and Cruz Hernández 2000). Previously infrequently used forms, such as bottles, kidney-shaped bowls, and trays, become more common in several paste types. Large water jugs, called *cantaros*—as well as appendages such as handles, lugs, and vessel supports—also appear more frequently in the Yucuita phase, compared with previous phases.

Yucuita phase potters employed a smaller palette of slips. Red slips become more common, and sometimes a red slip or wash is applied in bands to create a complex design, such as the possible vegetal motifs painted on the small olla (Object 2) from Burial 2 (Figure 7.13). In addition to red slips, tans, oranges, and browns appear on

Figure 7.12 Yucuita phase vessel shaped like a squash from Burial 2 (Object 8 in Table 7.2). Height = 12 cm.

brownware vessels. Distinct red and black slips, often with a "graphite" quality, first appear in the Yucuita phase and continue into the subsequent Early Ramos phase. Many distinct slips of the Middle Cruz and Late Cruz phases, including, for example, many different white and gray slips, disappear. Gray slips unique to the Yucuita phase appear primarily on graywares.

Slip often covers less surface on conical bowls during the Yucuita phase. While previously potters slipped both the interior and exterior, Yucuita phase brownware bowls are often slipped (if at all) only on the interior—a practical, labor-saving production step. Furthermore, a band of red slip along the rim (and sometimes also along the base) provides the sole decoration on many conical bowls; vertical bands of slip occasionally connect these bands. In such cases, the underlying paste color shows through. Another technique employed more frequently in the Yucuita phase is juxtaposing bands of red and brown slips.

Brownware vessels are rarely decorated with incisions or other subtractive techniques. When they are, the designs are usually less intricate, not as well-executed and not confined to the area around the rim as those on fine brownwares. There is one new technique of decoration introduced during the Yucuita phase, especially on the interior of brownware vessels that have either a red slip or no slip—a kind of decorative burnishing (Figure 7.14). During the Yucuita phase, the individual burnishing streaks are arranged to form designs, generally large "X" designs.

A probably unintentional design occurs on the bases of several brownware sherds as well as two bowls included in Burial 3. The bases of Objects 3 and 6, both conical bowls, bear the impression of a reed mat, or *petate;* potters placed these vessels on a mat at some stage in the production process. The nearly identical petate impressions

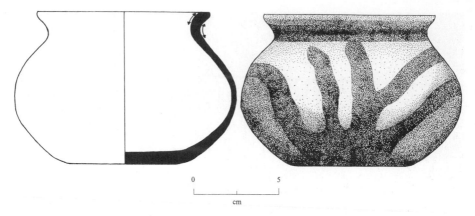

0   5

cm

Figure 7.13 Two views of the same small Yucuita phase olla from Burial 2 with a design painted in red on the exterior (Object 2 in Table 7.2). On the left is the shape and profile of the vessel, while the right shows its decoration and contours. The arrows in the rim area on the left show the location and extent of red bands painted on the exterior and interior. © 2003, J. Blomster.

on these Burial 3 vessels may indicate they were constructed at the same time. Other vessels have human palm impressions on both the interior and exterior. Both petate and palm impressions are known from the Valley of Oaxaca, where they have been defined on the *interior* of graywares (respectively referred to as G.32 and G.33) as decoration used during Monte Albán I (Caso, Bernal, and Acosta 1967:41).

Fine Brownwares

Fine brownwares become more frequent than in the final Cruz ceramic phase, showing a greater range in decoration. Fine browns often have a black or red slip, and the slip always covers all of the vessel's interior, sometimes continuing onto the exterior. Conical bowls, generally with rims everted away from the angle of the vessel's body, are the most frequent shape. The lips are often decorated with incised lines, sometimes forming double-line breaks with or without circular elements at the break. Designs appear limited to the rim/lip area on conical bowls as well as on vessels with restricted orifices. Bottles increase greatly in frequency, and fine brownware bottles appear in a variety of slips and lip shapes.

Fine brownware vessels nearly identical to those from Etlatongo and Yucuita have been documented in the Valley of Oaxaca (type K.6). In fact, the dissimilarity of these ceramics to local Valley of Oaxaca wares has long been considered evidence that they were imported from the Mixteca Alta (Caso, Bernal, and Acosta 1967:52, 54). Recent INAA of samples from Monte Albán and Mixteca Alta sites such as Etlatongo support this interpretation, demonstrating their compositional similarity (Winter and Cruz Hernández 2000). While the ultimate source for these ceramics within the Nochixtlán Valley has not been determined (Thieme 2002, personal communication), Mixtec villages both imported and exported ceramics to the Valley of Oaxaca—the movement of ceramics was not one-way.

Figure 7.14 Burnishing in the shape of an "X" diagnostic of the Yucuita phase at Etlatongo, on the interior of a conical bowl, EA-1.

Graywares

Graywares come in a variety of forms, including some unusual shapes closely associated with the Valley of Oaxaca, such as Object 4 from Burial 1 (see Figure 7.5). This small and squat form, which has been referred to as a "bule" (Caso, Bernal, and Acosta 1967:185, 189), has incised decorations stylistically associated with the Monte Albán I phase.

Decorations applied to the vessel also change from the previous phase. The Late Cruz technique of differential burnishing, used to juxtapose lustrous and matte designs, appears less frequently; instead, differential burnishing, sometimes combined with differential firing, is used to create patterns of darker versus lighter bands. The common incised Late Cruz decoration—the banner—disappears, replaced by a variety of designs appearing primarily on a few vessel shapes. While designs appear on conical grayware bowls, such as the zigzags or double "S" motifs on Object 1 from Burial 3, and an incised cross appears at the base of a plate (Object 10) from Burial 2 (Figure 7.15), two grayware forms are invariably decorated: vases and cylindrical bowls with everted lips. As noted earlier, cylindrical bowls are much less common during the Yucuita phase; when they appear, they are usually decorated graywares. Vases are vessels with a generally wide orifice, but the wall does not remain straight; the vessel widens above the base. If not for the basal widening, vases would be cylindrical bowls with everted rims.

Some of the most elaborate Yucuita phase designs appear on these vessel shapes. One vase, found in over 70 pieces scattered in an EA-1 midden context,

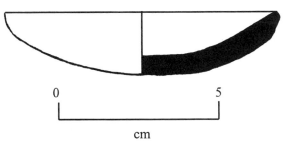

0   5

cm

Figure 7.15 Incised cross motif, with circle in the center, at the base of a small grayware dish from Burial 2 (Object 10 in Table 7.2). Two irregular lines frame the motif below the interior rim. © 2003, J. Blomster.

bears a complicated series of designs, including zoned cross-hatching in bands along the top and bottom of the vessel, with two wavy lines in the space between (Figure 7.16). The interior of the vessel, shortly below the lip, is largely unslipped and unburnished. This design is similar to those on early Monte Albán I graywares; INAA would resolve if this particular vessel has a Valley of Oaxaca origin.

While some graywares are imports, others may be local products. Grayware probably began to be manufactured in the Mixteca Alta as early as the Middle Cruz phase (see Chapter 6). Some Yucuita phase designs on Etlatongo graywares do not have correlates in published examples from the Valley of Oaxaca. One everted rim cylindrical bowl has a complex "sunburst" design, very shallowly incised, with additional bands of designs (Figure 7.17).

Some elements introduced during the Yucuita phase continue into the subsequent Early Ramos phase, while others (such as distinct incised designs and Valley of Oaxaca creamware vessels) vanish. New design motifs, stylistically associated with the late Monte Albán I phase, appear. Perhaps the most frequent example of this is what has been labeled at Monte Albán a G.12 (Caso, Bernal, and Acosta 1967:25), a conical grayware bowl with comblike incisions on the interior base. In Mixteca Alta

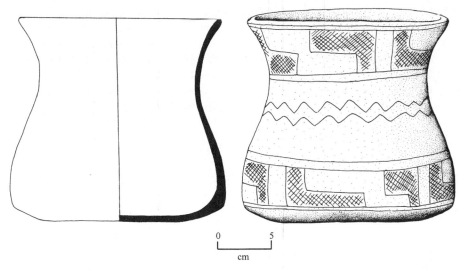

Figure 7.16 Found in many pieces in several adjacent EU-1 units, two views of a reconstucted Yucuita phase grayware vessel with an elaborate incised decoration. Visual inspection suggests it may be a Monte Albán import. © 2003, J. Blomster.

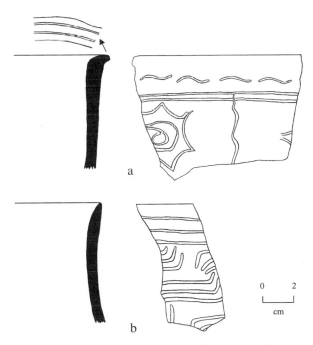

Figure 7.17 Two decorated Yucuita phase grayware sherds from EA-1, Feature 7: (a) this vessel probably had a series of unusual spirals or sunburst designs on it, separated by wavy vertical lines. The arrow points to two incised lines on the sherd's rim. (b) represents a vessel with a shape similar to that in Figure 7.16. The incisions on both "a" and "b" are extremely shallow. © 2003, J. Blomster.

variants, Margaret Houston discovered years ago that corncobs could be used to produce the pattern impressed on some of these bowls (analogous to G.12s). True G.12 vessels are absent in the Yucuita phase, but are well documented at later sites in the Mixteca Alta such as Monte Negro (Caso, Bernal, and Acosta 1967:29). A full analysis of the Early Ramos phase, as well as the Late Ramos phase (approximately equivalent to Monte Albán II in the Valley of Oaxaca), will be enriched by analyses of primary contexts from more than one Nochixtlán Valley site.

SUMMARY

The accidental discovery of a Late Formative burial resulted in the excavation of a larger robotage unit in the northern section of Area 2. Due to this excavation, it has been possible to reconstruct the movements of a series of houses probably occupied by generations of the same family line through time, as houses were occupied, abandoned, and then the location of a previous house built upon. This "corkscrew" pattern extends in time at least as far as the Middle Cruz occupation of Etlatongo (see Chapter 5). A cylindrical stone chamber served to physically and symbolically connect later occupants with those who first inhabited this portion of Etlatongo. By using both whole vessels from these burials, as well as fragments from related contexts at Etlatongo and contemporaneous ones at the site of Yucuita, it has been possible to outline a new ceramic phase—the Yucuita phase. By further subdividing the long Ramos phase (see Table 1.1), this research contributes to aiding other projects, especially surveys, in more accurately estimating chronological occupations of sites.

8/Conclusions
Complexity and Interregional Interaction at Etlatongo

The social landscape in which Middle Cruz Etlatongo lay situated included emerging social complexity and interregional interaction. Chapters 3 through 6 sample relevant Middle Cruz data generated by the 1992 Etlatongo excavations. Based on this limited data set, here I summarize and present interpretations about the formation of social complexity and the impact of interregional interaction on Early Formative social organization. I also place these data and observations on two larger scales. The first involves a comparison with contemporaneous Valley of Oaxaca villages. As detailed in Chapter 2, the Mixteca Alta has often been characterized as "peripheral" in terms of social developments and interregional interaction to the Valley of Oaxaca. For the second context, I extend the geographic range even farther, comparing both the Mixteca Alta and the Valley of Oaxaca with the Gulf Coast Olmec, returning to the questions of scale of social organization and interaction between these regions introduced in Chapter 1. Finally, I examine the prospects for future research at Etlatongo.

COMPLEXITY, INEQUALITY, AND PRESTIGE GOODS AT ETLATONGO

In Chapter 1, I defined social inequality and stratification as differential access to goods, services, and knowledge within society. One faction within society controlling access to basic raw materials, necessary for daily life, marks increasing stratification. Through this social transformation, basic sociopolitical institutions emerge. What evidence is there for social inequality and complexity at Middle Cruz Etlatongo?

Higher Status

In Chapters 4 and 5, I identified higher status based on both house construction and access to goods, particularly exotic prestige goods. As with the higher-status residences observed in earlier and contemporaneous villages in the Soconusco area to the south (Lesure and Blake 2002), villagers constructed higher-status structures at Etlatongo on platforms. These platforms elevated the structure lying atop up to half a meter above surrounding structures and land. In contemporaneous Valley of Oaxaca villages, platforms have been associated solely with public structures (Flannery and Marcus 1994).

Occupation 1, in EA-2, represents the earliest residential space (Structure 2-5) exposed at Etlatongo. The platform associated with Occupation 1, comprised of bedrock chunks, earth, and stone, appears to be on a different—and smaller—scale than that documented for Unit 1. This first EA-2 platform elevates Structure 2-5 between 30 and 50 centimeters above surrounding bedrock. Stones probably formed the base of Structure 2-5, although few of these remain *in situ*. I interpret Occupation 1 as a higher-status residence (as opposed to public space) due to the clear evidence of domestic activities visible on Structure 2-5 supported by the platform; ultimately differences in the functions of superstructures remain difficult to distinguish without a much larger database.

I interpret both Occupations 1 and 2 in EA-2 as higher status not only due to construction techniques but also because of the diversified assortment of artifacts and exotic materials encountered with these occupations. These villagers constituted a different social status or role than other contemporaneous villagers by their consumption and display of prestige goods. The occupants of these earliest contexts from EA-2 controlled exotic and imported items, including pottery demonstrated through instrumental neutron activation analysis (INAA) to have been exported from the Gulf Coast. In addition, unusual and exotic items come from contexts associated with these occupations: a large Olmec-style mask or bust (Figure 8.1), a cylinder seal, a large hollow figurine, and part of a large baked clay sculpture. The piece of this sculpture encountered in Feature 26 appears to be a life-sized representation of a feline paw (see Figure 8.2). If this paw were attached to a larger body, and the evidence indicates this was the case, the Occupation 2 villagers would have had an awe-inspiring item for display. This item may have had ritual importance and also could have had an impact on negotiations of social differentiation. Such objects have not been documented at this early date elsewhere in contemporaneous Valley of Oaxaca and Mixteca Alta villages.

The villagers associated with Occupations 1 and 2 as well as Feature 3, Unit 23, controlled greater amounts of storage space than did other members of the community, and certainly more than "normal" occupants of contemporaneous Valley of Oaxaca villages. The bell-shaped pits from Occupation 1 (EA-2) and Unit 23 constitute the largest of these features documented at Etlatongo, allowing for storage of accumulated lucre. While some of the items stored in these features undoubtedly were subsistence materials, the ability to store more reflects that these occupants achieved a privileged position in terms of reciprocity and accruing social debts among other villagers. The disposal of a dog at the base of Feature 3, Unit 23, may represent a prestige display, and the Olmec-style hollow baby encountered in this feature links these inhabitants with a style and underlying iconography and ideology foreign to the Mixteca Alta. I interpret both the size of these storage pits, as well as the disproportionate amount of ritual paraphernalia lying within, as reflecting social ranking. Additional excavation and analysis of contemporaneous households at Etlatongo will support or disprove this interpretation.

While there appears to be a relationship between access to ritual paraphernalia and exotic prestige goods, the evidence for economic differentiation remains limited. Households at Etlatongo probably provisioned their own chert and other raw materi-

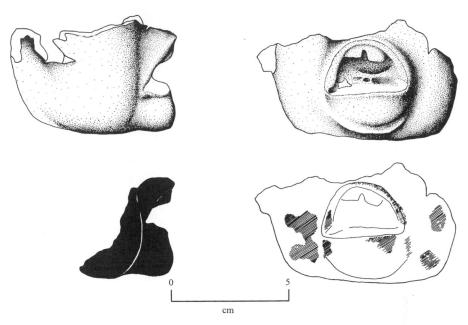

0   5
cm

Figure 8.1 Drawing of an Olmec-style ceramic mask or bust fragment from Feature 26, EA-2. The bottom view, left, shows a cross-section of the object, while the vertical lines on the bottom right view show where red paint remains visible. Areas without stippling on the front and side views on top are broken. © 2003, J. Blomster.

Figure 8.2 Photographed immediately upon disco-very, this baked clay "paw" (black arrow) comes from Feature 26, Occupation 2, EA-2. This paw is a fragment of a much larger sculpture. White arrow points to magnetic north; scale is 30 cm.

als for stone tools. Obsidian, a volcanic glass imported from the highlands to the north and west, and to a lesser extent from Guatemala to the south, does not appear to have been centrally controlled. While higher-status households appear to have had exclusive access to some sources, obsidian from at least a few sources was generally available to ancient villagers. Thus, we do not see control over basic raw materials at Etlatongo. The prestige goods controlled by certain households accentuate the noneconomic aspects of interregional interaction. There is no evidence of economic domination or vertical relations of production. The larger storage space associated with the higher-status households may have enabled these individuals to store additional subsistence goods, some of which may have been redistributed in times of emergency. As noted previously, these spaces also may have housed prestige goods when they were not being displayed, or may have stored materials that may have been redistributed in acts of ritual generosity, such as during feasts or through other tactics, that accrued social debts among those unable to return this "generosity."

Employing a practice perspective (see Chapter 1), viewing ancient villagers as constituting social roles defined within their societal context, early aggrandizers at Etlatongo appear to have been negotiating a higher social status through displays and ritual performances. Rather than a coercive class linked with economic powers, initial expression of social inequality may have been tied with access to sacred knowledge and control over community rituals. Part of this authority appears to be connected with foreign iconographic systems. Residential structures on small platforms expressed and manifested the occupants' different status within society. Rituals that encompassed an entire corporate group or groups larger than the immediate household may have been centered on these platforms. The occupants associated with these platforms maintained ritual paraphernalia from such rituals. More inclusive public rituals, incorporating factions that cross-cut kin groups, may have been centered on the large platform exposed in Unit 1 (see text that follows). Ultimately such connections between access to ritual knowledge and access to exotic goods may have been transformed into heritable economic advantages.

Public Space and Ritual

As noted in Chapters 4 and 5, archaeologists assiduously attempt to differentiate contexts as representing either higher status or public space. I interpret several contexts at Etlatongo as blurring these distinctions, a pattern also observed in the Soconusco region of Chiapas (Lesure and Blake 2002). In contemporaneous Valley of Oaxaca villages, platforms demarcated public space (Flannery and Marcus 1994). At Etlatongo, the situation appears more complex. I interpret smaller platforms as elevating higher-status structures, although the occupants of these structures appear inexorably linked with ritual paraphernalia, foreign symbols, and community rituals.

Unit 1 at Etlatongo offers the best evidence of possible public space and ritual. After several earlier and smaller platforms, a large platform (Mound 1-1) elevated Floor 2 approximately 1 meter above the surrounding land. From the beginning of utilization of this space, villagers selected a natural outcrop already substantially elevated above surrounding space. The construction of this platform involved the reutilization of midden deposits as platform fill; these deposits contained disproportionately high quantities of obsidian blades and figurine fragments. While these objects may initially have been utilized in rituals on the household level, a communitywide effort to sanctify this space involved depositing this material to elevate Floor 2. Unfortunately, the limited excavations conducted at this part of the site failed to expose the structure, if any, lying atop Floor 2.

Coordination of the labor to build such a large platform may have further constituted the claims to power or authority of early aggrandizers based on access to sacred knowledge. Rituals at a larger scale, perhaps involving a majority of the community, may have been centered on such large platforms as Mound 1-1. Objects utilized in such rituals may have been under the control of the occupants associated with the higher-status contexts discussed earlier. While this reinforces the blurring of conventional categories in early villages, it also supports the kind of social inequality based on control of esoteric knowledge and ritual paraphernalia suggested previously. As noted in the Soconusco region, platforms and the architecture atop may signal more formalized activities (Lesure and Blake 2002). I suggest these would have been directed and controlled by a small faction within society. Control over exotic symbols and iconography often enhances prestige, especially with an increase in the amount of distance to the place from which foreign symbols come (Helms 1979).

INTERREGIONAL INTERACTION AT ETLATONGO

In Chapter 6, I noted that many of the discussions about the movement of foreign symbols have been based purely on stylistic assessments. Many of these interpretations rest on underdeveloped conceptions of style and a poor definition of the Olmec style in particular. While Olmec-style iconography has often been tied stylistically with Gulf Coast Olmec archaeological sites, critics have argued that there are no quantifiable data to support movement of ceramic objects, and further that Etlatongo and the Nochixtlán Valley did not participate in the kind of interregional interaction occurring throughout Mesoamerica, lagging behind in sociopolitical developments (Drennan 1983; Flannery and Marcus 2000; Marcus 1989). In terms of both interaction and sociopolitical development, the 1992 Etlatongo Project proved that such characterizations are inaccurate. The Nochixtlán Valley manifests similar sociopolitical processes and transformations as those in the Valley of Oaxaca, and fully participated in San Lorenzo horizon interregional interaction. In addition to stylistic comparisons, robust data for interregional interaction comes from INAA of ceramics from Etlatongo and contemporaneous sites throughout Mesoamerica.

Ceramic fragments subjected to compositional analysis from Etlatongo, Valley of Oaxaca sites, San Lorenzo, as well as Central Mexico, reveal that the San Lorenzo Olmec exported pottery. In some cases, these vessels include fine kaolin clays, manufactured to represent shapes such as squashes. The fineness of the clay body has long distinguished such sherds in ceramic assemblages; it is now possible to link these with a Gulf Coast Olmec manufacturing locus. Such objects were not common at villages such as Etlatongo and appear to be associated with higher-status contexts.

In direct contradiction to models that promote primarily local manufacturing and interpretation of Olmec symbols (Flannery and Marcus 2000), vessels with distinct Olmec-style designs such as Calzadas Carved and Limón Incised (see Chapter 6) were, in fact, manufactured with Gulf Coast clays and exported to places such as Etlatongo. The INAA demonstrates that while local villagers produced some vessels with Olmec-style designs, a significant proportion of those at Etlatongo originated in San Lorenzo. Olmec exports include iconography and symbols. Further implications of these data will be considered in the following text.

In terms of style, the discovery of a nearly complete Olmec-style hollow baby figurine in Feature 3 (a large, bell-shaped pit), Unit 23, has led to revisions on both the distribution and function of these objects (see Figure 8.3). Inspired by the discovery of the Etlatongo example, my investigation of hollow babies revealed that numerous intact examples have been reported from throughout Mesoamerica, interpreted as being primarily Central Mexican and serving a funerary context (Flannery and Marcus 2000; Reilly 1995). An examination of purported hollow babies reveals that many remain inconsistent with a robust definition of Olmec style, and no intact hollow babies (what I refer to as Group 1) have been found in a meaningful stratigraphic context (Blomster 1998b, 2002). In order to better understand the nature and distribution of such objects, the literature must be purged of the promiscuous labeling of objects as "Olmec style."

Although looking at intact figurines allows for definition of this artifact type and delineation of how they differ from other contemporaneous hollow figurines, whole hollow babies provide little data on context. Instead, I examined fragments from documented archaeological excavations throughout Mesoamerica. By looking at fragments, it is possible to see that hollow babies are rare and are more associated with San Lorenzo, the important Olmec center, than with Central Mexico. By focusing only on Olmec-style hollow babies, rather than examples probably crafted to emulate that style—what I have referred to as "Group 2" figurines (Blomster 2002)—the distribution appears focused on large, regional centers. These figurines are present only at certain sites; the majority of villagers would have had no access to hollow babies. While more frequent than hollow babies, Group 2 figurines also appear to be uncommon and may represent another dimension of sociopolitical complexity in terms of access.

The discovery of the Etlatongo hollow baby in a large bell-shaped pit feature also supports an interpretation that such objects were not simply funerary goods. I interpret hollow babies as elements of ritual paraphernalia and regalia, used to negotiate rank or standing within a social group. The presence of the Etlatongo hollow baby in a higher-status context further supports that aggrandizers exhibited a different status encoded in ritual knowledge. Use and manipulation of ideology represents one source of power within society. The utilization of foreign imagery may represent an association with some of the sacred propositions represented by Olmec-style symbols. The discovery of an Olmec-style mask or bust in Feature 26 (see Figure 8.1) appears particularly significant; perhaps the EA-2, Occupation 2 villagers actually impersonated ancestors or supernatural forces mediated through the Olmec style. Such objects, of course, would have been multivalent in their meanings, depending on context and actors; they could have signaled information as well as constituted social identities.

I note as a cautionary tale that interpretations based both on style and compositional analysis can be taken only so far. For example, if archaeologists of the future were to examine the number of foreign appliances and automobiles found in typical American houses, and compositional analysis revealed an Asian genesis for many of these products, they might propose interpretations ranging from invasion to cultural domination. This demonstrates that such data must be viewed within a larger context.

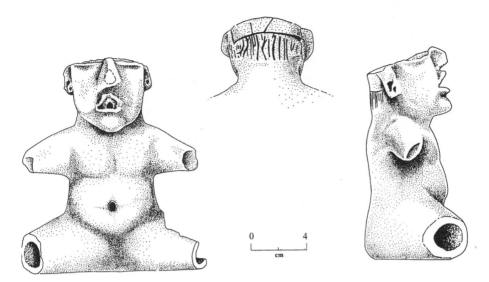

0 ———4
cm

Figure 8.3 Front, back, and side views of the hollow baby found in Feature 3, Unit 23, at Etlatongo. Areas without stippling are broken. © 2003, J. Blomster.

At Etlatongo, no evidence has been encountered for a coercive force behind inter-regional interaction. Although the settlement shift from Yucuita to Etlatongo appears dramatic (see text that follows), it does not appear to have been accompanied with violence.

Transformation in Middle Cruz Settlement Pattern

Limited social inequality, as documented earlier, appears approximately at the same time as evidence for interregional interaction in prestige goods such as imported ceramics and Olmec-style ritual paraphernalia. These correlate with a major change in social organization at Etlatongo, which shifted from being sparsely populated to being the largest village in the Middle Cruz settlement hierarchy of the Nochixtlán Valley. A two-tier settlement type characterized the preceding phase, the Early Cruz (Spores 1972). One large village, Yucuita, lay amongst scattered hamlets comprised of several households (Etlatongo may have been one of these hamlets, although no primary Early Cruz occupations have been documented). While Yucuita was larger than other villages, it remains unclear whether it actually had any administrative role, which is critical for the sites to actually form a settlement hierarchy. Apparently, Etlatongo, situated at an extremely advantageous locale for settlement, did not contain a significant population prior to the Middle Cruz.

Early in the Middle Cruz phase, Etlatongo grew to encompass an area of at least 26.2 hectares, comparable in size to San José Mogote in the Valley of Oaxaca (see Chapter 3, Figure 3.9). Etlatongo was transformed from a nearly invisible Early Cruz occupation to the top of a three-tier site typology, with several smaller villages and hamlets scattered throughout the Nochixtlán Valley. The presence of possible public space, higher-status residences, and imported prestige goods in higher frequencies than those reported in the limited documentation available from other contemporaneous Nochixtlán Valley sites suggests the presence of at least a two-tier hierarchy based solely on size—one large village (Etlatongo) versus several small villages and even smaller hamlets (Spores 1972). While there may have been an additional size class between Etlatongo and the smallest hamlets and even some secondary administrative functions present at smaller villages (this cannot be determined with existing data), there does not appear to have been a tight integration within this settlement system throughout the Nochixtlán Valley. Archaeologists usually associate a state level of political organization with a tightly integrated site hierarchy of three or four levels (depending on whether the smallest units are included as a "level"), with some administrative, ritual, and coordinative functions integrated through these tiers. This happens later in the Valley of Oaxaca with the Monte Albán state, and the Uruk state in southwestern Iran represents another oft-cited example (Wright and Johnson 1975).

Based on the available data, I interpret Etlatongo's influence as extremely limited throughout the Nochixtlán Valley, similar to the situation with contemporaneous San José Mogote, which controlled only part of its subvalley rather than all of the Valley of Oaxaca. Understanding Etlatongo's role throughout the Nochixtlán Valley necessitates excavations at other contemporaneous sites, to determine the presence of public and higher-status structures as well as access to imported prestige goods. At any rate, Etlatongo's dramatic transformation had a negative impact on Yucuita, which lost a significant portion of its population at this time (Plunket 1990; Winter 1989). What differentiated Etlatongo from Yucuita?

The earliest contexts exposed at Etlatongo clearly show the presence of foreign goods and exotica. While these may have been used to negotiate social identity—part of chiefly power is the ability to display foreign symbols (Helms 1979)—this link with foreign iconography and imagery also may have led to an advantageous position for Etlatongo. Throughout time and space in Mesoamerica, ruling houses attempt to associate themselves with a mystical, suprahuman race or noble lineage. Perhaps in the Nochixtlán Valley the origins of this lay in Middle Cruz Etlatongo, where early aggrandizers may have enhanced their own prestige through association with foreign symbols and ideology (Brumfiel and Earle 1987:7). As noted previously, the appearance of limited social inequality does not immediately appear to be linked with highly differentiated economic power; instead, higher-status individuals claimed access to sacred knowledge not shared by a majority of the community.

Social complexity in the Mixteca Alta certainly was an indigenous process—neither Zapotecs nor Olmecs created Mixtec complexity. Contact with and manipulation of Olmec symbolism, however, gave a "jump start" to the efforts of early Mixtec aggrandizers and may have imposed a unifying ideology connecting these disparate regions. A practice theory perspective privileges the role of self-interested social actors. The model sketched earlier, however, sounds too much like older "emulation" models and fails to account for why these specific symbols appear in Oaxaca. While much of the reasoning behind early aggrandizers at the Etlatongo level has been discussed, the motivations of the other party in this—the Olmec or their intermediaries—have been neglected. Such a topic is beyond the scope of this volume, but perhaps placing this in a world systems perspective can suggest some possibilities. Unlike systems theory perspectives (Flannery 1968; Flannery and Marcus 2000), which focus primarily on internally driven and neoevolutionist functional explanations (how a system "adapts" to the environment and maintains equilibrium), a world systems perspective encourages consideration of the impact of external interaction on sociopolitical organization.

A WORLD SYSTEMS PERSPECTIVE: MIXTECS, ZAPOTECS, AND OLMECS

The concepts involved in a world systems perspective (as opposed to world systems theory) have been summarized in Chapter 1. I consider this perspective merely a framework or paradigm through which to explore a larger context of interaction. Although I consider economic linkages, we must look beyond those in order to better grasp the nature of this interaction.

Typically, world systems perspectives define different sites and regions as cores, semiperipheries ("middlemen"), and peripheries. In order to identify a core, it should accumulate surplus, produce items for trade using skilled labor, and have some central political organization (Peregrine 1996). Peripheries, then, feature weaker political organization, supply raw materials, and import consumer products manufactured in the core. In prestate societies, cores may dominate peripheries by controlling access to prestige goods. Of course, establishing boundaries poses a challenge. In one study of Cahokia, a major center in the American Midwest, the site corresponded with a general definition of a core, but its extent was hard to define, leading the author to reject it as a core (Jeske 1999). Similar problems plague the current application, emphasizing how this perspective must be loosely defined—if used at all—in order to incorporate prestate societies. Here I attempt to apply this perspective at two different levels—within Oaxaca and between Oaxaca and the Gulf Coast.

The Nochixtlán Valley and the Valley of Oaxaca

In examining the relationship between the Nochixtlán Valley and the Valley of Oaxaca, the literature specifies that the Mixteca Alta "lagged" behind the Valley of Oaxaca in terms of sociopolitical complexity and interregional interaction (Drennan 1983; Marcus 1989). While never analyzed in terms of a world systems perspective, clearly the Nochixtlán Valley would be the periphery to the core centered at San José Mogote, in the Etla branch of the Valley of Oaxaca. Of course, this perspective may be inappropriate at this level, as San José Mogote exerted only minimal control over this northwest branch of the Valley of Oaxaca. Etlatongo may have exercised similar influence in its sector of the Nochixtlán Valley—there really are not enough data to determine the nature and extent of this relationship (see previous text).

If we do apply this perspective, clearly the Nochixtlán Valley was not a periphery of the Valley of Oaxaca. As explicated in Chapter 6, the ancient inhabitants of Etlatongo engaged in interregional interaction independent of the Valley of Oaxaca and had access to Olmec-style pottery diagnostic of the San Lorenzo horizon (Limón Incised and Conejo Orange-on-White), rare or absent in the Valley of Oaxaca. Analysis of graywares, long associated with the Valley of Oaxaca (Flannery and Marcus 1994), provides the biggest surprise—none of the graywares excavated at Etlatongo come from the Valley of Oaxaca, *contra* expectations and predictions (Flannery and Marcus 2000). Instead, the grayware pottery originates either from San Lorenzo, or some of it was probably locally made at Etlatongo. Thus, Valley of Oaxaca villages did not provide Etlatongo with any of the symbols or imported

Middle Cruz pottery. Ancient Etlatongoans apparently did not view San José Mogote as a source of iconographic and ritual, or even economic, power. Instead, they selected symbols tied in with Olmec symbolism deriving from the more distant Gulf Coast. Etlatongo villagers also participated in networks independent of those in the Valley of Oaxaca to obtain some of its obsidian (Blomster and Glascock 2002).

The only robust evidence of contact between Etlatongo and San José Mogote is a mirror fragment. While the 1992 Etlatongo excavations encountered several iron-ore mirror fragments, spectral analysis of a previously collected sample revealed that the magnetite derives from a geologic source at Loma los Sabinos, in the Zimatlán branch of the Valley of Oaxaca (Pires-Ferreira 1975:50). Fragments of ore from this source were found at San José Mogote, indicating that this mirror may have been manufactured in the mirror-producing "residential ward" at San José Mogote (Flannery 1968).

Etlatongo transformed into a large regional center during the Middle Cruz phase, comparable to San José Mogote. Like that Valley of Oaxaca village, it probably controlled a sector of the Nochixtlán Valley. Both of the "polities" represented by these villages are diffuse at best, and it would be difficult to bound them. Thus, it would be inappropriate to apply a clearly bounded world systems perspective. What emerges, however, is that these villages were comparable in terms of sociopolitical complexity; one was not a periphery of the other. Further, the Mixtecs appear to have had a wider involvement in the realms of Olmec symbols and pottery than did San José Mogote.

The Olmec and Oaxaca

The Olmec have lurked at the margins of this book. Although understanding the true nature of the Olmec lies beyond the scope of this volume, it is important to revisit the comparative sociopolitical systems of San Lorenzo and San José Mogote. As noted in Chapter 1, the perspective of researchers working in the Valley of Oaxaca has been that San Lorenzo and San José Mogote were similar in terms of sociopolitical organization (Flannery and Marcus 2000). I view this conclusion as inaccurate. One problem is the emphasis on the Olmec as a chiefdom rather than a state, as if proving this typological argument would deny any possible influence coming from the Olmec. Rather than becoming mired in determining which sociopolitical level best suits the Olmec, I emphasize the great organizational differences between the Olmec and other contemporaneous societies, which is reinforced by new evidence continuing to emerge from San Lorenzo (Cyphers 1996).

A San José Mogote leader lived in a thatched roof, wattle and daub (cane and mud) house somewhat larger and better plastered than all other houses at that village (Flannery and Marcus 1994:388). I envision the leaders of Etlatongo living in similar structures, although probably elevated by low platforms. Additional evidence from Etlatongo suggests that the interior of some structures may have featured painted designs (Blomster 1998a). San Lorenzo leaders lived on the heights of the site in the so-called Red Palace, with basalt columns and a stone drainage system— an extravagant use of basalt, a scarce and imported resource at San Lorenzo. While some households at San José Mogote may have controlled aspects of shell or iron-ore mirror production, elite households at San Lorenzo controlled monument carving and recycling—clearly a difference in scale (Cyphers 1996; Flannery 1968). Artists carved colossal heads that probably depicted actual Olmec rulers—an emphasis on individual power not expressed in Oaxaca. While Oaxaca exhibits early public architecture, the massive modifications of the San Lorenzo plateau dwarf any con-temporaneous public construction at San José Mogote. Further, San Lorenzo shows a level of integration in its regional settlement pattern and exploitation of its hinter-land absent in either the Valley of Oaxaca or the Nochixtlán Valley (Symonds 2000).

Was the Olmec a core? Not to sound too much like a former United States pres-ident, but it depends on how you define *core*. Clearly San Lorenzo controlled and exploited a large region surrounding it, although how far the control went within the Gulf Coast may have been limited—it probably did not extend as far as the Tuxtla Mountains, the source of much of the basalt (Arnold 2000). How far can we extend this core? Certainly not all the way south to Oaxaca; just as there are problems in using the term *horizon* with the Olmec because the spread of Olmec-style materials is not consistent across Mesoamerica (see Chapter 1), the same problem precludes viewing the Gulf Coast and Oaxaca as a contiguous unit. Olmec-style artifacts con-centrate at regional centers or villages along important trade routes. I focus here on comparing three sites—San Lorenzo, San José Mogote, and Etlatongo.

Turning to the criteria for a core outlined previously, San Lorenzo—referred to by some as an incipient state (Symonds 2000)—is most consistent with this defini-tion in terms of its level of political complexity and integration as compared to San José Mogote and Etlatongo. Surplus is more difficult to assess with the available data. The final issue, exportation of manufactured products, however, can be exam-ined. INAA has documented that the Olmec at San Lorenzo produced well-crafted ceramics exported throughout Mesoamerica. What is particularly remarkable about the INAA is the lack of imported ceramics at San Lorenzo. A larger project that ana-lyzed over 1,000 samples of both archaeological ceramics and modern clays failed to find a single piece of imported pottery at San Lorenzo (Neff and Glascock 2002:Table 8). In fact, sites in the Valley of Oaxaca, the Mixteca Alta (Etlatongo), the Basin of Mexico, and the Soconusco region received pottery only from San Lorenzo, not from each other. This seems to be a clear case of exporting finished products. While some raw materials—in this case, magnetite and ilmenite—at San Lorenzo came from Chiapas (Agrinier 1989), it remains unclear what raw materials the Olmec received from other parts of Mesoamerica. The only two mirrors made of Oaxacan magnetite that have been documented at San Lorenzo are from a post–San Lorenzo horizon context (Pires-Ferreira 1975:60). Despite these data, I resist label-ing the Gulf Coast Olmec as a core in the economic sense.

While ongoing research at San Lorenzo and other contemporaneous sites contin-ues to illuminate the economic aspects of Olmec relationships throughout Mesoamerica, we must move beyond the purely economic to understand this inter-action. This contact often emphasized iconography; in fact, interaction with the Mokaya of the Soconusco region resulted in the large-scale replacement of the pre-Olmec iconographic system—a process referred to as "olmecization" (Clark and Pye 2000). While such large-scale replacement does not characterize Etlatongo, there is probably great sociopolitical importance associated with the Olmec-style ritual para-phernalia. The possible Olmec mask found in Feature 26 (see Figure 8.1) suggests that it was advantageous to physically manifest the trappings of Olmec symbolism and ideology. Although no evidence of an actual Olmec person from the Gulf Coast has been found at Etlatongo, one such example may be present at San José Mogote—an individual marked as different from contemporaneous Zapotecs by both the type of cranial modification and the style of burial (Flannery 1968).

Like the Uruk of Mesopotamia, the Olmec civilization flourished in an area with high agricultural productivity but with scant mineral resources. It appears that they imported raw materials and primarily exported finished goods and services. In addition to ceramic vessels, it has been suggested that they exported rubber, portable sculptures, and possibly feline pelts (Diehl and Coe 1995:23). They also, however, exported ideology and symbolism, as seen in the iconography of Olmec-style vessels and hollow figurines, at least one of which has been traced to San Lorenzo through INAA (Blomster 2002; Neff and Glascock 2002:Table 1). While earlier models argue that the Gulf Coast Olmec were simply one of many groups creating this symbolism (Flannery and Marcus 1994), it appears that the Olmec had an important innovative role in creating a model for expressing supernatural and related concepts. Indeed, it seems unlikely that independent societies spread throughout Mesoamerica could devise such a consistent abstract symbolic system (Stark 2000).

Although summarizing the relationships between the Olmec and different regions of Mesoamerica remains beyond the scope of this book, I believe this interaction varied from region to region. Rather than proposing a monolithic model, the interaction within each region must be examined. Some patterns, however, do emerge. Major sites in select regions appear to demonstrate the largest spectrum of Olmec symbolism. In the Nochixtlán Valley, Etlatongo represents the focus of Olmec iconography; elsewhere in the Mixteca Alta, Santa Cruz Tayata may represent another such locus in the Huamelulpan Valley (Crohn 1998). While I do not believe the Gulf Coast Olmec can be defined as an economic core in Formative Mesoamerica, they did export both finished products and iconography. These Olmec-style symbols represented more than just status markers; they connected "those who were entitled to use them to the ultimate sacred propositions of Olmec religion" (Drennan 1976:358–359). The fact that so much of this interaction appears to involve distribution of ritual paraphernalia suggests to me that much of the interaction involved ideology, which is consistent with a regional cult (Blomster 1998a).

Regional cults reside at an organizational level between local cults and world religions (Werbner 1977a:ix–xxxiii). Though far-reaching, regional cults remain less inclusive than world religions. Regional cults can be both exclusionary and inclusive; they spread across ethnic, political, and linguistic boundaries as they promote transcultural rituals (Burger 1992; Van Binsbergen 1977; Werbner 1977b). While cults are expansive religions, they are not necessarily spread through force, nor do they necessarily proselytize and actively try to convert. Regional cults are often spread along preexisting communication paths and trade routes (Butt Colson 1985:104). In Mesoamerica, there was clearly contact and interaction between groups prior to the San Lorenzo horizon; the Olmec took advantage of these earlier networks in their interaction with other regions.

At Etlatongo, this contact may have been important in stimulating an already emerging social complexity, but it appears to have had very little lasting impact on Mixtec culture. In looking for the origins of the distinctive elements of Mixtec culture, the search begins and ends in the Mixteca Alta. Olmec-style developments in the subsequent La Venta horizon, such as the double-line break on ceramics, seem to have made less of an impact on the Nochixtlán Valley than in other regions of Mesoamerica. There are many problems in the application of a world systems perspective to prestate societies, such as recognizing how variable a periphery may be and determining its impact on the core. The regionalization that parts of Oaxaca experienced after the Middle Cruz phase precludes additional deployment of this perspective until the emergence of the Monte Albán state.

Informed by this perspective, it is appropriate to examine what the Olmec received from this interaction. Actually, in this case it is easier to determine what they did *not* receive. No raw materials (or finished products, such as ceramic vessels of figurines) from the Mixteca Alta, or even the Valley of Oaxaca, have yet been identified at San Lorenzo. While archaeologists have long argued that local elites may have benefited from contact with foreign symbols (Flannery 1968; Helms 1979), to understand how the Olmec benefited from interaction in places such as Etlatongo we may have to look beyond models developed from Western economic perspectives. Some scholars see Olmec symbols outside of the Gulf Coast as signaling trading relationships or proclaiming certain rights to resources (Earle 1990). Although clearly many sites exhibiting Olmec symbolism lie situated along important trade and communication routes—a pattern that is especially well developed in the subsequent La Venta horizon—the appearance of Olmec symbols at Etlatongo do not, at least based on current research, correlate with a specific raw material extracted from the Nochixtlán Valley. Until we determine specific resources that ancient Etlatongoans offered to the Olmec or their intermediaries, the extensive and varied nature of Olmec symbolism at Etlatongo argues against seeing the site simply as some node in a larger exchange network. To understand the location of some sites with Olmec symbolism, alternatives that include the importance of iconographic spread of a self-interested cult must be considered, rather than solely economic motives.

ETLATONGO AND THE FUTURE?

So far this volume has considered only the past of Etlatongo. What about the future of the site and additional research? Future archaeological research at Etlatongo holds the potential to further enrich our understanding of the past and challenge established points of view. One of the more positive outcomes of the 1992 project may have been raising awareness of the great time depth and regional importance of the site among contemporary San Mateo Etlatongo residents. Villagers report extensive looting of the site by outsiders in the decades prior to the 1992 project but, at least to me, did not express this in terms of loss of cultural heritage. Due to years of economic, political, and cultural repression, many villagers appeared reluctant to express much connection with the site and a sense of Mixtec identity, itself a complicated concept that varies based on situation and an individual's position or social role. Many villagers expressed surprise that I was interested in the ancient Mixtecs. Part of the ongoing hegemonic legacy of the Aztecs has been their promotion by the government, as part of the forging of national identity, as *the* remarkable Mexican civilization prior to the Spanish invasion. After their involvement in the 1992 investigations, many of the villagers who helped as field assistants or watched the excavations developed an additional perspective about their village's ancient predecessor, expressing a strong interest both in preserving the site and in learning more about the past of this place.

Archaeology (and anthropology as well) has often been referred to as an "imperialist" discipline, where investigators travel to distant places, harvest the local patrimony, and (in some cases) exchange and transform these data into lucrative careers. What can archaeologists do to benefit the living people? I hope this question elicits many and varied responses from readers. In addition to preservation of cultural patrimony, archaeologists should also ask the local community what they would like to see result from the research. While I continue to learn how to improve my own contributions, during the fieldwork I gave many informal lectures, from my perspective as an archaeologist, on the occupation of the site and its regional importance. Residents generously shared their knowledge of the site and region as well. Teachers and students proved to be interested audiences, and as noted in Chapter 3, the 1992 project has actually been incorporated into local textbooks. In addition to supporting efforts to eventually establish a community museum at Etlatongo, which could house both artifacts from archaeological projects as well as the material constantly turned up by farming of the site, I also submitted a report of the research, in Spanish, to the village council, and I continue to visit and talk about the site. I will also incorporate the interests of interested residents in any future research to make the process more of a dialogue and truly participatory. One approach, called "community archeology," closely integrates local interests and shows much promise (Geurds and Van Broekhoven 2003). While discussion about the issue of "who owns the past?" proves enlightening, in terms of preservation of the ancient village of Etlatongo, I believe the success of the living community in protecting this site will ultimately determine its future.

The research reported in this volume identifies unresolved issues from the original research design and generates new research questions that can only be clarified through additional excavations and data analysis. Perhaps the most pressing need remains establishing a larger sample of Middle Cruz houses. As noted earlier, the 1992 Etlatongo excavations exposed only fragmentary portions of non–higher-status houses—thus the reliance on comparative data from the Valley of Oaxaca. The substantial debris from later occupations atop all Middle Cruz houses, which precluded larger exposure during the limited scope of the 1992 excavations, remains a problem. In order to fully expose all sides of a Middle Cruz house, as well as related exterior features, at least 2 to 3 meters of later artifacts, structures, and features have to be responsibly excavated and analyzed. In fact, a more efficient alternative may be to document Middle Cruz structures at a Nochixtlán Valley site with less onerous overburden. Ronald Spores (1972) documented several potential sites in his survey.

A related problem centers on documenting the earliest, pre–Middle Cruz occupation at Etlatongo. Scattered fragments from this earlier occupation have been exposed, but always in later contexts. In order to understand the dramatic growth of Middle Cruz Etlatongo, a more accurate size of the earlier occupation must be projected. It may be the case that few, if any, households occupied this area prior to Middle Cruz Etlatongo. Additional excavations will clarify this.

While the first two suggestions for future research require additional excavation, a wealth of data, representing a variety of chronological periods, remains to be analyzed from the 1992 Etlatongo project. Unfortunately, the nature of grants and academic rewards tend to discourage the analysis and publication of all materials generated by an excavation. The pressure is for archaeologists to constantly initiate new field projects or new field seasons within established projects. The cream of the data collected by a project may generate a series of journal articles, critical in the "publish or perish" world of academic archaeology, but the rewards for full-length, data-rich monographs are few. In addition to time constraints, publishing costs conspire to preclude or delay the production of full reports. Much of the hard data generated by a project are relegated to reports issued to governments and granting organizations and/or dissertations. A positive development utilizes electronic media (Web sites or CD-roms) to store vast quantities of archaeological data, ensuring access and analysis at a reduced production cost (Varien 1999b).

The reanalysis of earlier archaeological projects has been a popular occupation among a new generation of archaeologists, and is possible due to the detailed nature and ready availability of such reports. Unfortunately, much of the data from major projects spanning the last 20 to 40 years remain unpublished. How is it possible to assess an archaeologist's conclusions about a given site if basic ceramic data remain unavailable for independent analysis? Archaeologists should be particularly aware of long-term patterns, but in this case short-term productivity and production have been privileged. As archaeologists, what kind of artifacts are we leaving for future scholars to analyze? What do *we* owe the past, present, and future? I recognize that I have just begun the production process and remain committed to additional analysis and publication of excavated materials. These data have served as a valuable training ground for students, and as they are reanalyzed and reinterpreted by different scholars, I hope they continue to contribute to archaeology in the future.

The issue of making data accessible is of primary importance in archaeology. Many archaeologists consider the discipline to be scientific, not only in the sense that results should be replicable (or able to be reproduced) by careful attention to contexts, but also in the sense that the discipline should serve as an example of how problems can be framed and data collected to support or reject given hypotheses. Robust, well-documented data allow archaeologists to apply different theoretical perspectives to them. In this sense, the Etlatongo project has been extremely successful. With a limited budget, the data generated by this project allow revision of ideas on the origins of social complexity and the impact of interregional interaction in an area once characterized as a "periphery." Utilizing a variety of theoretical perspectives, some conclusions have been offered and additional issues to be resolved by further research have been identified. While much work remains, the initial results contribute to understanding the human experience, giving voice to the accomplishments of Nochixtlán Valley villagers who lived over 3,000 years ago.

References

Acosta, Jorge R., and Javier Romero. 1992. *Exploraciones en Monte Negro, Oaxaca*. Instituto Nacional de Antropología e Historia, Mexico City.

Adams, William Y. 1968. Settlement Pattern in Microcosm: The Changing Aspect of a Nubian Village during Twelve Centuries. In *Settlement Archaeology*, edited by K. C. Chang, pp. 174–207. National Press Books, Palo Alto, California.

Adler, Michael A. 1989. Ritual facilities and social integration in non-ranked societies. In *The Architecture of Social Integration in Prehistoric Pueblos*, edited by W. D. Lipe and M. Hegmon, pp. 35–52. Occasional Paper 1, Crow Canyon Archaeological Center, Cortez, Colorado.

Adler, Michael A., and Richard H. Wilshusen. 1990. Large-scale integrative facilities in tribal societies: cross-cultural and southwestern U.S. examples. *World Archaeology* 22(2):133–146.

Agrinier, Pierre. 1989. Mirador-Plumajillo, Chiapas, y sus relaciones con cuatro sitios del horizonte olmeca en Veracruz, Chiapas y la costa de Guatemala. *Arqueología* 2:19–36.

Algaze, Guillermo. 1993. *The Uruk World System: The Dynamics of Early Mesopotamian Civilization*. University of Chicago Press, Chicago.

Arnold, Philip J., III. 2000. Sociopolitical Complexity and the Gulf Olmecs: A View from the Tuxtla Mountains, Veracruz, Mexico. In *Olmec Art and Archaeology in Mesoamerica*, edited by J. E. Clark and M. E. Pye, pp. 117–135. Studies in the History of Art, Vol. 58, National Gallery of Art, Washington, D.C.

Barth, Fredrick. 1966. *Models of Social Organization*. Royal Anthropological Institute of Great Britain and Ireland, London.

Bernal, Ignacio. 1967. La presencia olmeca en Oaxaca. *Culturas de Oaxaca* 1:1–24. Museo Nacional de Antropología, Mexico City.

———. 1971. The Olmec Region—Oaxaca. *Contributions of the University of California Archaeological Research Facility* 11:29–50. Department of Anthropology, Berkeley.

Blanton, Richard E. 1978. *Monte Albán: Settlement Patterns at the Ancient Zapotec Capital*. Academic Press, New York.

Blanton, Richard E., and Gary M. Feinman. 1984. The Mesoamerican World System. *American Anthropologist* 86:673–682.

Blanton, Richard E., Stephen A. Kowalewksi, Gary M. Feinman, and Jill Appel. 1982. *Monte Alban's Hinterland, Part 1: Pre-Hispanic Settlement Patterns in the Central and Southern Parts of the Valley of Oaxaca, Mexico*. Memoirs of the University of Michigan Museum of Anthropology, No. 15, University of Michigan, Ann Arbor.

Blomster, Jeffrey P. 1995. Microsettlement Patterning and Demographic Change at Etlatongo, Oaxaca, Mexico. Paper presented at the 60th Annual Meeting of the Society for American Archaeology, Minneapolis, Minnesota.

———. 1998a. *At the Bean Hill in the Land of the Mixtec: Early Formative Social Complexity and Interregional Interaction at Etlatongo, Oaxaca, Mexico*. Unpublished Ph.D. dissertation, Department of Anthropology, Yale University, New Haven, Connecticut.

———. 1998b. Context, Cult, and Early Formative Public Ritual in the Mixteca Alta: Analysis of a Hollow Baby Figurine from Etlatongo, Oaxaca. *Ancient Mesoamerica* 9(2):309–326.

———. 2002. What and Where Is Olmec Style? Regional Perspectives on Hollow Figurines in Early Formative Mesoamerica. *Ancient Mesoamerica* 13(2):171–195.

Blomster, Jeffrey P., and Michael Glascock. 2002. Obsidian Exchange in Formative Period Oaxaca: A View from the Mixteca Alta. Paper presented at the 67th Annual Meeting of the Society for American Archaeology, Denver, Colorado.

Boas, Franz. 1940. The Aims of Anthropological Research. In *Race, Language and Culture,* edited by F. Boas, pp. 243–259. Macmillan, New York [original 1932].

Bourdieu, Pierre. 1977. *Outline of a Theory of Practice.* Cambridge University Press, New York.

Brown, James A. 1975. Deep-site Excavation Strategy as a Sampling Problem. In *Sampling in Archaeology,* edited by J. W. Mueller, pp. 155–169. University of Arizona Press, Tucson.

Brumfiel, Elizabeth M. 1992. Distinguished Lecture in Archaeology: Breaking and Entering the Ecosystem—Gender, Class, and Faction Steal the Show. *American Anthropologist* 94:551–567.

Brumfiel, Elizabeth M., and Timothy K. Earle. 1987. Specialization, Exchange, and Complex Societies: An Introduction. In *Specialization, Exchange, and Complex Societies,* edited by E. M. Brumfiel and T. K. Earle, pp. 1–9. Cambridge University Press, New York.

Burger, Richard L. 1992. *Chavín and the Origins of Andean Civilization.* Thames and Hudson, New York.

Butt Colson, Audrey. 1985. Routes of Knowledge: An Aspect of Regional Integration in the Cirum-Roraima Area of the Guiana Highlands. *Antropologica* 63–64:103–149.

Byland, Bruce E., and John M. D. Pohl. 1994. *In the Realm of 8 Deer: The Archaeology of the Mixtec Codices.* University of Oklahoma Press, Norman.

Cancian, Frank. 1976. Social Stratification. *Annual Review of Anthropology* 5:227–248.

Caso, Alfonso. 1938. *Exploraciones en Oaxaca, quinta y sexta temporadas, 1936–1937.* Publicación 34, Instituto Panamericano de Geografía e Historia, Mexico City.

———. 1942. Resumen del Informe de las exploraciones en Oaxaca durante la septima y la octava temporadas, 1937–1939 y 1938–1939. *Actas y Memorias del XXVII Congreso Internacional de Americanistas,* Tomo II, Mexico City.

Caso, Alfonso, Ignacio Bernal, and Jorge R. Acosta. 1967. *La cerámica de Monte Albán.* Memorias del Instituto Nacional de Antropología e Historia 13, Instituto Nacional de Antropología e Historia, Mexico City.

Clark, John E. 1994a. *The Development of Early Formative Rank Societies in the Soconusco, Chiapas, Mexico.* Unpublished Ph.D. dissertation, Department of Anthropology, University of Michigan, Ann Arbor.

——— (editor). 1994b. *Los olmecas en Mesoamérica.* El Equilibrista, Mexico City.

———. 1997. Arts of Government in Early Mesoamerica. *Annual Review of Anthropology* 26:211–234.

Clark, John E., and Michael Blake. 1994. The Power of Prestige: Competitive Generosity and the Emergence of Rank Societies in Lowland Mesoamerica. In *Factional Competition and Political Development in the New World,* edited by E. M. Brumfield and J. W. Fox, pp. 17–30. Cambridge University Press, New York.

Clark, John E., and Thomas A. Lee, Jr. 1984. Formative Obsidian Exchange and the Emergence of Public Economies in Chiapas, Mexico. In *Trade and Exchange in Early Mesoamerica,* edited by K. G. Hirth, pp. 235–274. University of New Mexico Press, Albuquerque.

Clark, John E., and Mary E. Pye. 2000. The Pacific Coast and the Olmec Question. In *Olmec Art and Archaeology in Mesoamerica,* edited by J. E. Clark and M. E. Pye, pp. 217–251. Studies in the History of Art, Vol. 58, National Gallery of Art, Washington, D.C.

Coe, Michael D. 1965. The Olmec Style and Its Distribution. In *Handbook of Middle American Indians, Vol. 3: Archaeology of Southern Mesoamerica,* Part 2, edited by R. Wauchope and G. R. Willey, pp. 739–775. University of Texas Press, Austin.

———. 1977. Olmec and Maya: A Study in Relationships. In *The Origins of Maya Civilization,* edited by R.E.W. Adams, pp. 183–195. University of New Mexico Press, Albuquerque.

———. 1981. Religion and the Rise of Mesoamerican States. In *The Transition to Statehood in the New World,* edited by G. D. Jones and R. R. Kautz, pp. 157–171. Cambridge University Press, New York.

———. 1989. The Olmec Heartland: Evolution of Ideology. In *Regional Perspectives on the Olmec,* edited by R. J. Sharer and D. C. Grove, pp. 68–82. Cambridge University Press, New York.

Coe, Michael D., and Richard A. Diehl. 1980. *In the Land of the Olmec, Vol. 1: The Archaeology of San Lorenzo Tenochtitlán.* University of Texas Press, Austin.

Coe, Michael D., and Rex Koontz. 2002. *Mexico.* 5th revised edition. Thames and Hudson, New York.

Conrad, Geoffrey W., and Arthur A. Demarest. 1983. *Religion and Empire: The Dynamics of Aztec and Inca Expansion.* Cambridge University Press, New York.

Covarrubias, Miguel. 1946. *Mexico South: The Isthmus of Tehuantepec.* Alfred A. Knopf, New York.

———. 1957. *Indian Art of Mexico and Central America.* Alfred A. Knopf, New York.

Cowgill, George L. 1975. A Selection of Samples: Comments on Archaeo-statistics. In *Sampling in Archaeology,* edited by J. W. Mueller, pp. 258–274. University of Arizona Press, Tucson.

Crohn, Frank. 1998. The Huamelulpan Valley Survey Project: Evidence for Early Formative Sociocultural and Political Complexity in the Central Mixteca Alta, Oaxaca, Mexico. Paper presented at the 63rd Annual Meeting of the Society for American Archaeology, Seattle, Washington.

Cyphers, Ann. 1996. Reconstructing Olmec Life at San Lorenzo. In *Olmec Art of Ancient Mexico,* edited by E. P. Benson and B. de la Fuente, pp. 61–71. National Gallery of Art, Washington, D.C.

———. 1997. Olmec Architecture at San Lorenzo. In *Olmec to Aztec: Settlement Patterns in the Ancient Gulf Lowlands,* edited by B. Stark and P. Arnold, III, pp. 98–114. University of Arizona Press.

Dahlgren de Jordan, Barbro. 1966. *La Mixteca: Su cultura e historia prehispánicas.* 2nd edition. Universidad Nacional Autónoma de México, Mexico City.

DeMarrais, Elizabeth, Luis Jaime Castillo, and Timothy Earle. 1996. Ideology, Materialization, and Power Strategies. *Current Anthropology* 37(1):15–31.

Dennis, Philip A. 1987. *Intervillage Conflict in Oaxaca.* Rutgers University Press, New Brunswick, New Jersey.

Diehl, Richard A. 1989. Olmec Archaeology: What We Know and What We Wish We Knew. In *Regional Perspectives on the Olmec,* edited by R. J. Sharer and D. C. Grove, pp. 17–32. Cambridge University Press, New York.

Diehl, Richard A., and Michael D. Coe. 1995. Olmec Archaeology. In *The Olmec World: Ritual and Rulership,* pp. 11–25. The Art Museum, Princeton University, Princeton, New Jersey.

Drennan, Robert D. 1976. Religion and Social Evolution in Formative Mesoamerica. In *The Early Formative Village,* edited by K. V. Flannery, pp. 345–368. Academic Press, New York.

———. 1983. Ritual and Ceremonial Development at the Early Village Level. In *The Cloud People,* edited by K. V. Flannery and J. Marcus, pp. 46–50. Academic Press, New York.

Drennan, Robert D., and Kent V. Flannery. 1983. The Growth of Site Hierarchies in the Valley of Oaxaca: Part II. In *The Cloud People,* edited by K. V. Flannery and J. Marcus, pp. 65–71. Academic Press, New York.

Durkheim, Emile. 1938. *The Rules of the Sociological Method.* Translated from the French by S. Solovay and J. Mueller. Free Press, New York [original 1895].

Earle, Timothy. 1990. Style and Iconography as Legitimation in Complex Chiefdoms. In *The Uses of Style in Archaeology,* edited by M. W. Conkey and C. A. Hastorf, pp. 73–81. Cambridge University Press, New York.

Farrell, J. 1980. *Inventing the American Way of Death, 1830–1920.* Temple University Press, Philadelphia.

Fernández Dávila, Enrique, and Susan Gómez Serafín. 1997. Arqueología y arte: Evolución de los zapotecos de los Valles Centrales, periodo formativo. In *Historia del arte de Oaxaca, Vol. 1:*

Arte prehispánico, edited by M. Dalton Palomo and V. Loera y Chávez C., pp. 79–105. Instituto Oaxaqueño de las Culturas, Oaxaca City, Mexico.

Fernández de Miranda, María Teresa, Morris Swadesh, and Robert J. Weitlaner. 1960. El Panorama Etno-Lingüístico de Oaxaca y el Istmo. *Revista Mexicana de Estudios Antropológicos* 16:137–157.

Flannery, Kent V. 1968. The Olmec and the Valley of Oaxaca: A Model for Inter-regional Interaction in Formative Times. In *Dumbarton Oaks Conference on the Olmec,* edited by E. P. Benson, pp. 79–117. Dumbarton Oaks, Washington, D.C.

———. 1972. The Cultural Evolution of Civilizations. *Annual Review of Ecology and Systematics* 3:399–426.

———. 1976a. The Early Mesoamerican House. In *The Early Mesoamerican Village,* edited by K. V. Flannery, pp. 16–24. Academic Press, New York.

———. 1976b. Sampling by Intensive Surface Collection. In *The Early Mesoamerican Village,* edited by K. V. Flannery, pp. 51–62. Academic Press, New York.

———. 1976c. Contextual Analysis of Ritual Paraphernalia from Formative Oaxaca. In *The Early Mesoamerican Village,* edited by K. V. Flannery, pp. 333–345. Academic Press, New York.

———. 1983. Monte Negro: A Reinterpretation. In *The Cloud People,* edited by K. V. Flannery and J. Marcus, pp. 99–102. Academic Press, New York.

———. 1983. The Growth of Site Hierarchies in the Valley of Oaxaca: Part I. In *The Cloud People,* edited by K. V. Flannery and J. Marcus, pp. 53–64. Academic Press, New York.

———. 1994. *Early Formative Pottery of the Valley of Oaxaca, Mexico. Prehistory and Human Ecology of the Valley of Oaxaca,* Vol. 10. Memoirs of the Museum of Anthropology, University of Michigan, No. 27, University of Michigan, Ann Arbor.

———. 2000. Formative Mexican Chiefdoms and the Myth of the "Mother Culture." *Journal of Anthropological Archaeology* 19:1–37.

Flannery, Kent V., and Joyce Marcus. 1976. Formative Oaxaca and the Zapotec Cosmos. *American Scientist* 64:374–383.

Flannery, Kent V., and Marcus C. Winter. 1976. Analyzing Household Activities. In *The Early Mesoamerican Village,* edited by K. V. Flannery, pp. 34–47. Academic Press, New York.

Frankenstein, Susan, and Michael Rowlands. 1978. The Internal Structure and Regional Context of Early Iron Age Society in Southwestern Germany. *Bulletin of the Institute of Archaeology* 15:73–112.

Fried, Morton H. 1967. *The Evolution of Political Society: An Essay in Political Anthropology.* Random House, New York.

Gailey, Christine W., and Thomas C. Patterson. 1987. Power Relations and State Formation. In *Power Relations and State Formation,* edited by T. C. Patterson and C. W. Gailey, pp. 1–26. American Anthropological Association, Washington, D.C.

Gaxiola González, Margarita. 1984. *Huamelulpan: Un centro urbano de la Mixteca Alta.* Colección Científica 114, Instituto Nacional de Antropología e Historia, Mexico City.

Geurds, Alexander, and Laura N. K. Van Broekhoven. 2003. *Methodology, Trust and the Ñudzavui: Community-Based Archaeology in the Mixteca Alta.* Papers presented at the 68th Meeting of the Society for American Archeology, Milwaukee, Wisconsin.

Giddens, Anthony. 1979. *Central Problems in Social Theory.* Macmillan Press, London.

———. 1984. *The Constitution of Society: Outline of the Theory of Structuration.* University of California Press, Berkeley.

Glascock, Michael D., Hector Neff, K. S. Stryker, and T. N. Johnson. 1994. Sourcing Archaeological Obsidian by an Abbreviated NAA Procedure. *Journal of Radioanalytical and Nuclear Chemistry Articles* 180(1):29–35.

Grove, David C. 1984. *Chalcatzingo: Excavations on the Olmec Frontier.* Thames and Hudson, New York.

———. 1993. "Olmec" Horizons in Formative Period Mesoamerica: Diffusion or Social Evolution. In *Latin American Horizons,* edited by D. S.

Rice, pp. 83–111. Dumbarton Oaks, Washington, D.C.

———. 1997. Olmec Archaeology: A Half Century of Research and Its Accomplishments. *Journal of World Prehistory* 11(1):51–101.

Haas, Jonathan. 1982. *The Evolution of the Prehistoric State.* Columbia University Press, New York.

Hall, Thomas D. 1999. World-Systems and Evolution: An Appraisal. In *World-Systems Theory in Practice: Leadership, Production, and Exchange,* edited by P. N. Kardulias, pp. 1–23. Rowman & Littlefield, New York.

Hall, Thomas D., and Christopher Chase-Dunn. 1996. Comparing World-Systems: Concepts and Hypotheses. In *Pre-Columbian World Systems,* edited by P. N. Peregrine and G. M. Feinman, pp. 11–25. Monographs in World Archaeology, No. 26, Prehistory Press, Madison, Wisconsin.

Hayden, Brian. 1997. *The Pithouses of Keatley Creek: Complex Hunter-Gatherers of the Northwest Plateau.* Harcourt Brace College Publishers, New York.

Hegmon, Michelle. 1992. Archaeological Research on Style. *Annual Review of Anthropology* 21:517–536.

Hegmon, Michelle, James R. Allison, Hector Neff, and Michael D. Glascock. 1997. Production of San Juan Red Ware in the Northern Southwest: Insights into Regional Interaction in Early Puebloan Prehistory. *American Antiquity* 62(3):449–463.

Helms, Mary W. 1979. *Ancient Panama: Chiefs in Search of Power.* University of Texas Press, Austin.

Hill, James N. 1970. *Broken K Pueblo: Prehistoric Social Organization in the American Southwest.* Anthropological Papers of the University of Arizona, No. 18, Tucson, Arizona.

Hirth, Kenneth. 1992. Interregional Exchange as Elite Behavior: An Evolutionary Perspective. In *Mesoamerican Elites: An Archaeological Assessment,* edited by D. Z. Chase and A. F. Chase, pp. 18–29. University of Oklahoma Press, Norman.

Hodder, Ian. 1986. *Reading the Past.* Cambridge University Press, New York.

Hole, Bonnie Laird. 1980. Sampling in Archaeology: A Critique. *Annual Review of Anthropology* 9:217–234.

Jansen, Maarten, and Gabina Aurora Pérez Jiménez. 2000. *La Dinastía de Añute: Historia, literatura e ideología de un reino mixteco.* CNWS Publications, Vol. 87, Leiden University, The Netherlands.

Jeske, Robert J. 1999. World-Systems Theory, Core-Periphery Interactions, and Elite Economic Exchange in Mississippian Societies. In *World-Systems Theory in Practice: Leadership, Production, and Exchange,* edited by P. N. Kardulias, pp. 203–221. Rowman & Littlefield, New York.

Johnson, Matthew. 1999. *Archaeological Theory: An Introduction.* Blackwell, Malden, Massachusetts.

Joyce, Arthur A., and Raymond G. Mueller. 1997. Prehispanic Human Ecology of the Río Verde Drainage Basin. *World Archaeology* 29(1):75–94.

Joyce, Arthur A., and Marcus C. Winter. 1996. Ideology, Power, and Urban Society in Pre-Hispanic Oaxaca. *Current Anthropology* 37(1):33–86.

Kirkby, Michael. 1972. *The Physical Environment of the Nochixtlán Valley, Oaxaca.* Vanderbilt University Publications in Anthropology, No. 2, Vanderbilt University, Nashville, Tennessee.

Kluckhohn, Clyde. 1940. The Conceptual Structure in Middle American Studies. In *The Maya and Their Neighbors,* edited by C. L. Hay, R. L. Linton, S. K. Lothrop, H. L. Shapiro, and G. C. Vaillant, pp. 41–51. Appleton-Century, New York.

Kohl, Philip L. 1987. The Use and Abuse of World Systems Theory: The Case of the Pristine West Asian State. In *Advances in Archaeological Method and Theory,* Vol. 11, edited by M. Schiffer, pp. 1–35. Academic Press, New York.

Kolb, Michael J., and James E. Snead. 1997. It's a Small World After All: Comparative Analyses of Community Organization in Archaeology. *American Antiquity* 62(4):609–628.

Kreber, Jordan E. 1997. *Lambert Farm: Public Archaeology and Canine Burials along Narragansett Bay.*

Harcourt Brace College Publishers, New York.

Kristiansen, Kristian. 1987. Centre and Periphery in Bronze Age Scandinavia. In *Centre and Periphery in the Ancient World,* edited by M. Rowlands, M. Larsen, and K. Kristiansen, pp. 74–85. Cambridge University Press, New York.

Layton, Robert. 1981. *The Anthropology of Art.* Columbia University Press, New York.

Leach, Edmund R. 1965. *Political Systems of Highland Burma.* Beacon Press, Boston [original 1954].

Lesure, Richard G. 1997. Early Formative Platforms at Paso de la Amada, Chiapas, Mexico. *Latin American Antiquity* 8(3):217–235.

Lesure, Richard G., and Michael Blake. 2002. Interpretive Challenges in the Study of Early Complexity: Economy, Ritual, and Architecture at Paso de la Amada. *Journal of Anthropological Archaeology* 21:1–24.

Lind, Michael. 1996. Some Problems with the Monte Albán Chronology: Implications for Models of Interactions between Teotihuacan and Monte Albán. Paper presented at the 61st Annual Meeting of the Society for American Archaeology, New Orleans, Louisiana.

Lind, Michael, and Javier Urcid. 1983. The Lords of Lambityeco and Their Nearest Neighbors. *Notas Mesoamericanas* 9:76–111.

Lowie, Robert H. 1917. *Culture and Ethnology.* D. C. McMurtrie, New York.

Malinowski, Bronislaw. 1922. *Argonauts of the Western Pacific.* E. P. Dutton & Co., New York.

Marcus, Joyce. 1983. The Genetic Model and the Linguistic Divergence of the Otomangueans. In *The Cloud People,* edited by K. V. Flannery and J. Marcus, pp. 4–9. Academic Press, New York.

———. 1989. Zapotec Chiefdoms and the Nature of Formative Religions. In *Regional Perspectives on the Olmec,* edited by R. J. Sharer and D. C. Grove, pp. 148–197. Cambridge University Press, New York.

———. 1998. *Women's Ritual in Formative Oaxaca: Figurine-making, Divination, Death and the Ancestors. Prehistory and Human Ecology of the Valley of Oaxaca,* Vol. 11. Memoirs of the University of Michigan Museum of Anthropology, No. 33, University of Michigan, Ann Arbor.

Marcus, Joyce, and Kent V. Flannery. 1996. *Zapotec Civilization: How Urban Society Evolved in Mexico's Oaxaca Valley.* Thames and Hudson, New York.

Martínez López, Cira, Robert Markens, Marcus C. Winter, and Michael D. Lind. 2000. *Cerámica de la fase Xoo (Epoca Monte Albán IIIB-IV) del Valle de Oaxaca.* Proyecto Especial Monte Albán 1992–94, Contribución No. 8, Centro INAH Oaxaca, Oaxaca City, Mexico.

Matadamas, Rául. 2002. Cerámica del Preclásico en Yucunama, Mixteca Alta de Oaxaca. Paper presented at Taller de Cerámica: Tercera Mesa Redonda de Monte Albán, Oaxaca City, Mexico.

Mauss, Marcel. 1954. *The Gift: Forms and Function of Exchange in Archaic Societies.* Free Press, New York [original 1924].

McGuire, Randall H. 1983. Breaking Down Cultural Complexity: Inequality and Heterogeneity. In *Advances in Archaeological Method and Theory,* Vol. 6, edited by M. Schiffer, pp. 91–142. Academic Press, New York.

Metcalf, Peter, and Richard Huntington. 1991. *Celebrations of Death: The Anthropology of Mortuary Ritual.* 2nd edition. Cambridge University Press, New York.

Miller, Arthur G. 1995. *The Painted Tombs of Oaxaca, Mexico: Living with the Dead.* Cambridge University Press, New York.

Miller, Daniel, and Christopher Tilley. 1984. Ideology, power and prehistory: An introduction. In *Ideology, Power and Prehistory,* edited by D. Miller and C. Tilley, pp. 1–15. Cambridge University Press, New York.

Morgan, Lewis H. 1877. *Ancient Society.* Holt, New York.

Munsell Color Company. 1975. *Munsell Soil Color Charts.* Munsell Color Company, Baltimore, Maryland.

Murdock, George P. 1949. *Social Structure.* Macmillan, New York.

Neff, Hector, and Michael D. Glascock. 2002. Instrumental Neutron Activation Analysis of Olmec Pottery. Report on file at the Research Reactor Center, University of Missouri, Columbia, Missouri.

Nicholson, Henry B. 1971. Religion in Pre-Hispanic Central Mexico. In *Handbook of Middle American Indians, Vol. 10: Archaeology of Northern Mesoamerica,* Part 1, edited by R. Wauchope, G. Ekholm, and I. Bernal, pp. 395–446. University of Texas Press, Austin.

Niederberger, Christine. 1987. *Paleopaysages et Archeologie Pre-Urbaine du Bassin de Mexico.* Centre D'Etudes Mexicaines et Centramericaines, Mexico City.

Ortiz, Ponciano, and Ma. del Carmen Rodríguez. 1994. Los espacios sagrados olmecas: El Manatí, un caso especial. In *Los olmecas en Mesoamérica,* edited by J. E. Clark, pp. 68–91. El Equilibrista, Mexico City.

Ortner, Sherry B. 1984. Theory in Anthropology Since the Sixties. *Comparative Studies in Society and History* 26:126–166.

Paddock, John. 1966. Oaxaca in Ancient Mesoamerica. In *Ancient Oaxaca,* edited by J. Paddock, pp. 87–240. Stanford University Press, Stanford.

Pasztory, Esther. 1989. Identity and Difference: The Uses and Meanings of Ethnic Styles. In *Cultural Differentiation and Cultural Identity in the Visual Arts,* edited by S. J. Barnes and W. S. Melion, pp. 15–38. Studies in the History of Art, No. 27, National Gallery of Art, Washington, D.C.

Payne, William O. 1994. The Raw Materials and Pottery-Making Techniques of Early Formative Oaxaca: An Introduction. In *Early Formative Pottery of the Valley of Oaxaca, Mexico,* by K. V. Flannery and J. Marcus, pp. 7–20. *Prehistory and Human Ecology of the Valley of Oaxaca,* Vol. 10. Memoirs of the University of Michigan Museum of Anthropology, No. 27, University of Michigan, Ann Arbor.

Paynter, Robert. 1981. Social Complexity in Peripheries: Problems and Models. In *Archaeological Approaches to the Study of Complexity,* edited by S. E. van der Leeux, pp. 118–143. University of Amsterdam, Amsterdam.

———. 1989. The Archaeology of Equality and Inequality. *Annual Review of Anthropology* 18:369–399.

Peregrine, Peter N. 1996. Introduction: World-Systems Theory and Archaeology. In *Pre-Columbian World Systems,* edited by P. N. Peregrine and G. M. Feinman, pp. 1–10. Monographs in World Archaeology, No. 26, Prehistory Press, Madison, Wisconsin.

Pires-Ferreira, Jane Wheeler. 1975. *Formative Mesoamerican Exchange Networks with Special Reference to the Valley of Oaxaca. Prehistory and Human Ecology of the Valley of Oaxaca,* Vol. 3. Memoirs of the University of Michigan Museum of Anthropology, No. 7, University of Michigan, Ann Arbor.

Plog, Stephen. 1976a. Relative Efficiency of Sampling Techniques for Archaeological Surveys. In *The Early Mesoamerican Village,* edited by K. V. Flannery, pp. 136–158. Academic Press, New York.

———. 1976b. Measurement of Prehistoric Interaction between Communities. In *The Early Mesoamerican Village,* edited by K. V. Flannery, pp. 255–272. Academic Press, New York.

Plunket, Patricia. 1983. *An Intensive Survey in the Yucuita Sector of the Nochixtlán Valley, Oaxaca, Mexico.* Unpublished Ph.D. dissertation, Department of Anthropology, Tulane University, New Orleans, Louisiana.

———. 1990. Patrones de asentamiento en el Valle de Nochixtlán y su aportación a la evolución cultural en la Mixteca Alta. In *Lecturas históricas del estado de Oaxaca, Vol. 1: Época prehispánica,* edited by M. C. Winter, pp. 349–378. Instituto Nacional de Antropología e Historia, Mexico City.

Pohl, John M. D., John Monaghan, and Laura Stiver. 1997. Religion, Economy, and Factionalism in Mixtec Boundary Zones. In *Códices y Documentos sobre México, Segundo Simposio, Volumen I,* edited by S. Rueda Smithers, C. Vega Sosa, and R. Martínez Baracs, pp. 205–232. Instituto Nacional de Antropología e Historia and Consejo Nacional para la Cultura y las Artes, Mexico City.

Preucel, Robert W. 2000. Making Pueblo Communities: Architectural Discourse at Kotyiti, New Mexico. In *The Archaeology of Communities: A New World Perspective,* edited by M. Canuto and J. Yaeger, pp. 58–77. Routledge, New York.

Pyne, Nanette. 1976. The Fire-serpent and Were-jaguar in Formative Oaxaca: A

Contingency Table Analysis. In *The Early Mesoamerican Village,* edited by K. V. Flannery, pp. 272–280. Academic Press, New York.

Rabin, Emily. 1981. Chronology of the Mixtec Historical Codices: An Overview. Paper presented at the Annual Meeting of the Society for Ethnohistory, Colorado Springs, Colorado.

Ramírez Urrea, Susana. 1993. *Hacienda Blanca: una aldea a través del tiempo, en el valle de Etla, Oaxaca.* Unpublished master's thesis, Escuela de Antropología, Universidad Autónoma de Guadalajara.

Redman, Charles L., and Patty Jo Watson. 1970. Systematic, Intensive Surface Collection. *American Antiquity* 35(3):279–291.

Reilly, F. Kent, III. 1995. Art, Ritual, and Rulership in the Olmec World. In *The Olmec World: Ritual and Rulership,* pp. 27–45. The Art Museum, Princeton University, Princeton, New Jersey.

Rice, Prudence M. 1987. *Pottery Analysis: A Sourcebook.* University of Chicago Press, Chicago.

Rivera Guzmán, Ivan. 2002. Cerámica de Tequixtepec. Paper presented at Taller de Cerámica: Tercera Mesa Redonda de Monte Albán, Oaxaca City, Mexico.

Robles García, Nelly M. 1988. *Las Unidades Domésticas del preclásico superior en la Mixteca Alta.* British Archaeological Reports International, Series 407, Oxford.

Rowlands, Michael. 1987. Centre and Periphery: A Review of a Concept. In *Centre and Periphery in the Ancient World,* edited by M. Rowlands, M. Larsen, and K. Kristiansen, pp. 1–11. Cambridge University Press, New York.

Sackett, James R. 1977. The Meaning of Style: A General Model. *American Antiquity* 42:369–380.

Sanders, William T. 1992. Ranking and Stratification in Prehispanic Mesoamerica. In *Mesoamerican Elites: An Archaeological Assessment,* edited by D. Z. Chase and A. F. Chase, pp. 278–291. University of Oklahoma Press, Norman.

Schapiro, Meyer. 1953. Style. In *Anthropology Today: An Encyclopedic Inventory,* edited by A. L. Kroeber, pp. 287–312. University of Chicago Press, Chicago.

Schneider, Jane. 1977. Was There a Pre-Capitalist World System? *Peasant Studies* VI(1):20–29.

Schortman, Edward M. 1989. Interregional Interaction in Prehistory: The Need for a New Perspective. *American Antiquity* 54(1):52–65.

———. 1996. Actions at a Distance, Impacts at Home: Prestige Good Theory and a Pre-Columbian Polity in Southeastern Mesoamerica. In *Pre-Columbian World Systems,* edited by P. N. Peregrine and G. M. Feinman, pp. 97–114. Monographs in World Archaeology, No. 26, Prehistory Press, Madison, Wisconsin.

Schortman, Edward M., and Patricia A. Urban. 1987. Modeling Interregional Interaction in Prehistory. In *Advances in Archaeological Method and Theory,* Vol. 11, edited by M. Schiffer, pp. 37–95. Academic Press, New York.

Service, Elman R. 1975. *Origins of the State and Civilization: The Process of Cultural Evolution.* Norton, New York.

Sharer, Robert J., and David C. Grove. 1989. Preface. In *Regional Perspectives on the Olmec,* edited by R. J. Sharer and D. C. Grove, pp. xix–xxiv. Cambridge University Press, New York.

Shutes, Mark T. 1999. Goodness of Fit: On the Relationship between Ethnographic Data and World-Systems Theory. In *World-Systems Theory in Practice: Leadership, Production, and Exchange,* edited by P. N. Kardulias, pp. 25–35. Rowman & Littlefield Publishers, New York.

Smith, C. Earle, Jr. 1976. *Modern Vegetation and Ancient Plant Remains of the Nochixtlán Valley, Oaxaca.* Vanderbilt University Publications in Anthropology, No. 16, Vanderbilt University, Nashville, Tennessee.

Smith, Charlotte Ann. 1993. *Prehispanic Mixtec Social Organization: The Architectural Evidence.* Unpublished master's thesis, Department of Anthropology, University of Georgia, Athens.

Smith, Mary Elizabeth. 1973. The Relationship between Mixtec Manuscript Painting and the Mixtec Language: A Study of Some Personal Names in Codices Muro and Sánchez Solís. In *Mesoamerican Writing Systems,* edited by E. P. Benson, pp. 47–98. Dumbarton Oaks, Washington, D.C.

———. 1988. It Doesn't Amount to a Hill of Beans: The Frijol Motif in Mixtec Place Signs. In *Smoke and Mist: Mesoamerican Studies in Memory of Thelma D. Sullivan,* edited by J. K. Josserand and K. Dakin, pp. 696–710. British Archaeological Reports International, Series 402, Oxford.

Spores, Ronald. 1972. *An Archaeological Settlement Survey of the Nochixtlán Valley, Oaxaca.* Vanderbilt University Publications in Anthropology, No. 1, Vanderbilt University, Nashville, Tennessee.

———. 1974. *Stratigraphic Excavations in the Nochixtlán Valley, Oaxaca.* Vanderbilt University Publications in Anthropology, No. 11, Vanderbilt University, Nashville, Tennessee.

———. 1984. *The Mixtecs in Ancient and Colonial Times.* University of Oklahoma Press, Norman.

———. 2001. Estudios mixtecos, ayer, hoy y mañana: Dónde estábamos, dónde estamos, hacia dónde vamos? In *Procesos de cambio y conceptualización del tiempo: Memoria de la Primera Mesa Redonda de Monte Albán,* edited by N. M. Robles García, pp. 167–181. Instituto Nacional de Antropología e Historia, Mexico City.

Stark, Barbara L. 1995. Problems in Analysis of Standardization and Specialization in Pottery. In *Ceramic Production in the American Southwest,* edited by B. J. Mills and P. L. Crown, pp. 231–267. The University of Arizona Press, Tucson.

———. 2000. Framing the Gulf Olmecs. In *Olmec Art and Archaeology in Mesoamerica,* edited by J. E. Clark and M. E. Pye, pp. 31–53. Studies in the History of Art, Vol. 58, National Gallery of Art, Washington, D.C.

Steward, Julian. 1955. *Theory of Culture Change.* University of Illinois Press, Urbana.

Stuiver, M., and P. J. Reimer. 1993. University of Washington Quaternary Isotope Lab Radiocarbon Calibration Program Rev. 3.03A, MAC Test Version #6. *Radiocarbon* 35:215–230.

Swadesh, Morris. 1967. Lexicostatistic Classification. In *Handbook of Middle American Indians, Vol. 5: Linguistics,* edited by N. McQuown, pp. 79–115. University of Texas Press, Austin.

Swidler, Nina, Kurt E. Dongoske, Roger Anyon, and Alan S. Downer (editors). 1997. *Native Americans and Archaeologists: Stepping Stones to Common Ground.* AltaMira Press, Walnut Creek, California.

Symonds, Stacey. 2000. The Ancient Landscape at San Lorenzo Tenochtitlán, Veracruz, Mexico: Settlement and Nature. In *Olmec Art and Archaeology in Mesoamerica,* edited by J. E. Clark and M. E. Pye, pp. 55–73. Studies in the History of Art, Vol. 58, National Gallery of Art, Washington, D.C.

Thieme, Mary S. 2001. Continuity of Ceramic Production: Examination and Analysis of Clay Materials from Santa María Atzompa. In *Procesos de cambio y conceptualización del tiempo: Memoria de la Primera Mesa Redonda de Monte Albán,* edited by N. M. Robles García, pp. 341–349. Instituto Nacional de Antropología e Historia, Mexico City.

Tolstoy, Paul, and Suzanne K. Fish. 1975. Surface and Subsurface Evidence for Community Size at Coapexco, Mexico. *Journal of Field Archaeology* 2:97–104.

Troike, Nancy P. 1990. Pre-Hispanic Pictorial Communication: The Codex System of the Mixtec of Oaxaca, Mexico. *Visible Language* 24(1):75–87.

Ucko, Peter J. 1969. Ethnography and the Archaeological Interpretation of Funerary Remains. *World Archaeology* 1:262–290.

Urcid, Javier. 1992. *Zapotec Hieroglyphic Writing.* Unpublished Ph.D. dissertation, Department of Anthropology, Yale University, New Haven, Connecticut.

———. 1998. Codices on Stone: The Origins of Writing in Ancient Oaxaca. *Indiana Journal of Hispanic Literatures* 13:7–16.

Van Binsbergen, Wim M. J. 1977. Regional and Non-regional Cults of Affliction in Western Zambia. In *Regional Cults,* edited by R. P. Werbner, pp. 141–175. Academic Press, New York.

Varien, Mark D. 1999a. *Sedentism and Mobility in a Social Landscape: Mesa*

Verde and Beyond. University of Arizona Press, Tucson.

————— (editor). 1999b. *The Sand Canyon Archaeological Project: Site Testing.* CD-ROM, Vers. 1.0. Crow Canyon Archaeological Center, Cortez, Colorado.

Wallerstein, Immanuel. 1974. *The Modern World System I.* Academic Press, New York.

Watson, Patty Jo, Steven A. LeBlanc, and Charles L. Redman. 1971. *Explanation in Archaeology.* Columbia University Press, New York.

Werbner, Richard P. 1977a. Introduction. In *Regional Cults,* edited by R. P. Werbner, pp. ix–xxxvii. Academic Press, New York.

————. 1977b. Continuity and Policy in Southern Africa's High God Cult. In *Regional Cults,* edited by R. P. Werbner, pp. 179–218. Academic Press, New York.

Whalen, Michael E. 1981. *Excavations at Santo Domingo Tomaltepec: Evolution of a Formative Community in the Valley of Oaxaca, Mexico. Prehistory and Human Ecology of the Valley of Oaxaca,* Vol. 6. Memoirs of the University of Michigan Museum of Anthropology, No. 12, University of Michigan, Ann Arbor.

Wheeler Pires-Ferreira, Jane. 1978. Shell Exchange Networks in Formative Mesoamerica. In *Cultural Continuity in Mesoamerica,* edited by D. L. Browman, pp. 79–100. Mouton Publishers, The Hague.

Willey, Gordon, and Philip Phillips. 1958. *Method and Theory in American Archaeology.* University of Chicago Press, Chicago.

Winter, Marcus C. 1972. *Tierras Largas: A Formative Community in the Valley of Oaxaca.* Unpublished Ph.D. dissertation, Department of Anthropology, University of Arizona, Tucson.

————. 1976. The Archaeological Household Cluster in the Valley of Oaxaca. In *The Early Mesoamerican Village,* edited by K. V. Flannery, pp. 25–31. Academic Press, New York.

————. 1982. *Guía zona arqueológica de Yucuita.* Centro INAH Oaxaca, Oaxaca City, Mexico.

————. 1984. Exchange in Formative Highland Oaxaca. In *Trade and Exchange in Early Mesoamerica,* edited by K. G. Hirth, pp. 179–214. University of New Mexico Press, Albuquerque.

————. 1989. *Oaxaca: The Archaeological Record.* Minutiae Mexicana, Mexico City.

————. 1994. Los altos de Oaxaca y los olmecas. In *Los olmecas en Mesoamérica,* edited by J. E. Clark, pp. 129–141. El Equilibrista, Mexico City.

Winter, Marcus C., Margarita Gaxiola González, and Gilberto Hernández. 1984. Archaeology of the Otomanguean Area. In *Essays in Otomanguean Culture History,* edited by J. K. Josserand, M. C. Winter, and N. Hopkins, pp. 65–108. Vanderbilt University Publications in Anthropology, No. 31, Vanderbilt University, Nashville, Tennessee.

Winter, Marcus C., and Lucina Cruz Hernández. 2000. La fase Yucuita y los orígenes del urbanismo en el Valle de Nochixtlán, Mixteca Alta, Oaxaca. Paper presented at the IV Simposio de Estudios Oaxaqueños, Oaxaca City, Mexico.

Wittfogel, Karl A. 1957. *Oriental Despotism.* Yale University Press, New Haven, Connecticut.

Wobst, Martin. 1977. Stylistic Behavior and Information Exchange. In *For the Director: Research Essays in Honor of James B. Griffin,* edited by C. E. Cleland, pp. 317–342. Anthropological Papers, No. 61, University of Michigan Museum of Anthropology, Ann Arbor.

Wolf, Eric R. 1982. *Europe and the People Without History.* University of California Press, Berkeley.

Wright, Henry T., and Gregory A. Johnson. 1975. Population, Exchange, and Early State Formation in Southwestern Iran. *American Anthropologist* 77:267–289.

Zárate Morán, Roberto. 1987. *Excavaciones de un sitio preclásico en San Mateo Etlatongo, Nochixtlán, Oaxaca, México.* British Archaeological Reports International Series 322, Oxford.

Zeitlin, Robert N., and Arthur A. Joyce. 1999. The Zapotec-Imperialism Argument: Insights from the Oaxaca Coast. *Current Anthropology* 40(3):383–392.

Index

Numbers in italic indicate a table or a figure.